Publishing Newsletters

Publishing Newsletters

Howard Penn Hudson   **Revised Edition**

Charles Scribner's Sons • New York

Z
286
.N46
H83
1988

Charles Scribner's Sons
Macmillan Publishing Company
866 Third Avenue, New York, NY 10022
Collier Macmillan Canada, Inc.

Library of Congress Cataloging-in-Publication Data
Hudson, Howard Penn.
　　Publishing newsletters/Howard Penn Hudson.—Rev ed.
　　　　p.　cm.
　　Bibliography: p.
　　Includes index.
　　ISBN 0-684-18954-2
　　1. Newsletters—Publishing.　I. Title.
Z286.N46H83　　1988
070.5—dc19　　　　　　　　　　　　　　87-32925
　　　　　　　　　　　　　　　　　　　　　　CIP

Macmillan books are available at special discounts for bulk purchases for sales promotions, premiums, fund-raising, or educational use. For details, contact:

Special Sales Director
Macmillan Publishing Company
866 Third Avenue
New York, NY 10022

10 9 8 7 6 5 4 3 2 1

Contents

092189

Acknowledgments

This book is dedicated to the thousands of newsletter editors and publishers who have freely shared their knowledge with me in discussions and through study of their newsletters over the past eighteen years. Some of them are mentioned in the text.

The Second Edition is dedicated to my wife, Mary Elizabeth Hudson, my business associate and a superb editor, who died July 25, 1987. She guided me through the First Edition.

I must also thank the following:

Paul Swift, managing editor, *The Newsletter on Newsletters,* for his patient reading of the manuscript, for his skillful introduction of new material into the text, and for his tenacity in pulling together the fragments of our joint efforts into a coherent entity.

Maureen Heuer, for producing the final manuscript with her usual aplomb in fielding seemingly endless last-minute revisions.

Helene F. Wingard, co-editor, *Hudson's Washington Directory,* and Margaret Leonard, editor, *Hudson's Newsletter Directory,* for their professional advice.

Herbert Messing, formerly of Compupower, Inc., Secaucus, New Jersey, and Walter G. Caroll, Publishers Computer Corporation, Teaneck, New Jersey, for much of the material in Chapter 8.

Richard L. Wambach, Wambach Communications Group, Inc., Rhinebeck, New York, editor, *Newsletter Design* newsletter, for much of Chapters 5 and 6. Dick, a judge for the past ten years in our Newsletter Awards competition, provided the graphics illustrations in the First Edition. He has now replaced most of them with fresh examples. He has also counseled me in presenting the new revolution in printing, desktop publishing, in the proper perspective for newsletter publishers.

And, far from least, my colleague and neighbor, Thomas J. Gilgut, Jr., former publisher of *Inter-Connection* and *Regulation News,* execu-

vii

tive vice president, The Newsletter Clearinghouse, who has continued to provide invaluable advice on my errors and omissions on the newsletter industry, my syntax, and even my arithmetic. I appreciate his never-flagging enthusiasm and encouragement.

Howard Penn Hudson
Rhinebeck, New York

For additional information on newsletters please write to:

Howard Penn Hudson
The Newsletter Clearinghouse
P.O. Box 311
Rhinebeck, NY 12572

Preface

This is the first comprehensive book about newsletters. Whether you want to publish a newsletter for fun or for profit, this book will tell you how to go about it. And it will show you, in the Gallery of Newsletters, sixty-eight examples of publications already in the field.

There are at least 100,000 professional and amateur newsletters in the United States—some estimate as many as 500,000—and they are read by millions of people. Newsletters are so much a part of your life that you may not realize how dependent you are on them for information.

Newsletters give you specialized information you can't get from newspapers, radio, television, or magazines—information you need to coordinate your activities and interests. Newsletters fit the fragmented nature of our society; they are the communications link for the thousands of small interest groups that are so prevalent.

In the course of our lives, most of us encounter hundreds of newsletters and bulletins put out by all sorts of groups. These informal little periodicals are used by every kind of group and organization in the country, including your congressman. Newsletters are used within corporations, associations, labor unions, and various nonprofit organizations as a fast method of communication. Some companies publish two hundred or more for both internal and external communication, including sales relations, public relations, and shareholder relations. Trade associations find the newsletter a basic membership communications tool. Many associations and labor unions publish a Washington, D.C., or state capital letter to give their members information on government actions.

Public relations practitioners have also found the newsletter a useful tool in reaching a designated audience. Unlike the press release, it is a controlled message that cannot be altered. The publicist may also find the newsletter editor receptive to receiving information. If an item is used in a newsletter, the high readership by an influential audience may more than offset the small circulation.

It is estimated that there are three thousand to five thousand paid-subscription newsletters, ranging in price from $1 to several thousand dollars a year. From 1970 to 1980 a thousand new subscription letters were founded. Certainly no other periodical print medium—newspapers or magazines—exhibits such a growth pattern.

Many newsletters, of course, are so inept and amateurish that they cannot be considered a form of journalism. Yet they are true relatives of the professional newsletters. The more common amateur newsletters often have formats similar to the subscription varieties; the difference is in the superior content and the writing in professional newsletters.

Newsletters are part of the $13.1 billion business-information industry. A report by Knowledge Industry Publications in 1986 predicted that this figure would reach $19.1 billion by 1990. According to Frederick D. Goss, executive director of the Newsletter Association, the international trade association for newsletter and specialized information publishers, for at least three reasons it's quite difficult to put a dollar estimate on the size of the newsletter business: (1) 98 percent of the companies in the field are privately held and divulge very little of their operating results. (2) Many newsletter companies are also extensively involved in ancillary ventures such as seminars, list rentals, and book sales. Should those revenues be counted? (3) What's a newsletter? For example, several large firms, Commerce Clearinghouse, Prentice-Hall, the Bureau of National Affairs, Inc., produce what they call "information services," which very much resemble what other publishers call "newsletters." Do you count them? Who decides? If you take a broad view on points 2 and 3, newsletter publishing is probably at least a $1 billion annual business, perhaps $1.5 billion. Defined closely, it is probably more like $500 million to $700 million.

Just as the invention of the rotary press helped bring about mass-circulation newspapers and magazines, the electric typewriter with carbon ribbon and the offset press contributed to the growth of newsletters. Now typewriters are being replaced (although not universally) by word-processing units and computer-aided micropublishing systems. Desktop publishing, as it has come to be called, is changing the face of established newsletter operations and introducing whole new populations to the newsletter phenomenon.

There are good career opportunities in the newsletter field. One person can make a comfortable living by publishing one or two newsletters.

There are also a number of multinewsletter publishers, some with dozens of publications. At the moment, the industry is dominated by small entrepreneurs, but more and more large firms are becoming interested. For that matter, the small entrepreneurs are becoming larger. In 1966 Kenneth Callaway founded Capitol Publications from scratch with *Economic Opportunity Report,* hiring students in his old college fraternity to stuff envelopes for all the beer they could drink. He built up Capitol Publications to over forty newsletters through launches and acquisitions, and sold it in 1984 for a reported $20 million. And in recent years Phillips Publishing, Inc., Potomac, Maryland, and CPA Services, Inc., Milwaukee, Wisconsin, have both appeared more than once on the *Inc.* magazine list of fastest-growing companies in the United States.

Newsletter companies employ writers, editors, graphic designers, business managers, marketing experts, and printing production specialists as well as clerical staff and experts in subscription promotion and fulfillment. There is an increasing need for people with data-processing, computer, and electronic communications knowledge. Free-lancers are also finding employment opportunities in newsletters, as are increasing numbers of newspaper and magazine journalists.

Newsletters may rekindle an interest in writing and the printed word. Much of the pleasure of writing is getting published, and with a typewriter or word processor and a photocopier anyone can publish a newsletter. This leads me to suggest another need the newsletter field might fulfill.

Many schools and colleges are making renewed efforts to teach writing skills to students—skills that are essential to the clear thinking and expression of thought vital to success in any career. Perhaps newsletters can provide the necessary spark of interest. Only a handful of students can work on the school newspaper, and most students can't start radio or television stations, but there is hardly any limit to the number of small newsletters that could be written and produced by groups of students. The only technical skill needed is keyboarding (typing), which enables one to operate a typewriter or a word processor linked to a computer or perhaps a laser printer as the desktop publishing revolution reaches the educational system.

Newsletter writing requires precision and discipline, two factors missing from much student writing. It has a purpose: the communication of information in an understandable form to others. Students preparing their own newsletters would have the fun of seeing their words in print, and would learn both writing and the role of computers in information processing. They would also acquire a pleasant hobby—and if they sought a career in journalism, they would have had several years of practical experience before their first job interviews.

I began doing newsletters in high school when I was presented with a very secondhand Underwood typewriter. At the University of Chicago, where I was editor of the daily newspaper, I also found time for several newsletters. In the army I converted various technical regulations into newsletter form for easier comprehension. In my public relations work I found newsletters valuable tools, and later I began preparing newsletters for other organizations on a contract basis.

Then, in 1968, I began publishing *The Newsletter on Newsletters* and found that I had stumbled on the last unorganized industry in America—just when it was beginning the growth surge that still continues. Through writing for eighteen years about the developments in the field; holding numerous seminars for subscription, association, and corporate newsletters; editing seven directories of newsletters; founding international conferences and the Newsletter Association; and through the Newsletter Awards program started fifteen years ago, as well as private consulting here and abroad, I have had a unique inside look at the field. And, doubtless, the opportunity to look at more newsletters—many, many thousands—than has anyone else, ever.

In this book, then, I share this experience—my enthusiasm for the field and the people who inhabit it and the tricks of the trade I have learned.

Publishing Newsletters

1 The Newsletter Phenomenon

When Did Newsletters Start? Newsletters are an old medium brought up-to-date. The first known examples are believed to have been developed by Count Philip Edward Fugger (1546–1618) of Augsburg, Germany. They were loose, handwritten sheets that reported business news gathered by various agents in trade centers of Europe and overseas ports. They later became known as *Fugger–Zeitungen*. (*Zeitung*, which means "tidings," later became the German word for "newspaper.") Also found in the Fugger collection were news reports that were sold to paying subscribers. Here we have the basic characteristic of newsletters—specialized information prepared for a subscription audience.

English newsletters started in Amsterdam about 1620. Van Hilten, George Veseler, and Pieter Van de Keere were three printers who put out what were called "corantos." These were one-page sheets about commercial and political affairs that were translated into English and sold in London. In 1631, William Watts introduced *The Continuation of Our Weekly News from Forraine Parts,* much of it drawn from the Dutch letters. When Charles I prohibited all printing of newsletters in England, Van Hilten prepared and sent English newsletters from Amsterdam. By 1641, censorship in England had been abolished and London became a news center once more.

The first American newsletter, the *Boston News-Letter,* which has also been called the first newspaper, was published in 1704. The growth of newspapers and the advent of magazines in the nineteenth century signaled the rise of mass media but the fall from popularity of newsletters. But by 1900, newsletters began to bounce back. Many business and financial people were ready for more specialized news than they got from the popular press. They showed an interest in the opinions of people with expert knowledge and in forecasts of what might happen to their investments. First to meet the need was Roger W. Babson of Wellesley, Massa-

1

chusetts. His *Babson's Reports,* founded in 1904, appears to be the first investment advisory letter, with analyses and forecasts that found instant acceptance. It continues today, along with a host of other publications by the same publisher.

The Modern Newsletter   The first modern newsletter was the *Whaley-Eaton Report,* founded in 1918. In 1923, Willard M. Kiplinger launched the *Kiplinger Washington Letter* (Fig. 1). In 1980, his son, Austin, purchased Whaley-Eaton and merged it into the Kiplinger organization (Fig. 2; page 4). Willard Kiplinger invented a style and format that have been widely imitated. His newsletter is considered a classic, occupying a niche of its own.

Despite the success of Kiplinger, other publishers were slow to follow his lead. A few began in the 1930s—William H. Wood, Chicago, 1933, whose National Research Bureau developed forty-one newsletters; Fred W. Henck, *Telecommunications Reports,* Washington, D.C., 1934; *Pratt's Letter,* Washington, D.C., 1934; and *Doane's Agricultural Report,* St. Louis, 1938. Others began publication in the next decade—Ruth Finley, *Fashion Calendar,* 1941; George Armstrong, *The Investment Reporter,* Toronto, 1941; and Denny Griswold, *Public Relations News,* New York, 1944. Still others emerged after World War II, but the field really began to move only in the 1960s—and erupted in the 1970s. As I said earlier, there are more than 100,000 today. Gale Research Company's *Newsletters Directory*—which *excludes* house organs, publications of strictly local interest, and those distributed by hand—lists 8,000 newsletters. The 1987 *Oxbridge Directory of Newsletters* lists 13,500. The subscription area is much smaller, however, with about 3,400 such publications listed in the sixth edition of *Hudson's Newsletter Directory.*

Clear benchmarks show the newness of the field: the industry publication *The Newsletter on Newsletters* was started in 1964; the industry's Newsletter Association, in 1977; and this book, the first comprehensive one on the subject, was originally published in 1982. The field, however, is maturing rapidly. Not especially in numbers of professional letters (in fact, Newsletter Clearinghouse research reveals that 1984 saw the peak of new letters launched in any one year, 215), but in their acceptance and influence. In areas such as public health, law, corporate activity, and technology, our nation's leading magazines and newspapers increasingly cite, quote, and interview appropriate newsletter editors because they are the authorities (and often because they have already scooped the mass media on the information).

Newsletter editors and publishers are also taking their place among the ranks of fellow journalists. The membership of SDX, the Society of

THE KIPLINGER WASHINGTON AGENCY

ALBEE BUILDING

WASHINGTON, D. C.

NEW YORK OFFICE 15 PARK ROW

WILLARD M. KIPLINGER
MELVIN RYDER
E D MURPHY
HENRY UTLEY MILNE

BUSINESS REPRESENTATION
GOVERNMENT PRACTICE
SALES INVESTIGATION
UNPUBLISHED INFORMATION
LEGISLATION REPORTS
FOREIGN BUSINESS
TRADE PRESS CLIPPINGS

THE KIPLINGER WASHINGTON LETTER   Sept. 29, 1923   ISSUED WEEKLY TO CLIENTS

Rumors of an international German loan are renewed - a loan to revive the mark. Bankers take them seriously in a few cases, but they are foolish. No German loan will come without plenty of advance notice and the paper mark will not come back. Begin to watch for the decline of the franc, too.   Expiring Coal Commission recommends government regulation of the coal industry by the Interstate Commerce Commission. It will take legislation, and that probably won't come at the next session, opening in December. It will take a longer period of talk.   An important case before the Supreme Court, which opens its fall session Oct. 1 is that of the First National Bank of St.Louis, involving the question of whether national banks may legally establish offices, or branches, within the same city; re-argument scheduled for Nov. 12.   Muscle Shoals is still an issue, though the Gorgas steam plant was sold to the Alabama Power Co. Henry Ford's offer will remain to be fought over.   The revenue act will be revised at the coming session of Congress, but mainly on technical phases.   Washington will not give the farmers much relief; it can't. The proposal for a government-financed wheat exporting corporation probably means subsidy is an emergency shot-in-the-arm constitutionally good, or isn't it?   Country bankers plan a suit to test the par collection rules of the Federal Reserve Board. In the end, they won't get anywhere.   A report on the history of electric light is published by the Smithsonian Institution. It is significant of what museums can do for business, if "business" only knew what to ask for.   Radio, what a lot of valuable research by government departments is available on this popular subject! But government documents suffer under their age-old reputation for mustiness.   The Japanese disaster means more business for American interests. It also means better relations between the two nations. Those are the two high points in the situation, so far as Washington is concerned, sentimentally barred.   Every banker who looks ahead should read the story of what labor banks are doing, embodied in the book, "Labor's Money", by Richard Boeckel, Harcourt, Brace & Co., $1.50. Read it whether you believe in the labor banks or not.   Another good book for banks, or foreign traders to have, is "WHO'S WHO IN WORLD TRADE", a directory and hand book of foreign agents, forwarders, attorneys, published by the International Bureau of Trade Extension, Washington.   Mexican claims: Nothing much can be done about them for six months or but every effort should be made now to get them in good shape for pressing.   Bankers meeting in Atlantic City at the convention of the American Bankers Association recommend amendment of the federal reserve act to eliminate politics from administration of the system.   The recommendations are interesting and meritorious, but they will not be embodied in legislation very soon.   Banks are getting ready to ask Congress for legislation to remove the tax exemption privileges from building and loan associations.   They probably won't succeed.
FULLER REPORTS ON ANY OF THESE SUBJECTS WILL BE FURNISHED ON REQUEST.

This is a reproduction of the first Kiplinger Washington Letter

OUR THIRTY-FIFTH ANNIVERSARY
1923-1958

THE KIPLINGER WASHINGTON LETTER

Circulated weekly to business clients since 1923—Vol. 64, No. 33

THE KIPLINGER WASHINGTON EDITORS

1729 H St., N.W., Washington, D.C. 20006 Tel: 202-887-6400

Cable Address: Kiplinger Washington D.C.

Dear Client: Washington, Aug. 14, 1987.

A gentle note of caution on interest rates seems to be in order.
We think that rates are headed higher for the rest of this year
and well into next year...something you ought to crank into your plans.
Fairly moderate increases, not another interest rate crisis.
Up 1% or so by the middle of 1988, cooling the economy, not choking it.
Perhaps falling later in '88, but that's too far to see now.

A stronger economy is the main reason for expecting higher rates.
Not a boom, but enough of a pickup to increase borrowing needs broadly.
Economy will grow about 3% this year and a little more than that in '88.
Export gains are the big plus, and business investment will expand too...
strong points that will offset softness in housing and consumer spending.
Another reason, worse inflation. Probably 4½% to 5% this year,
5% or so next year. Making lenders worry about even steeper increases.

Expect the Federal Reserve to tighten credit, nudge rates upward,
although very cautiously so as to avoid pushing the economy off a cliff.
It will probably act this fall, hiking the discount rate from 5½% to 6%.
The Fed feels obliged to rein in the economy before it overheats.
Fears inflation...business growing too fast, driving prices and wages up,
triggering a bust. Besides, higher rates keep the dollar from plunging.

Here's what we see ahead on the key interest rates:
Prime will end 1987 near 9%...then rise to 9½% or 9¾% next year.
Treasury bills (13 weeks), a bit over 6% this year, 6½% next.
Treasury bonds (30 years), 9% at year end, 9½% or so by mid-'88.
Municipal and corporate bonds...up almost 1% in the next year.
Mortgages...10½% this year and 11% next year on fixed rates.
Savings CDs, 1% higher by spring. Credit cards, about as-is.

And here's what you can do about it:
Stick to short-term certificates of deposit now...up to 6 months.
Next year, you should be able to lock in higher rates with long-term CDs.
Borrow sooner rather than later. Costs will go up if you wait.
Consider an adjustable-rate mortgage if you're buying a house
because interest rates will average lower than now over the long haul.
If you prefer a fixed rate, don't delay long...higher rates by late '87.
Remember, bonds will look better next year, after prices slip.

Is the stock market too high? A great many investors fear it is,
so we've been rechecking our sources and have come to this conclusion...
The market FACTS support further increases the rest of this year.
Still plenty of money around...and stocks look as good as anything else.
Foreigners will keep investing...our stocks are cheap by their standards.
Good profits, justifying higher prices without stretching price-earnings.
And bigger dividends...thus more buying to get in on the melon-slicing.

Figure 2

Professional Journalists, counts 6.6 percent of its membership from newsletters—far below daily newspapers' 30 percent but well above broadcast and trade journalists. In 1986 the National Press Club in Washington, D.C., enthusiastically accepted for its library the Hudson Collection of sixty-four volumes of three thousand newsletters listed in the Newsletter Clearinghouse's directory.

In 1985 the *Encyclopaedia Britannica* finally included "newsletter" among its entries: "*newsletter,* informal publication, often simple in format and crisp in style, that provides special information for a defined audience. Newsletters are ordinarily but not always issued regularly. They offer varieties of personal journalism and seldom carry advertising."

Indicative of the mainstream recognition of the newsletter field is the increasing use of the word "newslettering." Senator Daniel Patrick Moynihan of New York wrote in his letter, "I would especially welcome comment about this adventure into newslettering," but language pundit William Safire took him to task. "Lettering," according to Safire, "is a legitimate verb, and an honorable line of work for people who paint legible signs, but 'newslettering' is new." I told Safire, whom I've known for years, that Denny Griswold was quoted in the 1971 book *How to Make $25,000 a Year Publishing Newsletters,* "Newslettering is basic free enterprise." And I drew his attention to the descriptive tag on the front page of *Editor & Publisher,* "The Only Independent Weekly Journal of Newspapering." Many people, including myself, refer to those engaged in newslettering as "newsletterers."

The 1980s also saw newsletters gain a victory for freedom of the press with a Supreme Court decision that toppled the Securities and Exchange Commission's jurisdiction over who can and who cannot publish investment advisory letters. *Lowe* v. *SEC* gave newsletters the bona fide status that newspapers, magazines, and journals enjoy—excluding them from SEC regulation. It was a sweet victory for Glen King Parker, who spearheaded the Newsletter Association's support of the appeal to the Supreme Court. NA garnered financial and editorial support from the nation's leading mass media publications, and in doing so showed the world the maturity of both the association and the industry.

In fact, "maturity" is the one word that most characterizes the newsletter field at this time, according to NA past president Thomas L. Phillips, who was the keynote speaker at the 1987 NA international conference in Washington, D.C. He noted that the novelty of the newsletter phenomenon is wearing off and now newsletters are becoming more legitimate in the eyes of government, the mass media, and the general public. Renewals are up, and yesterday's hot new ideas are now established publications. Phillips also observed that such maturity is bringing new competition from outside the field—magazine publishers, for example, who are targeting specialized audiences traditionally served by newsletters. He said that survival is contingent on growth; newsletter publishers cannot stand still but must grow, not only in the number and size of their letters but in the format of providing information.

Newsletters are increasingly popular not only in the United States but also in Canada (where Toronto is the home of a number of major publishers) and the United Kingdom (which supports more than 250 newsletters) and Japan (where Nikkei–McGraw-Hill, among others, is launching Japanese letters and translating U.S. ones into Japanese). There are many reasons for their rise in popularity. First of all, very few people read everything in a newspaper or magazine. Some read only certain sections. Some read the ads in contemplation of a purchase. Others enjoy the illustrations and artwork. Newsletters can be read fast. More and more people today prefer to get their information in the capsule size of a newsletter. Readers like the portability of newsletters and the typewriter composition, which is what business people read most each day (although this is undergoing a change with the advent of desktop publishing's ease of producing typeset-like material). People have the satisfaction of finishing the whole publication at one sitting. In fact, some publishers incorporate newsletters in their magazines. *U.S. News & World Report* contains five separate newsletters, all designed to look as if they were typewritten. (The founder of *U.S. News,* the late David Lawrence, also created the newsletter and binder service now known as the Bureau of National Affairs. It has sales of $122.6 million, the largest such publisher in the field.) Many newspapers, too, are taking on some of the characteristics of newsletters. *USA Today* managing editor Nancy Woodhull, for example, told *Editor & Publisher* magazine: "We think of ourselves as a daily newsletter. The three or four paragraph style of many *USA Today* stories has been difficult for some reporters to get adjusted to and some have returned to whichever Gannett Co. newspaper they worked on before moving over to *Today.*"

A second reason for newsletter popularity is that people today want more specific information about their interests. It was not television alone that killed the two giant magazines, the original *Life* and *Look.* Readers felt they were too generalized. Even the television industry, with the growth of satellites and cable, is now developing "narrow-casting" in addition to broadcasting.

In the early 1970s, Ray E. Hiebert, then dean of the School of Journalism at the University of Maryland, said that the age of mass communications had ended and the future belonged to personal communications. He said that we were going back to the style of an earlier day when communications were less formal and more personalized. This certainly fits many newsletters. In magazines and newspapers, on the other hand, the editor does not intrude except on the editorial page; there are often strong objections when a newspaper appears to editorialize in its news columns. But the newsletter editor considers editorializing to be part of the job.

Willard Kiplinger set the style in 1923, using the newsletter as a jumping-off point for telling his readers the significance of the news. He interpreted it and advised his readers on what actions they should take in their own lives in light of the news. Even today, the name of his original newsletter remains the *Kiplinger Washington Letter*. It deliberately does not use the word "news," his son, Austin, says, because it does not report the news as such; the editors write about it. Other newsletter editors emphasize the highly editorial and opinionated aspect of what they do by attaching their names to the publication. The *Lundberg Letter* (on oil), the *McKeever Strategy Letter* (on investments), *Jack O'Dwyer's Newsletter* (on public relations), and the *Gallagher Report* (on advertising) are just a few examples. Some even carry a photo of the editor. Other newsletters prefer a more straightforward descriptive title. Perhaps they recall the fate of *I. F. Stone's Newsletter,* which once had a very large following. When Mr. Stone wished to sell his newsletter, no one would buy it because no one else could be I. F. Stone. Regardless of name, however, a personalized style and editorial commentary are characteristics of many newsletters.

Newsletters pride themselves on giving inside information. Because the editor is a specialist who becomes an expert in his chosen narrow field, he tends to uncover much more than the more generalized newspaper reporter. This is why we frequently see newsletters quoted in news stories as the source of information. Editors interpret, counsel, take stands, and make predictions. They show their authority in their style and write with a certainty that is not usually found in the daily press. And this attracts readers.

The difference in the editorial styles—and the readers' expectations—of newsletters and the mass media was graphically provided in the mid-1980s by Esther Dyson. As the young and intelligent editor of *RELease 1.0,* she held an enviable position of respect and authority in the computer industry. Then she sold the newsletter to Ziff-Davis and joined the trade newspaper *Computer Industry Daily* as founding editor. The newsletter subscriptions were fulfilled by the *Daily,* but readers reported that they "found it interesting but rarely compelling." The *Daily* went out of business in three months. Dyson said at the time: "It turned out that eight pages of daily news about the industry was more than most people needed. And what they wanted, daily analysis, is what we didn't really give them."

The Computer Letter editor Richard Shaffer summed up Dyson's and Ziff-Davis's experience this way: "People paid money for *RELease 1.0* because they wanted to buy into Esther's mind. Even when they thought she was wrong, infuriating, or off-base, she was always interesting. And in the *Daily,* there wasn't enough of what she does best."

Esther Dyson, by the way, is certainly not the first woman to make her mark in newsletters. Women have traditionally held strong positions within the field—both as successful, independent business persons and as influential leaders in the development of the newsletter industry. Denny Griswold's *Public Relations News*—a seminal publication in the PR business—dates from 1944. Ruth Finley's *Fashion Calendar* goes back to 1941. Shirley B. Alexander, publisher of the 1954-founded *Downtown Idea Exchange,* was one of the original members of the organization that became the Newsletter Association, and she served as NA president in 1979. At this writing, Karen Fine Coburn, head of Cutter Information in Arlington, Massachusetts, is president of NA. Wanda J. Sablonski founded *Petroleum Intelligence Weekly,* New York, in 1961; subscription price is currently $1,045 per year. The major newsletter firm ATCOM, Inc., founded by the late Ed Brown, NA's first president, is now run by Beverley Walker, a black woman. Susan Baka is publisher at one of Canada's principal newsletter publishers, Corpus Information Services. These are just a few of the hundreds of women who have found newsletters to be an equal opportunity industry.

Many newsletters are popular because they carve out a niche by, in effect, becoming a selective digest of other publications in a given field. Perhaps there are fifty other magazines and trade papers in one area. The newsletter editor will follow them closely, then report to his or her readers what he or she believes to be the most significant information. The readers are saved the time and expense of reading all the publications themselves. There are many fine digests, particularly in the investment field. But if we were asked to name only one, it would be *Boardroom Reports,* a business newsletter founded in 1972 by Martin Edelston, currently with 101,000 subscribers. It is a trendsetter both in editorial concept and graphics.

Some newsletters try to fill the void that has existed since lengthy correspondence between relatives and friends went out of style—the kind of chatty letter that brought the family together to hear read out loud. Charles Aronson, in *Peephole on People,* sounds off each month about his views on everything from making money, writing, and cooking to the actions of public figures. He attracts letters from readers, reprints these, and gets into arguments. And certainly Howard Ruff's *The Ruff Times* is highly personalized throughout.

Whether staffed by a board of editors or one person, newsletters are the personalized journalism of which Dean Hiebert spoke.

Characteristics of a Newsletter   The normal page size of a newsletter is 8½ " × 11"—the same size as a business letterhead. The legal size, 8½ " × 13½ ", is less common, although it is more prevalent in Britain than the United States. A few newsletters appear in other sizes, larger or smaller, presumably to attract attention. I do not favor this. Unusual sizes are effective for advertising brochures and fliers, but newsletters are a journalistic vehicle. Most newspapers and magazines have established sizes that are recognized; newsletters should be the same. Further, on a practical note, most file folders and binders are designed to fit 8½ " × 11" paper.

Newsletters do not contain advertising—other people's, that is. Subscription newsletters survive on their subscription revenue, not advertising. In other words, they are unsubsidized publications, and are priced accordingly. (In contrast, if the *New York Times* contained no advertising, its price would be prohibitive.) A 1987 survey of the publications listed in *Hudson's Newsletter Directory* revealed $95.50 as the average price—not the average exactly, but the median subscription price, since the results of figuring the average would be skewed by the twenty-six newsletters priced at more than $1,000. Tim Baskerville's monthly *Video Marketing Surveys and Forecasts* topped the list at that time at $4,500. The reason newsletters do not take advertising is that if you are charging a hefty price for a four- or eight-page newsletter, you are defrauding your subscribers if you devote even an inch to someone else's ad. Further, to some people, your editorial content will be considered more reliable because of the absence of advertising. And there just isn't that much space available for both editorial and advertising material. However, there is no reason why a newsletter can't enclose additional sheets advertising books, seminars, or other products related to the subject matter. In fact, this can be a service to the reader. Certain chamber of commerce–type publications do take small ads from community businesses, but this is an exception.

Newsletters, unlike magazines, do not have covers. They rarely have more than twelve to sixteen pages. Again, there are exceptions. Sometimes you have to apply a negative test. Ask yourself whether the publication is clearly a magazine or a tabloid newspaper. If so, it can't be a newsletter. Occasionally, however, someone will bind fifty pages into a cover and call it a newsletter. Such compilations cannot fulfill the functions of a true newsletter.

Many newsletters are written like letters—all the way across the page—a style known as full measure. Others are divided into two columns. Either way is suitable for typewriter composition, but if you aspire to three columns, the newsletter should be set in type and headlines placed above the stories. At this stage you have moved from the "pure" newsletter format into a hybrid publication, too small to be termed a newspaper or a magazine. Some people call these "magaletters." Magaletters are more frequently found in the nonsubscription category, where the emphasis is more on "news" than on "letter."

There are also highly technical publications that come in loose-leaf form, $8\frac{1}{2}" \times 11"$, designed to be filed in binders for reference. These are called binder services. Although they differ from typical newsletters, they are sold by subscription and so belong, in this sense, in the newsletter field.

Whatever their physical appearance, there is one unifying characteristic of newsletters: *they provide specialized information.* They are informal publications, created to serve designated audiences or universes rather than a mass audience. Many times the audience served is a narrow segment of a universe that wants information in depth. For instance, the universe might be engineers; the audience, electrical engineers. We are really, then, talking about specialized information as opposed to the general information provided by the mass media.

There are four principal categories of newsletters.

Subscription Newsletters

Investment Letters   These are sometimes called "investment advisories" or "market letters." The term clearly defines the audience—investors and business people in finance. Some are purely statistical, heavy with charts and graphs; others are forthright and opinionated. Advisories rise and fall with the market. At this writing, mutual funds are dominant. The largest letter by far is *Mutual Fund Forecaster,* 260,000 circulation. Other major investment letters with estimated circulation: *Value Line,* 120,000; *Personal Finance,* 100,000; *Ruff Times,* 80,000.

Business Letters   These make up the bulk of the subscription newsletters and help meet the increasing need of business for information. They provide this information much more cheaply than each company could on its own. In the past much of this data was obtained through trade magazines (specialized publications in various aspects of business). At the end of the 1960s, when advertising revenues for trade magazines declined, publishers started to shift to newsletters. The publishers had the editorial background and could repackage their information into the small, easy-to-produce newsletter format. Today newsletter editors and publishers are considered experts in their own right and, as mentioned earlier, are quoted more and more as sources by the mass media.

Business newsletters embrace a wide variety of specialized interests, such as economic conditions, finance, chemicals, environment, and publishing. A special category of business letters is Washington-based and follows the activities of the federal government in all sorts of special fields and regulations. The *Kiplinger Washington Letter,* for instance, specializes in telling business people about government actions that affect them. It also has a circulation larger than most, 425,000.

Consumer Newsletters These are aimed at a large, general audience and cover subjects with a broad appeal, yet again provide specialized information. Examples (those having a circulation of more than 200,000) are the *Contest News-Letter,* which gives information on contests and tips on winning them; *Growing Child,* aimed at parents of children up to the age of six; the *Harvard Medical School Health Letter,* one of many on health. There are also many newsletters about travel, cooking, and restaurants.

Affinity Newsletters These are a variation of consumer newsletters and link together disparate groups that share a passion or an interest, such as stamp collecting, needlework, or skiing. *The Avant Gardener* is one such newsletter whose title readily comes to mind.

Probably the ultimate affinity letter is the one directed to members of particular families. *Hilborn's Family Newsletter Directory* lists over 1,500 families publishing newsletters on their own family name, history, and genealogy. Montreal-based Robin Hilborn says, "Back in 1978 I started my own family newsletter, the *Hilborn Family Journal,* which still sells well at $12 a year to 130 family members near and far." He told me his research over the years turned up hundreds of other people, almost all amateurs, doing the same thing, publishing their own family newsletters—mostly for love and curiosity but some for money. Hilborn turned his research into the *Directory.*

Instructional Newsletters These are more like correspondence courses or serialized self-help books. Examples are newsletters provided by employers for their clerical workers telling them how to be more efficient, and a series of letters on interior decorating. The series has usually been prepared in advance. Whenever you subscribe, you start with issue number one while your neighbor may now be receiving issue number twenty-one.

Nonsubscription Newsletters

Association Newsletters   These are published by various trade and professional associations for their members. Their cost is usually included in members' dues. Sometimes there is a subscription price for nonmembers. Occasionally large associations, such as the American Banking Association and the American Hospital Association, have a number of newsletters for which they charge for subscribing. These usually represent specialties of interest to only a fraction of the memberships.

Organizational Newsletters   These include publications of labor unions, government, and the country's many nonprofit organizations, such as churches, civic groups, service clubs, and citizen organizations—on local, regional, and national levels. The numerous health and education organizations in the United States are heavy users of newsletters to keep their donors and volunteers informed.

Corporate Newsletters   Thousands of corporations publish newsletters—internally for their employees and externally for their customers, stockholders, and sales prospects. In order to attract readers, many of these newsletters put great store in graphic design, often utilizing four-color art and photography, the megaletter or tabloid format, and coated paper stock. Rarely do these publications have a subscription price.

Franchise Newsletters   These are also known as syndicated or third-party publications. An example is a newsletter offering information about personal finance that is sold to banks. A bank buys the newsletter in bulk for its customers with the bank's name printed in the heading. Only one such newsletter is franchised in a given geographical area. Since physicians and dentists and other professionals have been allowed to advertise, many of them have chosen the giveaway newsletter as a way to keep in touch with their patients and reach out to new ones.

Public Relations Newsletters   These "uninvited letters" may be sent by a company or an association to prospective customers to tell them about a specific product. The letters are soft sell, providing information to the target audience to make it receptive to learning more about the product.

2 Finding Your Market

A newsletter starts with an idea—either for the publication itself or of an audience to be served. The nonsubscription letter publisher already knows the audience he or she wishes to serve—e.g., stockholders, customers, suppliers, employees, members. So nonsubscription newsletter people need not read this chapter. Instead, they should turn to Chapter 3, which deals with editorial content.

Finding a market is the starting point for the subscription newsletter. While all elements of newsletter operations must be well executed, the single most important success factor is the market. The most beautiful-looking newsletter in the world with the finest editorial content is worthless if no one will buy it. In the newsletter field, subscribers do not buy beautiful graphics and exquisite prose; they buy information. Therefore, you have to find out who wants and will pay for the information you have.

Ten Mistakes to Avoid When Launching a Newsletter Let's take a look at what copywriter and marketing consultant Stephen Sahlein says are the most common mistakes people make when getting into the newsletter business. Avoid these.

1. Desire to get into a new field, which always looks easier than the one you're in. (You usually do best when you remain in a field you know.)
2. "The competition is lousy; we can do a better job."
3. A "problem avoidance" newsletter. (You have the extra task of having to sell the problem.)
4. A "how to" newsletter.
5. Starting a newsletter for the wrong reason, e.g., "We want to get into the newsletter business."
6. You personally love the field.

13

7. Spending money on overhead, editorial, and a promotion package before you see if there are any lists in the field.
8. Going out with a split test before you have eyeballed the list itself.
9. The test brings poor results but you rationalize and go ahead with the launch anyway.
10. Giving the people what they need—that is, what *you* think they need. (To be successful, you must give them what they *want.*)

Using "Hudson's Pyramid"   For a quick understanding of the market possibilities and pitfalls, see Figure 3, which is known as "Hudson's Pyramid" because of its use in my seminars over the past decade. It is a device you may want to use when you study the market for a newsletter.

The pyramid represents all of the adult population in the country. I divide this universe into four sections: business, affinity, organizations, and consumer. (The total numbers of people within the sections are not important. I am simply showing the advantages and disadvantages of these groups as prospects for your newsletter.)

Business   This segment of the pyramid is by far the smallest, a fraction of the entire universe. Yet business is the biggest user of information in the country, so it is no surprise that the preponderance of newsletters is aimed at the business audience. Business feeds on information to survive—technical information, policy trends, marketing, government actions. Companies need to know about anything that can affect their type of business. Big companies, of course, have their own research staffs. But such are the complexities of today's world that these staffs alone cannot keep up with the mountains of information available. They need the help of outside experts, with broader and less partisan perspectives. They get a lot of such expert help from newsletters.

As government becomes more pervasive, businesses must know how events in Washington, D.C., will affect them. The federal government is, in effect, a vast warehouse of information that gets larger every day. All kinds of information can be found in Washington—data on imports and exports, research, scientific experimentation, patents, and, always, statistics in bewildering array. Except for security matters, government data are public property, and the government hires large staffs to disseminate information. The Government Printing Office is the world's largest book publisher, with an output so vast that very few people can keep up with it. And Washington has the largest concentration of journalists in the world—more than 3,700 newspapers, radio and television stations, and

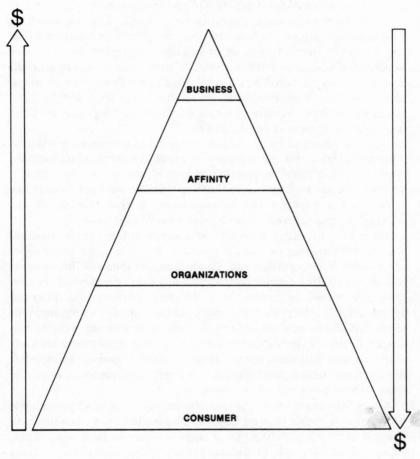

"HUDSON'S PYRAMID"

$

BUSINESS

AFFINITY

ORGANIZATIONS

CONSUMER

$

Figure 3
How various segments of the total universe value information (see text).

periodicals are represented there by more than 3,900 correspondents. However, even with such massive efforts to collect and distribute information, only a fraction of the material ever gets to the public, let alone to the business people who need it most.

This situation is ideal for newsletters, which is why we sometimes call

Washington, D.C., the cradle of newsletters. A Washington newsletter first selects a special field. Then its staff gathers daily material pertaining to that field, gets to know policy-making officials, and translates the information it gathers into terms business people can understand. Much government material is written in infuriating gobbledygook. As one Washington newsletter publisher said, "Our position is secure until the government learns to write in English. But that will not happen in our lifetime, if ever." (The Reagan administration's policies of deregulation, however, took the bloom off the rose for some Washington newsletters that interpreted various regulations.)

You don't have to be in Washington to write a business newsletter, however. There are many segments of business—automotive, banking, chemical, manufacturing, research and development—where pertinent information can be found. Newsletter publishers who are experts can work and live wherever they please as long as they can provide the information and the authoritative advice needed by business.

There are two other attractive advantages in tapping the business market. Take another look at the pyramid (Fig. 3) and the arrow on its left, which points to a dollar sign. This indicates graphically that business will pay more for information than will any other segment of the universe. Also, businesses are sophisticated users of information. They understand that it is hard work to condense a mass of information into four pages that are readily understandable, and they will pay well for this service. Further, a newsletter is a business expense. While there are some obvious limits, businesses are not price resistant. Whatever a newsletter costs, it is less than would be spent by an individual company to get the same information from other sources.

A company bases its buying decision on how necessary the available information is, rather than on its price. You couldn't sell a newsletter to General Motors for $1.50 a year if there were no business need. Thus, selling on price and special discounts is not as prevalent in the business market as elsewhere.

Affinity The next segment of the pyramid represents affinity groups. As mentioned before, these are people from all walks of life—members of the clergy, doctors, housewives, teachers—whose affinity is sharing a passion for a sport or hobby or avocation. For example, there are some 600,000 people interested in scuba diving, half of them serious enough to go somewhere every year to indulge their interest. Travel is another such area, and there are many newsletters covering all its aspects.

There are large markets available in the affinity area. However, they must be examined carefully. First of all, do not confuse this market with the consumer market discussed below. Just because millions of Americans share an interest in, say, football or baseball, that does not make them an affinity group. There are so many people in such groups that mass media are sufficient for their needs; they don't require any further specialized information. Once in a seminar the participants and I examined the possible market for a citizen-band-radio newsletter when CBs first became a craze. It was quickly obvious that this group, while sharing an interest, satisfied its needs with talk, not literature. A successful affinity market, then, is much smaller than the mass market, and its common field of interest must require that it obtain specialized information not otherwise available. Since members of an affinity market usually pay out of their own pockets, they will pay less, as the pyramid shows, than business people, but generally more than consumers with less intense interests.

Organizations These are the numerous business associations, professional groups, and educational and nonprofit organizations in health, education, and social services, fraternal groups, alumni associations, and state and local governments. At first glance, the figures are staggering— thousands of organizations with hundreds of thousands of members, sometimes even millions, as in trade unions. And all of these groups need information. But their needs are less intense than those of the business and affinity groups. Most members already receive information from their organizations in the form of magazines, reports, and newsletters. Few have a burning desire for additional information in their fields, particularly if they have to pay for it. This, too, is indicated on the pyramid.

For the commercial newsletter publisher, then, the key to the organizational market is through the leadership hierarchy. The average member behaves much like those in the consumer group, but the leadership has informational needs similar to business's. These leaders also must know about government actions, about economic and business trends that can affect their organization, and about better ways to operate their group. They buy goods and services and must understand financial planning. So newsletters to education leaders or health care specialists, for instance, can be a fruitful field, as many publishers have discovered. But remember, this market is less willing to pay for information. Revenues come from dues and taxes; since there are sometimes budget squeezes, newsletter publishers in this area are often affected.

Consumer In looking at the pyramid, it's clear that the consumer segment is by far the largest. Actually, it's even larger than portrayed there. The consumer segment also includes members of the business, affinity, and organizational groups when they are not in their daily occupations. This means *everybody*—and it's the group that the mass media have courted throughout their existence. Radio, television, and magazines attract this market in the many millions. Not all of this group likes to read, yet *Reader's Digest* has found 17 million of them who pay for the privilege.

It's understandable that newsletter publishers, having tasted the delight of starting a newsletter at $95 and obtaining 2,000 subscribers in a small market, look to a much bigger market. They dream of a low-priced newsletter that would attract hundreds of thousands of readers out of this vast consumer segment.

Yet until 1982 no consumer letter had reached the circulation of the business-oriented *Kiplinger Washington Letter,* which at the time averaged 556,000 copies. (*Moneysworth* claimed 800,000 subscribers some years earlier, before it converted to a tabloid newspaper taking advertising.) With Roger and Carolyn Tyndall's *Contest News-Letter,* marketing expert Richard Benson not only surpassed Kiplinger in circulation but went on to achieve the first 1 million circulation for any newsletter. Benson pushed *Contest* on toward the 2 million mark and then sold it to McCall's, which now claims 750,000 subscribers.

Only a handful of others have gone beyond a 200,000 circulation— *Growing Child, Harvard Medical School Health Letter, University of California, Berkeley Wellness Letter* (Dick Benson again), and *Mayo Clinic Health Letter,* for instance.

A major obstacle to taking a $5 newsletter into big numbers is the sheer cost of obtaining subscribers. As explained later, many publishers have to settle for a 1 percent return on their promotion mailings. On a $5 item, you'd never get your money back. Of course, if you had lots of money to invest to get into the high numbers, your newsletter might become profitable. But it's not a recommended way to make money.

The reason why the consumer market is generally unattractive for newsletters is shown in the pyramid. Look at the arrow on the right pointing down. It reveals that while the consumer segment is the largest, its members will pay the least. The consumer will pay big money for pleasure—sports, gambling, travel, restaurants, stereos—but puts little monetary value on information. He or she is used to the newsletter *format*—through church bulletins, newsletters from organizations, schools, the chamber of commerce, a bowling league. The consumer reads newsletters as a company employee or a union member. But these newsletters are free. When you ask readers to pay for them, their attitudes may change.

First of all, there is dismay at the price. *You* may think it's low, but the consumer may think it's high. The reaction of an average reader to a monthly four-page newsletter, typewriter-composed, at $24 or $39 a year is one of outrage. He thinks you are trying to defraud him. Unlike the business person, the consumer must pay out of his own pocket and thus is inclined to measure value by the pound. Whereas the person in business is delighted to get information from you in only four pages, the consumer may point out that he can get *Reader's Digest*—more than two hundred pages a month—for something less than $6 or $8, depending on the special offer.

So in dealing with the consumer market we are locked in by the basic function of a newsletter as a small publication, with information in depth, at a relatively high price, uncluttered and unsubsidized by advertising. It is difficult to believe, then, that a newsletter will ever maintain a circulation of 1 million, or that many will get over the 100,000 mark. This may happen through electronic transmission, but that's still down the road.

Is there no way to crack the consumer market? Of course there is. I am simply pointing out that once you stray from the business segment, so ideal for newsletters, you find increasing resistance and more problems to overcome. The one way to reach the consumer market in any degree is not through information per se, but through emotional appeals. In my seminars I sometimes find this statement greeted with disbelief or a feeling that I am overly cynical about humankind. People forget, because they do it so regularly, that most of their buying decisions are made emotionally, not rationally. Aside from the necessities, we react to sales pitches with our viscera, not our minds. Often this can make us terribly resistant, or terribly enthusiastic. Direct mail copywriter and newsletter consultant Stephen Sahlein stresses the point that successful sales are based more on what people *want* rather than on what they need.

Direct mail copywriters learned this long ago. Everything they write has emotional and psychological impact. The most effective appeals are to greed, avarice, fear, or profit, not necessarily in that order. So we can understand why a newsletter telling how to win contests and sweepstakes, or how to make use of supermarket coupons, would have great potential. People worry about their health, so a newsletter on health has an audience. Investment letters, which are also distributed largely to the consumer segment, appeal to people's desire for profit, if not their greed.

And the consumer newsletter *Sex Over Forty,* implying that there may be problems yet offering solutions, has the double enticement of fear and (sexual or personal) profit.

The irony about the consumer newsletter market is that it attracts many people with little capital who want to moonlight by starting a newsletter. They think that, given the millions of people in this country, there must be many thousands who would gladly pay only $5 to $7 for a newsletter. If your aim is to develop a paying hobby, that's one thing. But if your aim is to establish a business, forget it.

The Limited Market/High Price Newsletter versus the Broad Market/Low Price Newsletter   Another step in determining the market for your newsletter is to examine two sharply conflicting concepts of newsletter publishing. They are known as the limited market/high price newsletter and the broad market/low price newsletter. James J. Marshall, a Washington publisher who is biased in favor of the limited market, has prepared an economic model to make his point. He admits that this model is biased, that it is only an exercise and not a real situation. Yet a study of it is instructive. It is a single page that I have reproduced as Figure 4. You should go over it line by line and then ponder the significance of the conclusion.

Pay special attention to each of the four sections. Section A describes three newsletters, with universes in the 10,000, 50,000, and 100,000 range. Newsletter number one is priced high; the other two are low. The frequencies of publication are different—two weekly and one monthly. For purposes of the model, the response rate to subscription mailings is arbitrarily set at 1½ percent. This is not real, but it is reasonable and does not affect the outcome. The next line shows how many more subscribers you can obtain from a large universe. And the last line, income, shows that both number one and number three gross the same; number two, considerably less.

Section B deals with the promotional costs of obtaining the subscriptions. Now we begin to see the benefits of the smaller universe—fewer mailing pieces, hence lower printing, postage, mailing, and list charges.

For example, I visited with a newsletter publisher in Colorado who said he had a universe of 1,000. While many newsletterers have a subscription list of 1,000, based on a universe of, say, 30,000, what can one do with a universe of 1,000? This publisher confounded me even more by saying that actually his universe was nearer 300. But out of this he had more than 50 percent market penetration—160 subscribers to be exact. But no nickel-and-dime business is his. Each subscriber paid $910, with total revenue of $145,600.

A Subjective Look at the
Limited Market at a Higher Price
by
James J. Marshall

A. Newsletter	# 1	# 2	# 3
Universe (potential subscribers)	10,000	50,000	100,000
Subscription price—per year	$250.00	$25.00	$25.00
Frequency	Weekly	Weekly	Monthly
Response rate	1½%	1½%	1½%
# of subscribers	150	750	1,500
Income—per year	$37,500.00	$18,750.00	$37,500.00
B. Promotion Cost (for one mailing)			
Printing	$2,500.00	(3X) $7,500.00	(5X) $12,500.00
Postage	(1st) $1,500	(8.4) $4,200	(8.4) $8,400.00
Mailing charges ($15 per 1,000)	$150.00	$750.00	$1,500.00
List rental ($35 per 1,000)	$350.00	$1,750.00	$3,500.00
Promotion costs	$4,500.00	$14,200.00	$25,900.00
C. Expenses			
Printing	$7,800 ($150 per issue)	$13,000 (250)	$4,800 (400)
Postage	$780.00 (15¢)	$ 5,850 (15¢)	$2,700 (15¢)
Billings ($2 per year)	$300.00	$1,500.00	$3,000.00
Overhead	$10,000.00	$10,000.00	$5,000.00
	$18,880.00	$30,300.00	$15,500.00
D. Total Income	$37,500.00	$18,750.00	$37,500.00
Total Expenses	$23,300.00	$44,500.00	$41,400.00
Profit or Loss	(+)$14,200.00	(– 25,750.00)	(–3,900.00)

Figure 4

It's the money income, not the subscriber volume, that makes the worth of a newsletter. In other words, it is not what's up front that counts, it is what's left in the end.

Section C refers to the costs of producing the newsletter—printing, postage, billing charges, and overhead, which here means editorial costs. Note that number three is the winner in this section. Because it's a monthly, its production costs are much lower and there is not so much editorial time (and cost) involved.

Section D shows the winner. Number one grosses $37,500, spends $23,300, and nets $14,200. Number two grosses only half that, $18,750, and has an immense expense of $44,500 because of its high production costs due to weekly publication (Section C). Therefore, number two has a loss of $25,750. And number three, while having much lower production expense (Section C), cannot use this to advantage because of higher promotion costs and low price. Number three, then, loses $3,900.

Remember that the response rate for each letter is deliberately the same. It is conceivable that number three, with a low price and a large universe, might attract a larger response rate, which would put it into the winner's column. Those are variables that will be discussed later. Meanwhile, when you are considering the business and consumer markets, put your own figures into this model form. It will help you make your decision on facts, rather than gut feelings.

Market Penetration   With business newsletters, you should get 5 percent of your market for subscribers within the first two or three years. This is a realistic objective. Of course you would like more, and some older newsletters have 70 to 90 percent of their markets. But if you can't get even 5 percent, obviously you are not an effective force within your market. I am more confident of this figure in business letters because you can usually get some accurate numbers of the people within your universe. Farther down the pyramid, however, where the universe numbers are larger, it is more difficult to evaluate which lists are truly prospects and which are marginal. When you get to the big numbers of the consumer market, 5 percent of a universe of 5 million sounds great. But it's anybody's guess, usually, whether 5 million represents reasonable prospects for your newsletter.

Evaluating the Market   Once you have selected a market for your newsletter, you must learn as much as possible about its characteristics and behavior. Paul J. Bringe, a direct marketing consultant and himself a newsletter publisher, identified five market types that are suitable for a newsletter audience. Here they are with my comments.

The market is broad and is served by many periodicals but with too much lag between writing and publishing. Some years ago, Joel Frados was working on a magazine that served the large plastics industry. He participated in writing and planning major stories about the field. These would sometimes take months before publication. So he started a weekly newsletter, *Plastics Focus.* He found a welcome reception because he brought his readers the news while it was fresh. Also, whenever he learned of a new development he would check with industry leaders and have a story in print that week, rather than a month later. There have been many examples of such spin-offs of newsletters from magazines. In most cases, the subscriber continues to read the magazine for its more encompassing features while turning to the newsletter for the essentials needed right away.

The market is narrow with few or no periodicals serving it. The reason there are few periodicals in such markets is that their small size makes them unattractive to advertisers. And magazines need advertising. This kind of market is what Jerry Steinman found when he started *Beer Marketer's Insights.* His universe is minuscule compared with many others, but he has managed to saturate it in a way that few other publications have.

The market is professional or semiprofessional, requiring information not generally available elsewhere. Again, we are talking about a market that advertisers spurn, either because of the size or because of the nature of the people or organizations within it. Advertisers want to reach people who need a variety of products and who authorize their purchase. Look for professionals who receive only general information from magazines, find out what information they need that they can't get, and you may have a newsletter.

The market is fast moving, with last week's or last month's information largely useless today. The usual characteristic of such a market is a need for figures and statistics, such as oil prices. McGraw-Hill's *Oilgram* is an example of a newsletter that meets such a need. Such is the demand for immediate delivery of the information that the *Oilgram* is widely received by computer.

The market is highly specialized with intense interest in the subject within a relatively small group. For such a market, look for people who are in technology, then for some who are specializing within the technology. The many newsletters in the electronic and computer field are examples.

Your Newsletter Premise and Positioning   At the beginning of this chapter, I described the kinds of markets available. Obviously, you are examining markets because you have a newsletter idea and you want to know where it will fit. George Wein, of Select Information Exchange, which serves the newsletter field, prepared a paper on this problem several years ago. To answer the question of whether your newsletter premise is basically correct, he says you must first answer satisfactorily a variety of questions. Here are some of them.

Will the newsletter be generally acceptable to prospective subscribers?
What kind of information are prospective subscribers seeking?
How much money will they pay to get it?
Who exactly would use the newsletter?
What are they like?
What income class are they in?
What are the uses of the newsletter?
What are the buying habits of the prospective subscribers?
Will they buy through direct mail and mail order solicitations?
Do they buy multiple subscriptions?
Who makes the buying decision? The treasurer of a company or the president? A husband or wife?
What is the direct competition for the newsletter?

Wein warns against launching a new newsletter unless it has a real point of difference that can be perceived by the prospective subscribers. He concedes that if a particular market category is rapidly growing, such as the energy field, or has very few newsletters covering it, it is possible to introduce a "me too" newsletter successfully, but the risks are great. He notes that *Moneytree* and *Money* made it after *Moneysworth* grabbed some 700,000 subscriptions from that market. However, he says, this market was unusually large and its readers unusually hungry for that type of information.

Other questions that should be answered about the newsletter premise are

Why should prospective subscribers want to buy your newsletter?
What advertising media are available?
In which magazines and newspapers could the newsletter be successfully advertised? Are they good mail order media? How large are their circulations?
Could the newsletter be advertised on radio or television?
How many good mailing lists are available for rent?
What size are the mailing lists?
Will you have to compile your own mailing lists?
What type of advertising appeals and presentations work best for the newsletter?
What price can you charge?

Satisfactory answers to these questions are essential, says Wein. If your newsletter premise is incorrect, all the promotional and business expertise in the world will not make the newsletter successful.

Positioning Your Newsletter   According to Wein, the next step is positioning—the process by which you determine the answer to the question, What is it about your newsletter that you want your prospective subscribers to perceive? Positioning is at the center of any successful advertising campaign. Here are some examples he gives.

The Newsletter Itself   The design and graphics of your newsletter, what you say in it, and how you say it will help position your newsletter, expressing both its promise and your personality.

- Make sure your newsletter meshes with the personality you are trying to build for it.
- Make your newsletter reflect the wants of your prospective subscribers.
- Put your advertising promise at the helm of your newsletter in the same words your advertising uses.
- Don't skimp on design and graphics. Eventually you are going to invest in them anyway—so why not do so at the beginning?

The Newsletter Name   A good name will also help position your newsletter and spell out its promise, as well as reinforce your advertising.

- Choose a name that helps position your newsletter, for example, *Moneysworth* rather than *The Ginsberg Letter,* or *Newsletter on Newsletters* rather than *The Hudson Letter.*
- Put your advertising promise in the name, again like *Moneysworth.*
- Make the name memorable, again like *Moneysworth, Moneytree,* or even *Money.*
- Choose a name that identifies the newsletter subject quickly. Don't pick a name that is so vague that it could apply to almost anything.
- Choose a name that is easy to pronounce.

Again, the name is extremely important in selling newsletter subscriptions and a lot of thought should be given to choosing it. Watch out for negative connotations in the name, or you might turn off prospective subscribers. You might consider testing two or more names before you actually proceed.

Remember that names should be descriptive. If you can't think of something both clever and descriptive, settle for something descriptive. There must be at least twenty newsletters named *Impact.* Impact on what, or for whom? Magazine-type names like *Life* and *Look* don't belong in newsletters. You want your prospects to know what field you are covering. In the field of energy newsletters, it is becoming increasingly difficult to choose an original name because it's essential that the word "energy" be prominent. Thus there are *Energy Analects, Energy and Housing Report, Energy and Mineral Resources, Energy Conservation Digest, Energy Conservation News, The Energy Daily, Energy Design Update, Energy d'Etente, Energy Forecaster Report, Energy Pricing News, Energy Regulations Report, Energy Report, Energy Research, Research Bureau Letter, Energy Research Reports,* and *Energy Today.* (Note, if you are interested in being quickly identified in an index, that these newsletters' *key* words are also their *first* words.) Consider the names of some of the older, established newsletters, such as *Television Digest* or *Telecommunications Reports.* The emphasis is on description, not cuteness. Perhaps my favorite name is from Business Publishers, Washington, D.C., which has a host of environmental newsletters. It is called simply *Sludge.* Now, that's impact!

The Journalistic Approach versus the Marketing Approach   The journalistic approach is to pick a topic that you know well, or perhaps have already written about, figure out how to develop it into newsletter format, and then find a segment of a market you can serve. Many fine newsletters have started this way. The journalist, however, is not trained in marketing and management. Journalists must either learn the business side or find a partner who is an expert. Most journalists don't like business details but many succeed in learning.

One successful publishing formula is a combination of a journalist and a business type (editor and publisher) with fifty-fifty ownership and fifty-fifty sharing of profits. It is a simple division. In magazines and newspapers, which sell advertising space as their major means of support, three major departments are needed: editorial, circulation, and space sales. Also needed are substantial supporting departments for sales promotion, printing, production, and accounting.

A newsletter needs only two major departments, editorial and circulation. Production is simple, so the editorial department can handle it. Bookkeeping can be done by the circulation department. If the editor does not want to collaborate with another person, he or she can hire an outside agency or a free-lancer to assume the circulation and business duties.

The marketing approach is just the opposite of the journalistic approach. You look for a market where you think a newsletter would be welcome. Then you develop such a newsletter, and if necessary, hire a journalist to do the editorial duties.

Either way, you follow the same procedure in finding the market.

How to Determine Whether There's a Market for Your Newsletter The first thing to look for is other publications, particularly newsletters, that may be serving your market. The fact that a trade newspaper or magazine is in the market is not necessarily a deterrent. As noted earlier, newsletters function differently from the more traditional publications. If you conclude that a newsletter can coexist with other publications, find out if you can obtain mailing lists of the subscribers to the other publications. Usually there are ways, but you must be sure.

What if you find other newsletters? Competition is not necessarily bad. The relatively small field of public relations is served by four newsletters, all of which appear to prosper. They all have their special approaches to the subject. What seem to be small differences can be important to readers. This is why so many supermarkets in a community, which seem to sell the same goods at similar prices, can flourish. In a major area such as energy, there are hordes of newsletters. Such are the stakes that business people in the field feel they must protect themselves with every bit of information offered. Newsletters are noted, of course, for the swiftness with which they cover a new market that demands serious information. The months following the outbreak of Acquired Immune Deficiency Syndrome in the United States saw the launch of *AIDS Alert, Executive AIDS Watch,* and *AIDS Policy & Law*—followed within the year by *The AIDS Record, CDC AIDS Weekly,* and *AIDS Prevention.*

Once a field diminishes in importance, however, there will be a shakeout. While competition isn't always a disadvantage, it must be studied carefully. There have been various newsletters over the years that have tried to imitate Kiplinger, but their names have been forgotten. It is important when entering a field that is heavily populated to calculate what share of the market will content you and how much money you need to spend to get that share.

What if there is no competition? You have to find out why. If you're operating on a shoestring, you may find the niche you are seeking by being there first. But the larger publisher is wary. He wants to see other footsteps in the forest and he wants to know what happened to those who entered before him.

Finding Your Universe The word "market" has various shades of meaning. What you are really seeking is what I call your universe—the number of people who appear to be reasonable prospects for your newsletter. Here you must start dealing with specifics. It is not enough to say that your newsletter is aimed at people who are interested in money. You have to find these people by name and address. Here is where mailing lists are essential. *In fact, if you can't get names and addresses of actual people in your field of interest, you do not have a universe.* Some years ago, a very bright man started a newsletter entitled *Home Office Report.* Its purpose was to provide useful material to people who had offices in their homes. He knew there must be a lot of them, perhaps millions. But he did not know who they were. He started by writing a book on the subject. He advertised it and sold quite a few copies. These buyers became the basis of a list. But he still couldn't find the many others. Even when he walked up and down the streets, he couldn't determine which house had an office inside and which didn't. So he began to advertise with small space ads, offering three issues of his newsletter for $1. He got responses and these names were added to the list. Eventually he had a respectable universe of fifty thousand names. Only then did he find that the universe was not particularly interested in his newsletter. All of this cost a lot of time and money. However, I said he was bright. He offered his list for rental to other publishers and this was profitable. But he ended up selling the newsletter, which the new owner discontinued in a short time.

On the other hand, if you come up with an idea clearly aimed at lawyers, accountants, chemists, or any one of the numerous categories where good lists can be found, selling your newsletter is much easier.

Tips on Locating a Universe
- To find out if there are other newsletters in your field, consult the latest edition of *Hudson's Newsletter Directory.* (See the Bibliography for the address of this and other publications discussed in this book.) This lists approximately 3,400 subscription newsletters divided into subject categories. Even though no directory is 100 percent accurate, this is the single best way to find out about possible competition.
- As a further check on who is covering your field, consult the latest edition of *Ulrich's International Periodicals Directory.* This contains some 70,750 entries—mainly magazines. Like *Hudson's Newsletter Directory,* it is divided into subject categories. It won't take long to get an understanding of what is offered to people in your universe. *Bacon's Publicity Checker* is also useful because it lists only the most prominent of the publications in each industry.
- Get a copy of the Standard Rate & Data Service's *Direct Mail List Rates & Data.* This contains descriptions of more than 100,000 mailing lists that are available. Look in your area to see what is obtainable. Also, become familiar with the offerings of various list brokers, list management firms, and compilers of lists. They, too, will help you to understand your universe. Some of their catalogs will provide the

number of names available in every Standard Industrial Code (SIC). These codes were developed by the U.S. government as the official descriptions of the categories within industries. For instance, SIC 2000 stands for food and 2011 for meat-packing plants. A study of the quantity within these categories can pinpoint segments of an industry that might be large enough to be served by a newsletter.

- The Standard Rate & Data Service also publishes *Business Publication Rates & Data* and *Consumer Magazine Rates & Data.* These list all magazines published according to subject or industry. If you want sample issues, apply to the magazine's advertising department, for you might well want to advertise your newsletter in the magazines in your field. You will receive the advertising rate card and research material on the industry with the sample, including major companies and executives.
- Check Gale's *Encyclopedia of Associations* to find out which trade associations serve the industries you are researching, for many of these provide useful information to their members.
- After you have a better understanding of these specifics, you may want to make an informal survey of some of the companies within your universe. Select two hundred at random and send them a short questionnaire. Ask what they are now reading. Ask what kinds of information they want that they are not getting from these publications. You will not get a tremendous response, but you will get valuable clues. Or you may want to make a telephone survey.
- Subscribe to a clipping service to find out what is now being said in print about your subject area. Or engage a data base research company such as FIND/SVP, a division of the Information Clearing House, which can produce a bibliography of your subject area.
- Finally, when you have located your universe and you have learned what competing publications are in it, you might consider the merits of acquiring one or more of these newsletters rather than starting your own. Perhaps the present owner wants to sell.

When you are doing your research, don't be biased. Look for the facts, pro and con. It is a mistake to assume when you go into a new market you will get a precise answer—either you will receive lots of subscriptions or your effort will flop. If it flops, you will simply cut your losses by abandoning all further efforts. However, it is more likely you will get a mixed response that will keep you hanging on month after month. You can reduce the chance of this happening by doing good initial research in your universe.

3

Managing Your Editorial Content

What to Do Before You Start to Write Your Newsletter Your first step is to define your editorial content. Take a large pad of paper. Write down short items describing the kind of editorial material you will publish. Think of unique characteristics wherever possible. Lay out boundary lines—you will cover these areas, you will never cover other areas. Describe what you will treat differently from others covering your field. Put down the sources you will use for obtaining your news. Develop an editorial posture—whether you will advocate, dissent, or remain objective regarding your chosen field.

When you get through, you ought to have twenty-five to fifty items on your list. Make a photocopy and put it in a folder marked "Subscription Promotion." (You will find out why in Chapter 7.) Now go over your list again and try to make a short statement of purpose for your newsletter, perhaps twenty-five words. (If you can't describe your newsletter in twenty-five words or fewer, maybe it's not a good idea in the first place.) Keep this close to you until you know it by heart. It will be invaluable when you are describing your newsletter to other people, such as employees, or in news releases you send out about your newsletter. Your overall list will doubtless keep changing; it should not be engraved in marble. Eventually, it will become a policy guide that your editors will use in coming years. And it will be the basis of your advertising promises.

The importance of this first step can best be seen in the sad experience of a major newsletter publisher a few years ago. The publisher, through research, found an area of a large industry that was not being covered by the dominant publication in the field. Research revealed that many people in the industry had noted the gap and were eager to have someone fill it. The newsletter publisher rushed into production. An editor was hired and told to produce the first issue. The promotion department went to work on a mouth-watering letter and a large mailing was made to the target audience. The response exceeded their greatest expectations. Many people sent in checks. There was an enthusiastic emotional response from others who telephoned their orders. Elated, the publisher pushed forward the launching date and out went volume one, number one. Again there was an immediate and also emotional response, but this time it was negative. Subscribers were outraged. They demanded their money back. They used harsh language. They claimed the newsletter they received did not live up to the promise of the promotional letter. The publisher, in his haste, paid little attention to the editorial content and didn't realize that the editor had gone off in another direction and missed the entire concept. The newsletter had to be killed on the spot.

Since it is the promotion material, and not the newsletter, that attracts new subscribers, the editor must understand what new subscribers perceive the newsletter to be and what they want. One way to do this is to send potential subscribers a questionnaire asking their interests and what other publications they read.

If the publisher wants to make sure the editor is on the right track, he should ask him or her, as an exercise, to write a promotion letter. This will reveal what the editor perceives to be the central points of the newsletter and will help the publisher resolve any misunderstandings.

This same lesson on making sure that editorial content fulfills the publisher's promises applies to every type of newsletter. A person who wants to start a newsletter for employees or association members usually has to get approval of a board. If you are in this position, be enthusiastic about what the newsletter will accomplish, but be sure you can deliver. The board will judge the final result on your promise.

Where Will You Get Your Material?   You have information in mind when you plan your newsletter. Make sure that you have a plan for getting a regular supply. If yours is a digest publication, you need to subscribe to the various publications that you will digest. Ask companies in your field to put you on their press release lists. Send an item to *PR Aides' Party Line* newsletter describing your subject area, and you will receive additional news releases from people in the field. If yours is a Washington letter, you may want to subscribe to a messenger service that will pick up government releases from agencies important to you. If there are books in your field, buy them and keep them close at hand. Don't be caught on deadline with an essential fact missing so that you have to go to the library. Have a supply of good reference books and a reliable dictionary on hand. Above all, keep in touch with your readers and let them guide you to stories.

An imaginative editor can often find a gold mine of information in the special reports that association and company committees prepare. Many readers don't have time to review such reports in detail. A brief summary in a newsletter can be helpful and can signal the availability of a report to those who need to go through it in detail.

Speeches by members of an association or by authorities in a particular field can provide newsletter copy. The editor should also be on the alert for books, pamphlets, and reports from different sources that could be helpful to readers. The newsletter should tell where copies are available and the cost, if any.

I mentioned clipping services earlier in connection with your market research. They can also provide useful material in your subject and let you know what is being written around the country in the field. When subscribing, you give the clipping service some key words in your subject area. The service will send you clippings of stories in newspapers and magazines in which these words appear. Since you pay per clip, be as specific as possible. If you are writing about property insurance, specify this rather than just insurance, which will produce more clips than you need.

Focus groups are sometimes used when seeking a market or in establishing editorial content. Various advertising agencies and research organizations can provide the service. A group of people in your subject area is formed (they are paid for their services) and a professional discussion leader asks questions and gets suggestions of needs for editorial coverage. You, as client, can sit behind a one-way mirror to observe and listen. You are also given a transcript of the discussion. Some newsletter producers who have used this technique say that it is useful but caution not to accept the findings 100 percent.

Can You Use Material From Other Publications?   The general answer is yes—but with caution. The last thing you want to be involved in is copyright infringement, which could make you liable for damages. First, brief yourself on the general regulations. One matter is very clear— you should not use extensive material verbatim from a copyrighted article or book without permission from the copyright owner, or at least without crediting the original author. Unless you are reviewing a work, which makes your material more "scholarly" or "academic," you should limit the length of any quotation.*

---

*Different publishers have different rules on quoting their copyrighted material. Obviously, quoting 500 words from a 100,000-word work is not as significant as quoting the same amount from a two-page pamphlet. Therefore, if you have any doubts, you should query the publisher.

But this is not what concerns the newsletter editor. What do you do about the newspapers, magazines, and specialized periodicals you read to find out what's going on? All of them are copyrighted. First of all, you wouldn't have much of a newsletter if you merely quoted directly from other publications. Your first use of material from other sources is as a lead for your own stories, which you will write in your own distinctive way. If you borrow an idea from another publication, rewrite it in your style and give your interpretation of the significance of the item to the reader. A basic reading of the copyright law plus some common sense should enable you to stay within the law.

If you need standard illustrations to flesh out your content or for department headings, you can purchase them from *clip-art* services, ready for reproduction. There are also *cartoon* services and *filler* services.

The 1976 booklet from the TOWERS Club Bookstore *How to Start Publishing Newsletters* recommends getting the annual directory of the Associated University Bureaus of Business and Economic Research, which describes all material pertaining to business and industry published by various business administration schools. It also suggests *The Monthly Catalog of United States Government Publications* and the *Monthly Checklist of State Publications.*

Gershon Fishbein, *Environews,* Washington, D.C., has some specific views on gathering material:

In terms of editorial content and approach to coverage, newsletters operate somewhat differently from newspapers—and ex-newspapermen often find this hard to learn. (I had typical withdrawal symptoms after years with the *Washington Post* and AP and had to unlearn some old tricks and learn some new ones.) You simply can't sell a newsletter (for $60, $70, or $100 and up) with news which is nothing more than a rehash of what's in the daily papers. You must go on the assumption that your readers also have access to the papers; because you are addressing an "inside" audience with daily responsibilities in the field you cover (unlike the general public), your stories must talk directly to that need. That means either exclusive stories which nobody else touches or shooting angles on significant stories in the dailies.

That doesn't mean those deadly "how-to" stories which clutter the trade magazines. (One thing guaranteed to send a newsletter publisher into anaphylactic shock is to compare his product with a trade publication!)

A newsletter also covers the news differently. Press conferences are generally a waste of time for newsletters. They're primarily for the dailies and wire services with tight deadlines, and rightly so. Newsletters should mop up later with interviews and think pieces.

New York newsletter publisher Samuel Grafton offers these pointers:

- *Read many Sunday newspapers.* They have many wonderful stories about people. When you find a story in your field, call the person involved. It'll lead you to your own story.
- *Check out sources in other parts of the country.* Call the local newspapers and find out who the reporters are in your subject matter. They'll gladly help—or if you need something special, pay someone a moderate amount to do a story for you.
- *Utilize the government agencies in Washington.* Start with the public information officer—find out from him or her key people who are expert in your field. They'll help.
- *Use your readers as news sources.* Ask them what they want to know—and get the story for them.
- *Use stringers around the country.* Check with trade associations. Go to conventions. But look for *people* who are knowledgeable and interesting. They will lead you to your story.
- *Do questionnaires of small groups.* Write a story on the findings. People like judgmental questions; they like to rate things. Leave room for comments.
- *Get a group together for a discussion and tape it.* Don't identify the people but use what they say in a story.
- *Don't trust a printed story or release.* Do your own checking and chances are you'll end up with a better story.

Establish a Style   It is up to the editor to establish the style of the newsletter. It can be sober and purely factual; contentious and argumentative; personalized; institutional; controversial (good for any newsletter if it can be brought off successfully); predictive (forecasting trends is a valuable characteristic of many newsletters); "inside" (everyone likes to read "inside" information); interpretative (explaining complicated material in simple form is good for any newsletter); or humorous on occasion (but not at the expense of other people.) There are plenty of options. Just make sure that your choice fits you.

Brian Sheehan, in his book *How to Make $25,000 a Year Publishing Newsletters* (1971), wrote, "Newsletter subscribers prefer facts to unfounded judgments. They like problems solved in print; never enjoy having a problem handed back to them. They admire newsletter editors who take positions, right or wrong, and stick to their guns." Style is so important that Chapter 4 is devoted to the subject.

Establish a Stylebook A stylebook is a compilation of preferred usages covering punctuation, capitalization, forms of address (Mr., Mrs., Ms.), hyphenation, and so on, to ensure that all reporters on a publication's staff follow the same usage. The simplest procedure is to review several newspaper stylebooks, pick one you like, and then add any items that are peculiar to your field.

Develop a Publications Calendar This applies to every newsletter. First, go over the calendar month by month, noting holidays that have a bearing on your editorial content. Every employee letter has to have a Christmas issue, or at least a message. Plan ahead so that you have something pertinent to say, not just the usual banalities. Then go over the calendar from the point of view of the industry you are covering. When is the annual convention? When do many plants take a holiday? Do key people you want to interview have known vacation periods when they can't be reached? When are major decisions on budgeting likely to be made? There are dozens of items that should be noted on your calendar. The editor must make plans and schedules for fitting these seasonal matters into his or her editorial planning.

Hiring and Training Editors and Reporters A newsletter editor should be able to interpret the forces at work that affect a particular trade or line of business or profession and analyze the significance of those forces. The editor can say, in effect, "Here are the facts. From our perspective and from what we learn from people long experienced in our field, this is what these facts mean to you." That can be a most important role, and the newsletter editor who fills it satisfactorily is providing a tremendous service for readers.

Hiring editors is not easy. Of course you will want them to have some experience. Even a college graduate at entry level should have a journalistic background or some writing experience. But a file of clipping books won't guarantee success. Most newsletter publishers find that a trial period of up to six months with no commitment is necessary.

Some publishers advertise for editors in newspapers, a tedious process if there are many replies. Some ask other publishers for suggestions. And some try to hire people away from other publishers.

Wayne Kelly, *Congressional Quarterly,* Washington, D.C., provides a writing test for prospective employees. He has learned that many good reporters can't write a newsletter. McGraw-Hill, which hires on a six-month trial basis, has found that one in three will not make it. It will be well worth your effort to take the time to hire good reporters and editors.

As to training, Albert Warren, *Television Digest,* Washington, D.C., advocates several steps. Give new employees plenty to do—show them that you expect a lot from them. Train new reporters to deal with top people when going after stories. Encourage reporters to lunch with their sources and to read avidly.

Eric Easton, *Business Publishers,* Silver Spring, Maryland, expects one editor to handle a weekly or two biweeklies.

The late Ed Brown, ATCOM, Inc., New York, had twelve newsletters. He personally wrote the first ones, then added editors. They both report and write—and are trained to write from the position of the reader, always as advocates. He looked for self-starters with enthusiasm and a good attitude.

The Free-Lance Editor as Entrepreneur   Many newsletter publishers find that their editorial needs can be satisfied by a free-lance editor. Particularly in the start-up phase of a newsletter, it's better to hire a free-lancer who's used to taking chances than to hire a full-time editor who may end up without work if the newsletter fails. Also, there are many newsletters that do not need an editor on the staff every day of the working year. By hiring a competent, professional free-lancer, the management or publisher gets the job done for less money than by taking on a salaried editor and more satisfactorily than by asking a secretary to take on the work as a second duty.

A free-lance editor can build a business by writing newsletters for others. There are many opportunities available because of the vast number of companies, associations, and organizations that use newsletters or would like to start one. To be successful, the free-lancer must understand all aspects of newsletters.

To start such a business a free-lancer should begin by developing a prospect list of companies that might use a newsletter. Then launch a campaign to get appointments with big executives in those companies. Be prepared to demonstrate what can be accomplished by the newsletter (employee morale, sales leads, goodwill for the company, regular communication to customers, and so on). You must be able to show samples to indicate what the newsletter might look like, and to discuss production and printing and mailing lists. And the free-lancer must put it all together in a package with a reasonable price tag.

I started such a service in New York in the 1960s under the name Newsletters Unlimited, and soon had more business than I could handle. If you learn the shortcuts and can work faster than the client thinks you can, it can be a rewarding business. One negative aspect, however, is that some clients, once they see what you have accomplished for them and how you did it, will replace you with the boss's nephew who just graduated from journalism school. However, there are always plenty more prospects for the enterprising free-lancer.

One person who has written about this facet of the newsletter field is Gerene Reid, who published an eighty-six page booklet, *How to Write Company Newsletters,* in 1985. "Everyone agrees that company newsletters lift the morale of the employees, encourage the sales force, and build goodwill among customers," she writes, "but everyone also seems to feel that writing a regular newsletter is a tremendous chore . . . one that's better postponed indefinitely than begun. They're right about the first consensus—but the second one is all wet. Most of my freelance income is earned writing company newsletters, and if it really were drudgery, you can bet I wouldn't have continued it for over ten years."

Her observations coincide with my experience, not only with companies, but also with associations and nonprofit organizations. Both sides can only gain when a competent free-lancer takes over as editor.

What Pay and Benefits Should You Offer?   There are going rates for journalists in all communities and you'll have to find out what they are. A survey made by the Newsletter Association in 1985 showed the average salary of executive editors to be $39,394. Other editors averaged $27,012. Reporters averaged $17,977. In New York and Washington the rates were higher. And there were major differences between large and small publishers. Although these figures are already out-of-date and will continue to change, they do indicate what newsletter journalism can pay.

Benefits vary from company to company. If you work for a large association or corporation, there will be experienced personnel directors who will help with your hiring and allocation of benefits. However, be prepared to defend the worth of your editors and reporters. Personnel people used to hiring engineers, for example, may want to downgrade editors below the going rate in the community.

Most employees expect insurance and pension benefits. If you are a sole owner, you should investigate a pension plan for your own needs. It will shelter profits and the additional amount for employees may not be burdensome.

William H. Wood was a strong proponent of sharing ownership. As he developed newsletter after newsletter (eventually forty-one) he became aware how dependent he was on his editors. The one thing he wanted to avoid was a good editor's moving on to another company. So if an editor performed well in his first two years, Wood gave him 5 percent ownership and told him to start thinking of the newsletter in ownership terms. He would not oversee the editor day by day but would be available for advice. The editor's share increased over the years and could eventually reach 45 percent.

Some Special Comments About Nonsubscription Newsletters Most of the above advice on editorial input applies to all newsletters. However, some additional comments may be helpful in particular to editors of association, organization, and corporate letters.

If an association or professional society is to justify its existence, it must continually communicate with its members. A newsletter mailed weekly, every two weeks, or monthly can be a logical and efficient way of doing that. Association members generally are busy people. If they receive too much information in too bulky a form, they will be discouraged from reading it; the longer the letter, the less likely that it will be read through with interest. Association members whose organization sends a well-prepared, concise, thoroughly edited newsletter will never be caught by surprise when something big happens in their business or profession or when there is a major development in government, politics, or an industry that has an impact on their own field. They will have been alerted in advance to trends.

Although not universal, the number one problem for these editors is getting clearance from a supervisor. Unless a workable procedure is established, the editor will probably fail and resign or be fired. It is a peculiar trap. The management will state when it wants a newsletter to be issued. It will also insist that someone in top management, often the chief executive, approve the copy. Yet when the editor shows up with the finished copy, the executive will sometimes delay and delay, because of other "more important" duties. There is only one solution. The editor must insist on a definite time for clearance or get the authority to take full responsibility without clearance, risking the consequences if there is a serious error. If the editor is good, the risk is minimal. And such an editor will have a better future.

How do you persuade your management to give you this authority? Point out that newspapers and magazines have this problem every day. Can you imagine the *New York Times* holding the presses for a week while the editor waits outside the publisher's office? Establishing a procedure with top management will take a careful presentation on the editor's part. It will not be easy. But if the editor cannot obtain the clearance procedure he desires, he might as well quit. If there are complaints about the letter's not going out on time, management will not accept culpability; it will blame the editor. Getting fired later rather than sooner is not much of a choice. Face up to the situation at the start. If you still don't believe this, start reading the *Ragan Report,* a newsletter for the nonsubscription editor. Issue after issue is filled with complaints from unhappy editors who have not learned to handle this reality.

Test Your Editorial Effectiveness—a Readership Survey If you really want to find out what your readers think of your newsletter, ask them. It is often said that the subscription newsletter doesn't need this kind of survey, since a subscriber's decision at renewal time is enough of an indicator of the newsletter's success. Still, this kind of negative response doesn't give any clues as to what you may be doing wrong. A readership survey can be helpful for all types of newsletters.

Many editors fear that such a survey would elicit so many negative responses that the newsletter's future would be jeopardized. Walter Anderson, who was a business communications authority, claimed this fear is unfounded. A survey he made of one hundred readership surveys showed that response, in fact, is mostly favorable. But the important point is that many readers also say what they would like more of and will rate the contents in order of usefulness. Such specifics will be of immense value in shaping future issues—and the overall favorable comments will be reassuring to the publisher or management. The survey should be mainly multiple choice with a few open-ended questions for the more articulate readers.

Robert Baker has also written about readership surveys in *Impact* (no. 236, 1981). He approves of the device but gives this warning: "A survey is not likely to spawn new ideas or unusual approaches. It is more likely to discourage editorial boldness, provide an excuse for mediocre performance. Editors must be creative spokesmen capable of developing and expressing opinions of their own in keeping with publication objectives. They can't function exclusively as a parrot of suggestions offered by others. The new idea, the unusual approach, attract readership often because they are new and unusual."

I caution against doing prepublication surveys. There are those who think the way to start a newsletter is to ask potential readers what they want. This approach is doomed because most readers don't know what they want. Part of an editor's job is to know what readers want. Also, if after studying the potential audience, an editor still doesn't know, he won't last long.

Proofreading People who are good writers or editors are not necessarily good proofreaders. If you can afford a trained proofreader, it's a good investment. If you have to proofread yourself, have another person read to you, line by line. Or if you have to do the proofreading alone, stand up at your desk and read out loud. This is not infallible, but it will help you to concentrate. If you think this posture makes you look foolish, think how foolish you'll look with a big error in the headline. Incidentally, professionals recognize that the reader is most likely to notice errors in a headline, in a title, in the first line, in the first paragraph, on the first page, and in the top lines of a new page. These are precisely the places where editors and proofreaders are most likely to miss errors.

If you use word processing and compose directly on a screen, you will have to be even more careful. You have nothing to check against, as you would when you read a proof against a manuscript. Again, it's better to get someone else to read what you have written.

In recent years, *The Editorial Eye* has offered superb advice on proofreading and has published a manual that should be in your reference library, *Mark My Words: Instruction and Practice in Proofreading,* by Peggy Smith. If you have a word processor, get a spelling program for it, which will indicate at the push of a key which words may be misspelled.

4

Newsletter Style

Excellence in style as well as editorial content is necessary for the success of any newsletter. If you intend to write a newsletter, remember that there is only one way to achieve a good style—by writing and rewriting. This is true whether you write the newsletter yourself or hire editors and supervise them. Therefore you must establish high standards and enforce them.

Some of the best advice I've seen comes from James M. Jenks, chairman of the Alexander Hamilton Institute, New York, publisher of a number of business newsletters.

How to write in newsletter style. Space availability is the first arbiter of newsletter style. The second is readability. Satisfying one brings only temporary prosperity. Satisfying both is essential to success.

Plunge right into your subject. Limited space allows no introductory or warming-to-the-subject paragraphs. Because brevity is one of the benefits newsletter readers buy, they, too, want to get to the heart of the matter in a quick rather than leisurely fashion. The narrow scope of the newsletter, another of its benefits, has prepared the reader for this kind of treatment.

Use short sentences. Sometimes one-word sentences. Sentences that are not grammatical sentences as these last two. Break long sentences into shorter ones.

Use strong nouns and verbs. Adjectives and adverbs are only helpers to weak nouns and weak verbs. Rather than use helpers, try to find stronger substitutes. You're not forbidden to use adjectives and adverbs. But limit their use.

Use the active voice. Passive? Taboo!

Metaphors? Forget them.

Use you. Remember, you are writing a letter to a reader. That's a singular you and a singular reader.

41

Some forgettable combinations and their substitutes:

Forget	*Use*
in order to	to
along the lines of	like
in case of	if
in the neighborhood of	about
on the basis of	by
with reference to	about
with the result that	so that
from the point of view of	for
for the reason that	since, because
inasmuch as	since, because
in the event that	if

Brevity Is Important but Not Enough   Remember, a newsletter should be a basic, hard-hitting means of communication that gets essential information to the reader in a form that is as concise and clear as possible. Brevity is essential. Editors who add a few more pages to a newsletter by including a lot of superfluous information are defeating the purpose of the publication.

Brevity is also a necessity because of space. The objective of newsletter writing is to make this limitation an asset. However, it's not enough just to condense—the end result should be better readability.

One of the greatest newsletter writers was Howard W. Mort, who wrote a newsletter for the University of Chicago community many years ago. In 1955, in a speech before the Society of Associated Industrial Editors in Omaha, he gave a graphic presentation of how to condense and yet maintain full meaning and readability. Figure 5 is an example of how he boiled down an article by Robert M. Yoder, a well-known journalist of the time with the *Saturday Evening Post.*

Another way to achieve brevity is to avoid redundant phrases. Here are some examples from an article in the newsletter *in black and white* on how to eliminate:

". . . a good variety . . ." (are there bad ones, too?)
". . . circulate around . . ." (where else?)
". . . advance warning . . ." (as opposed to warning after the fact?)
". . . the most unique . . ." ("unique" cannot be qualified—it stands
    alone)
". . . while at the same time . . ." (this is as redundant as "1 P.M. in
    the afternoon")

"HOW TO ACHIEVE READABILITY THROUGH BREVITY"---An Example
(Below, left, is an excerpt from an article "Is There Life After Forty?" Editorial
changes are shown, and the shortened version is to the right).

BEFORE

For some reason or another, and all of
                    40
them good, ~~the~~ age of forty is approached with dread and ~~is~~ a birthday in bold-
                      welcome
face type. Men and women are glad to
              21;
reach twenty-one, men at least like
            30;
reaching thirty, nobody minds being
          38   or
thirty-eight and nobody minds being
      42
forty-two. But forty hangs in the mind

like one of the big turning points, and

not for good, either. Forty sounds

like a turning point the way the fire
                              is
was a turning point for Chicago or ∧ like

a "Road Closed" sign on an auto trip.

That is how you think of forty before

you get there.
                  just   40
Well, the other day I ∧ reached ∧ the Jump-

ing-Off-Place and am now in a position

to report how forty looks from the other

side. I can report that it looks exact-

ly as advertised. Before reaching for-
          it loomed
ty you are likely to think of that birth-
          a
day as ∧ one of life's major division
                          Now
point~~s~~. Upon reaching forty ∧ you are

convinced that forty not only is a divi-

sion point on Life's Journey - why don't

they fix that roadbed? - but probably
it
~~is~~ is where the narrow gauge starts.

AFTER

The age of 40 is approached with dread-
a birthday in bold-face type. Men and
women welcome 21; men at least like 30;
nobody minds 38 or 42; but 40 is like a
ROAD CLOSED sign on an auto trip. That's
before you are 40.

I just reached it and can report it looks
as advertised. Before, it loomed as a
major division point. Now you are convinced it is where the narrow gauge
starts.

Figure 5

". . . extremely clear . . ." (as opposed to murkily clear?)

". . . will be a part of . . . in the future . . ." (could it be a part in the past?)

". . . the state of New Hampshire . . ." and ". . . the month of January . . ." (as opposed to the month of New Hampshire and the state of January?)

". . . starts over again . . ." (as opposed to starting under again or starting over the first time?)

". . . mandatory requirements . . ." (are there optional requirements?)

". . . new innovations . . ." (as opposed to old innovations?)

". . . we reviewed our successes and failures in the past . . ." (as opposed to reviewing those in the future?)

". . . all year round . . ." (which is different from all year square?)

". . . my own personal feelings . . ." (are there impersonal feelings?)

". . . highly complex . . ." (as opposed to lowly complex or simply complex?)

". . . traditionally in years past . . ." (as opposed to future traditions?)

". . . working in conjunction with . . ." (can you work separately with?)

". . . continuing to occur . . ." (this is like "already existing")

". . . successfully obtained . . ." (as opposed to unsuccessfully obtained?)

". . . the criterion was based on . . ." (it's good to have a "starting point to begin with")

". . . mutually supportive of one another . . ." (we need all the help we can get!)

". . . concurrently at the same time . . ." (and also simultaneously)

". . . two brothers from one family . . ." (rejoice over this one!)

". . . advance preparations . . ." (what do they follow after?)

". . . many myriads of colors . . ." (that's how you maximize rainbows!)

". . . revert back . . ." (this can be "reduced down")

"You Can Figure Out What It Says" Is Not Good Enough My friendly representative from the Phoenix Mutual Life Insurance Company sent me the following statements from insurance forms in which drivers attempted to summarize the details of an accident.

- I thought my window was down, but I found it was up when I put my head through it.
- I collided with a stationary truck coming the other way.
- A pedestrian hit me and went under my car.

- The guy was all over the road. I had to swerve a number of times before I hit him.
- In an attempt to kill a fly, I drove into a telephone pole.
- I had been driving for forty years when I fell asleep at the wheel and had an accident.
- My car was legally parked as it backed into the other vehicle.
- An invisible car came out of nowhere, struck my car, and vanished.
- I told the police that I was not injured, but upon removing my hat, found that I had fractured my skull.
- The pedestrian had no idea which direction to run, so I ran over him.

It is possible to discern what the writers are really trying to say in these humorous statements, but they are prime examples of imprecise writing. Newsletters cannot afford such laxity.

Since newsletters deal with straight information—often of a technical nature—and readers often make decisions on the basis of what is printed, there can't be any misunderstanding. Newsletter writers sometimes write their own promotion copy—at the least, they have to approve it—and this kind of writing, too, demands precision. For example, there must be no doubt about the meaning of a special offer. It must be clear whether the same price applies for domestic and overseas readers. A guarantee must be specific in just what is being guaranteed. "Guaranteed satisfaction" is quite different from "money returned if not satisfied." Many errors can be avoided simply by consulting a dictionary. Probably the three most frequently misused word groups in English are *your* and *you're; its* and *it's;* and *their, there,* and *they're.* Make sure you understand the correct use of these words. Misused or misspelled words damage your credibility.

Commonly Misused Words It is much more difficult than it once was to be an accurate writer and editor because of the mass of inaccuracies that surround all of us daily. Many of these imprecisions are proliferated by the daily press. Professor Philip Herzbrun of Georgetown University found that many of his students defended their misuses of language by saying that they had "seen it in the newspaper." He monitored the *Washington Post* and, sure enough, he found seventy-seven improprieties that coincided with those in freshman compositions. Each entry on his list is an example of the obliteration of a distinct meaning that Professor Herzbrun says "must be preserved if sanity is to prevail in the institution of language." As a start, make sure you understand the differences between the pairs of commonly confused words that follow.

THE HERZBRUN LIST
(in alphabetical order, mistaken word first)

abrogated—arrogated
adverse—averse
affect—effect
appraise—apprise
assignment—assignation
avoid—evade
beside—besides
bite—bight
compliment—complement
contemptible—contemptuous
council—counsel—consul
credible—creditable—credulous
defies—deifies
delusion—illusion
demure—demur
depreciate—deprecate
discrete—discreet
dispense—disburse
disprove—disapprove
dissemble—disassemble
distinguished—distinctive
economical—economic
emerged—immersed
eminent—immanent—imminent
enormity—vastness or hugeness
equivalence—equivocation
erring—errant
eruption—irruption
essay—assay
evoke—invoke
exalt—exult
excessively—exceedingly
exorcized—excised
expiate—expatiate
flaunt—flout
forthright—forthcoming
founding—foundering
fulsome—abundant
gentile—genteel—gentle

haul—hale (into court)
historical—historic
hitherto—heretofore
homogenous—homogeneous
imply—infer
indite—indict
inequity—iniquity
Jacobin—Jacobite—Jacobean
libel—liable
loathe—loath
luxurious—luxuriant
martial—marital
mislead—misled
moral—morale
obtuse—abstruse
omnivorous—omnifarious
oppose—appose
parameter—perimeter
peaceful—peaceable
persecuted—prosecuted
persistent—insistent
perspicuous—perspicacious
phase—faze
pour—pore
precipitous—precipitate
preclude—include
predominate—predominant
presently—now
presentment—presentiment
rebound—redound
sanguinary—sanguine
sensual—sensuous
site—cite
slight—sleight
specially—especially
toxin—tocsin
troop—troupe
verbiage—wording

Personalize Your Newsletter   As an editor, you can strengthen the impact of your newsletter by emphasizing "you" rather than "we."

Managements of large organizations like "we." And this is why so many communications from them sound so stuffy and why many people are turned off by them. The reader associates the "we" approach with the universally disliked braggart. When you use the "you" approach, you win the reader over to your side. You get reader involvement. Try to serve your readers. Deal directly with their self-interests.

Why not go a step further and emphasize the "letter" in "newsletter"? The miniature magazine or newspaper is favored in many organizations when reporting on news. But there are lots of areas where you can try the letter approach that Kiplinger pioneered. Each letter starts with "Dear Client" and is signed by Austin Kiplinger. This immediately makes the reader feel that the letter is written personally to him or her. Another good example of this approach is the *Shareholder Newsline* issued by the Sun Company to its stockholders, which replaced a magazine. The immediate favorable feedback to the newsletter format elated the president of the company, and presidents like anything that keeps shareholders happy.

The *Shareholder Newsline* is from a person, not the company. The company logo, a yellow sun, is subordinate to the photo of the writer, Ella W. Wright, director, shareholder relations. Just below the photo is her address and phone number. This newsletter clearly is from "Ella," which is how she signs the four-page letter. Throughout, the words "you" and "I" are used frequently. This makes the letter a truly personal communication, quite unlike the pomposities that emanate from too many corporations.

Ms. Wright reports that the response has been gratifying. Shareholders react in kind to the warmth of her letters, writing to her as "Dear Ella" and signing their own first names. Some tell her stories about how they bought their shares of stock and how they treasure them—all signs that the company is succeeding in its objective of being a collection of people, rather than an impersonal institution. Even large shareholders, "sophisticated investors," have reacted favorably.

Let's Retire "The President's Message" And "The Chairman's Corner" while we're at it. Many newsletters—particularly association, organizational, and corporate ones—set aside the left-hand column of the front page for an innocuous statement by the top person. This device has probably turned off more readers than any other single item. The sad thing is that the top person has a lot of value to say—he wouldn't be at the top otherwise—but far too often, all flavor and personality have been drained out and whatever "message" there was is now too bland to be creditable.

There are two things you can do to make this message significant. The first is to select topics that are *news-oriented,* hence amenable to more facts and less philosophizing. And the second is to put a *news head* on the item. Give the president a byline; run his or her photo if you want. But please, no more bland "president's messages."

Writing in Classic Newsletter Style   The classic newsletter style is often called the "Kiplinger style." Many editors have created their own variations; some have tried unsuccessfully to copy it; and others have developed a style of their own. However it is done, good newsletter writing is terse—it starts with a pointed statement rather than an explanatory, background paragraph. Some editors have learned that after they have written a story, it can often be strengthened by throwing out the first paragraph and leading off with the second.

For those who want to write in the classic way, much study and practice is required, using the *Kiplinger Washington Letter* as a guide. Here are some excerpts from the August 14, 1987, issue, with comments.

A gentle note of caution on interest rates seems to be in order. We think that rates are headed higher for the rest of this year and well into next year . . . something you ought to crank into your plans.

Fairly moderate increases, not another interest rate crisis. Up 1% or so by the middle of 1988, cooling the economy, not choking it.

Perhaps falling later in '88, but that's too far to see now.

(The first line is the so-called sweep line, which is really a topic sentence. It is a one-line statement. The next lines give examples. Your English teacher would say that these are not true sentences, with subject and predicate. Yet there is no difficulty in understanding what is written. These short statements would be no clearer if they were full sentences; they'd only be longer. This is how space is saved.)

A stronger economy is the main reason for expecting higher rates. Not a boom, but enough of a pickup to increase borrowing needs broadly.

(Now we have a specific bit of information. The second line adds a supporting fact.)

Economy will grow about 3% this year and a little more than that in '88. Export gains are the big plus, and business investment will expand too . . . strong points that will offset softness in housing and consumer spending.

<u>Another reason, worse inflation.</u> Probably 4½% to 5% this year, 5% or so next year. Making lenders worry about even steeper increases.

(This technique continues. Note also that the underlining, which substitutes for headlines, calls attention to key points.)

Other examples of the classic style can be found in each issue of *U.S. News & World Report.* David Lawrence, founder of the magazine, was also a pioneer in newsletters. As noted earlier, the magazine contains five newsletters, simulating typewriter type, which have very high readership.

<u>Now as to Underlining.</u> In the above examples, underlining is used to emphasize key phrases. In other cases, it may be used for key groups or important offices, such as <u>Labor, Farmers, Conservatives,</u> and <u>The President.</u> Underlining in these cases is a substitute for capitals or italics in type. Some editors underline the entire first line of a story, making it a kind of headline. Underlining also can substitute for boldface type. Keep in mind, however, that too much underlining can be an annoyance to readers. Caution: With desktop publishing providing a variety of typefaces, some publishers are substituting boldface for underlining. This is unattractive. Italics are the correct substitute.

What If Your Newsletter Is Not in the Classic Mode?   Suppose your design uses two or three columns. You can still adapt some of the classic newsletter techniques. Get as much of your story as possible into the headline. Then move right into your story, and avoid repetition. For instance, too many stories are like this:

HEAD: Henry Jones Elected 1988 President. LEAD: Henry Jones was elected 1988 president at the conclusion of the board of directors meeting.

Change the LEAD to: He praised his predecessor, John Smith, at the conclusion of the board of directors meeting, said he was setting a target of a 25 percent increase in the membership.

In this way, you can preserve the flow of the story and include additional specific information in a short space.

Finally, remember that when you move away from the traditional newsletter format, you will have layout considerations such as story placement, headline size, and continuation of stories on inside pages. Layout designers like to contemplate the overall appearance and then make the material fit their scheme. As editor, try to make the content control the design. If at all possible, avoid jumping stories from one page to another. Using the newsletter formula, you should be able to start and end your stories on the same page. Otherwise your readers may never finish the articles.

As the TOWERS Club monograph on newsletters says, "In writing a newsletter you are in effect writing a series of telegrams, not a series of essays."

Write precisely and to the point. Discard more data than you publish. That's a sign you're winnowing out the nonessential and saving the best for your readers.

Summary   Newsletter writing should be concise, precise, and personal. One point that writers and editors need to keep firmly in mind is that they are not in the business of providing entertainment. Your writing need not be stodgy or dull, but don't be overclever or flippant. Try to use actual examples and case histories. Exercise your editorial voice. Take a stand. Give advice. Inform your reader. But do it all with flair and brevity.

5 Designing Your Newsletter

Where Do You Start? Let's first look at the purpose of design in a newsletter. There seem to be two main schools of thought, both vocal. One group believes that design should receive major emphasis. The other side is hostile to design, graphics, and any mention of the subject.

To the first group I say, you must always remember that your message and how you say it is your first consideration. You should start with the content and not the design. To the second group I say, there's no way in the world you can avoid design. Even a lack of interest in how your newsletter looks is in itself a design decision. Once you have gone beyond a blank piece of paper, have decided to put words in print on that paper, and have added a heading and your address, you have taken the first step toward design.

Some people persist in calling design "art stuff" and say they don't want any part of it. I suspect they are reacting to what I would call "overdesign"—type, layout, and color used so extravagantly that the reader finds it difficult to decipher the words.

In 1972, *The Newsletter on Newsletters* started its annual Newsletter Awards competition to recognize newsletters with successful design. There are five categories for entrants, recognizing the different needs of newsletters: (1) subscription; (2) trade associations; (3) government and nonprofit organizations; (4) internal corporate communications; and (5) external corporate communications.

For the first competition three top graphic arts designers were chosen as judges. The letters soon began to arrive from subscription newsletter publishers. To quote one, ". . . visual appearance and graphic quality are the *least* important characteristics of a successful newsletter." After reading this and other such comments, I thought through my philosophy on newsletter graphics. In the October 1972 issue of *The Newsletter on Newsletters,* I agreed that graphics are the least important characteristic.

51

However, even as "least important," graphics are of some importance—and often neglected. Having reviewed thousands of newsletters which have filtered through this office, we come to these conclusions: 1. Regardless of content, some NLs [newsletters] are more attractive, "more readable" than others. 2. Some typefaces, including typewriter, are more pleasing than others. 3. Some headings express better the subject and flavor of the letter than others. 4. Some headlines and handling of body copy "grab" you more than others. 5. Some color combinations are more inviting than others. 6. Some printing is better than others. The simple 8½ " × 11" format of most NLs is capable of infinite variations. When we speak of graphics for NLs, we are not thinking of coated stock and four color illustrations. We are speaking of doing the most effective job within the given limitations. . . .

Subsequently I added two newsletter publishers to our judging panel to check the editorial content. And then we found what we think is the key word in newsletter graphics—"appropriate." What is appropriate for one newsletter may not be for another. It depends upon the purpose and the audience. Hence *The Newsletter on Newsletters* now uses the following criteria for awards: "overall excellence—superior editorial content enhanced by appropriate design and typography, photographic quality, and printing quality." This is exactly what you should be aiming for in your newsletter.

There is, of course, a justification for subscription newsletters to be less interested in graphics. The subscription newsletter is primarily interested in subscribers; once the sale is made the reader is going to read the newsletter for its information, not its appearance. The nonsubscription newsletter, on the other hand, is "uninvited"; the reader did not ask for it.

Design techniques can help attract attention and recognition. Just the same, I think you can go overboard on design to the exclusion of good content and sprightly writing—just as I think that some subscription letters get a little careless in their appearance.

Possibilities for greater interaction of content and graphics have been broadened dramatically as a result of the desktop publishing revolution. At no time has it been easier and more cost-effective to produce camera-ready pages in-house. This will have a tremendous impact on the newsletter industry today and in the future as the technology improves and costs decline.

Hardware and software technical capabilities of today's personal computer systems seem ready-made for newsletters, whether for the one-person operation or the multinewsletter publisher. There seem to be applications to suit all needs. This is especially true for publishers who already have a personal computer for other business functions. In most such situations the existing system can be modified with additional software to produce text and graphics.

On the other hand, the maze created by the choices and options encountered upon first exposure to this technology is mind-boggling to those who have decided to take advantage of the vast new opportunities. Many newsletter editors think they can solve all their design problems with desktop, while many designers resist moving away from the comfort of more traditional (and evidently more costly) methods of production.

I think profit and cost objectives of both groups can be served by using the new technology. The key to successfully implementing desktop advances in newsletter publishing can be found in closer working relationships between editors and designers. They should collaborate from the very outset of the creative process when developing a newsletter. The decisions made at the critical time will enable the available selection of tools for production perform best for you.

The layout and production capabilities offered by desktop systems have unfortunately moved many newsletter people—both amateur and professional—to imitate magazine or newspaper format. Three or four articles are begun on page one and jumped to inside pages. Magazines and newspapers begin many articles at the outset to attract the widest possible audience, and they continue the articles throughout the publication to satisfy advertisers who want to be near editorial. To those subscription newsletter publishers engaged in this growing trend of jumping articles, I say remember the "letter" in "newsletter."

Also, I think newsletters are more akin to books than to magazines in terms of reader expectation and perception. Newsletters and books are made for people to read straight through. Magazines are made for people to, at least initially, flip through. In fact, the word "magazine" comes from Italian and French words meaning "storehouse" and, from that, "department store." Serious newsletter readers are not shoppers. They have already bought your newsletter and—like book readers—want to read it without distraction.

In designing your newsletter, I recommend that you get a professional art director. Do it yourself only as a last resort. Consider carefully all recommendations made by your art director, but do what you think is best. Don't let yourself be talked into something you really don't want.

To help this decision-making process I have developed a checklist of the most common design decisions every newsletter publisher must face. Since what is appropriate for one newsletter may not be appropriate for the next, I do not intend to dictate what is "good" or "bad" graphics. The list is simply a guide for the questions that must be asked and answered before your first issue goes into production.

Decision 1: Your Logotype, or Nameplate This is the most important design element in your newsletter. Your logotype will appear issue after issue, to bring favorable recognition or to haunt you.

There are two elements involved. The first is the name of the newsletter, which must be drawn in a distinctive typeface that will identify your newsletter forevermore. The second element is a suitable design that symbolizes your subject matter or your organization to your reader. For organizations, it could be the grand seal. For a newsletter on oil, it could be an oil derrick. Decide what the symbol should be, then have your artist give it an imaginative twist.

One of the best examples is that of *Congressional Monitor.* Probably thousands of publications dealing with government matters have used a photo or drawing of the U.S. Capitol. But the designer for *Congressional Monitor* made a slight change. By partially lifting the "lid" off the Capitol, the designer created a unique logo, symbolic of the way the newsletter opens up the Capitol and releases the information stored within (Fig. 6). Some other logos that produce an instant visual play on title and content are shown in Figure 7.

The logo is especially important to newsletters because of the additional ways it can be used to attract attention to the product and the organization. On inner pages it can be reproduced in miniature to reinforce identification. It can be used on envelopes for promotion mailings and adapted for the company letterhead as well.

Figure 6

Figure 7

Consider color first in designing the logo. Most look better in color. Remember, one color is cheaper than two. An inexpensive way to use color is to have the printer reproduce a year's supply of your paper with the logo in one color. Then print or type the body of each issue on this form.

Sometimes an effective logo can be created by using a color band, with the type showing through in white. This treatment, known as a reverse, is created by making a negative image from a positive art source (Fig. 8; page 56).

A handful of newsletters follow a journalistic tradition started by the earliest newspaper columnists—a photo of the writer. There's nothing wrong with it, especially and obviously for a personalized newsletter. Both *Jack O'Dwyer's Newsletter* and *Cameron's Foodservice Promotions Reporter* carry headshots of their namesakes.

Your designer will recommend a variety of type styles, including, perhaps, one where the name of the newsletter is in lowercase (no capital letters). Keep in mind that if you choose this style you will have to describe your newsletter in print in the same style. Some newsletters do this, but I find it awkward when it appears in a line of type; for example,

NEWSLETTER

Figure 8A

Positive art source.

NEWSLETTER

Figure 8B

Negative image by reverse method.

newsletter on newsletters. It's all right to underscore or italicize. If you are quoted in other publications, which I hope will happen, underlining may look strange.

Robert Baker, editor of *Impact,* "a newsletter on trends, techniques, and tools for communicators," says there are certain attributes that your nameplate should have.

1. It should be unusual, preferably unique.
2. It should be simple in design, yet bold and clear in keeping with the publication objective.
3. It should display immediate and distinct identification of publication and sponsoring organization.
4. It should reflect an accurate "organizational image."
5. It should blend well with all front page or front cover treatments.
6. It should be "mobile" and fit anywhere on the page.
7. It should be adaptable to varying colors.
8. It should be expandable or reducible in size without endangering legibility, and the logotype itself should be "design flexible" (able to be produced in solid, reverse, outline, shadow, or in two colors).

There are certain attributes to avoid, Baker says, among them long and cumbersome names; overly common names such as "News" or "Bulletin" or "Journal"; "names that are trite, slangy, flippant or undignified."

Many newsletters carry the nameplate or logotype design to the inside pages. Without sacrificing too much editorial space, design adaptations of the name for folio or department headings can be very effective (Fig. 9).

Decision 2: Page Size and Column Width Since most newsletters are

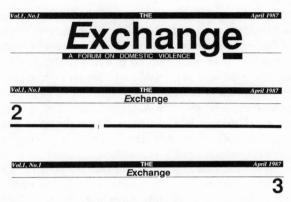

Vol.1, No.1 | THE | April 1987
Exchange
2

Vol.1, No.1 | THE | April 1987
Exchange
3

Figure 9A
Nameplate and folio using similar design.

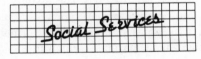

Figure 9B
Nameplate and department heading using similar design.

8½″ × 11″, I'll use that for my examples; I'll discuss other sizes later.

One column, or full measure, is typical of many newsletters (Figs. 10 and 11). How long should the lines be? Many editors like to use very narrow margins so that they can cram a lot of information into a small space. They claim that their readers want the information and don't care how crowded it is. Designers, however, maintain that long lines of type are hard to read in large doses. They advise keeping lines of type as short as possible so the reader's eyes don't tire and "double" (reread lines or skip lines when returning to the left-hand margin).

Designer Polly Pattison says that a good basic rule of thumb is forty to forty-five characters on a line, regardless of the size of type. This is a comfortable line length for the average reader and avoids eye fatigue. But it would indicate a two-column rather than one-column format. So, she adds, if for space reasons, you insist on long lines of type, it is very important that you have wide enough margins left and right (six picas on each side is a good rule of thumb) and adequate white space between paragraphs (two picas is recommended).

Let's see how the *Kiplinger Washington Letter* (Fig. 2; page 4) stacks up. The left-hand margin is seven picas, the right-hand margin is six picas, so there's ample room. And the longest line of type is thirty-six picas (six inches), which is very readable.

In working with full measure, you can shorten your lines by the way you place your headlines. If the headline is above the item (Fig. 15A; page 66), then you have the maximum per line. But if the headline is in the left-hand margin (Fig. 16A; page 68), then a shorter line is possible, but still longer than a two- or three-column line (Figs. 17A and 18A; pages 70 and 72).

The two-column format (Fig. 12; page 62) has two advantages. It allows more words per page and a line that the experts consider optimum. It also gives you opportunities for variations in layout and for the use of photos or charts.

The three-column format (Fig. 13; page 63) allows even more words per page, with a line length still acceptable to the typographic experts. It is virtually impossible to use typewriter type successfully in this format. (I have in my files a four-column format, typewriter composition. I stick by my statement: it is not successful.) This format calls for typesetting and justified right-hand margins—which means a different kind of publication, more of a miniature newspaper or magaletter than a newsletter. If you use this format, you'll have to master the rules of layout so that the reader can follow the copy without confusion. You'll have to figure out a number of variations so that you don't repeat the same layout each time. And you must give special consideration to your body type and headline type.

The August 1979 issue of *Editor's Workbook,* a monthly newsletter, was devoted to a description of the magaletter and had this to say:

> The MagaLetter could be described as the best qualities of a magazine blended with the best qualities of a newsletter in an inexpensive format.
> The two chief advantages of such a merger are: the clean, graphically pleasing look of a magazine instead of the cluttered look of a newsletter and the opportunity to give one-page display to important or interesting feature articles.

The chief disadvantage is the reduced space available for copy because of the "open" look inside and the magazine cover. However, this disadvantage can be offset by reducing wordy articles to "briefs" for the "newsbriefs" section. Research supports that readers have many demands on their time and short, succinctly written summaries may actually increase readership.

I've found, especially among organization and corporate newsletter categories, an increase in popularity of the tabloid design and format. Although I do not consider this to be in the true tradition of the newsletter, I see more of it each year in our Newsletter Awards competition. Incidentally, the desktop publishing revolution may naturally reverse this trend, since page makeup is most easily accomplished with the basic 8½" × 11" page format. To do an 11" × 17" page layout may require extensive electronic manipulation along with some manual cut-and-paste.

However, there is at least one example of an unusual twist on the use of the single 11" × 17" page format worth mentioning. That is to switch from horizontal to vertical layout to create a completely different format (Fig. 14; page 64). Not necessarily for you, but in this case the design innovation seems appropriate to the content.

Decision 3: The Use of Color   Color can be used in several ways. You can use color paper and print in black. You can use color paper and print in another color, but be very careful of your combinations. I have seen some horrendous results. On the other hand, I was pleasantly surprised by a newsletter that prints green type on green paper. You need an expert to guide you; be sure to see many samples before you decide.

The effective use of color requires a designer who understands the combinations and a printer who can carry out the specifications. This means that a quick copy shop may be adequate for a black-and-white job, but for color you need expert photo offset technicians. Here are twelve color combinations that have been ranked in descending order for legibility through psychological tests. Aesthetics were not considered.

1. black on yellow paper
2. green on white paper
3. blue on white paper
4. white on blue paper
5. black on white paper
6. yellow on black paper
7. white on red paper
8. white on orange paper
9. white on black paper
10. red on yellow paper
11. green on red paper
12. red on green paper

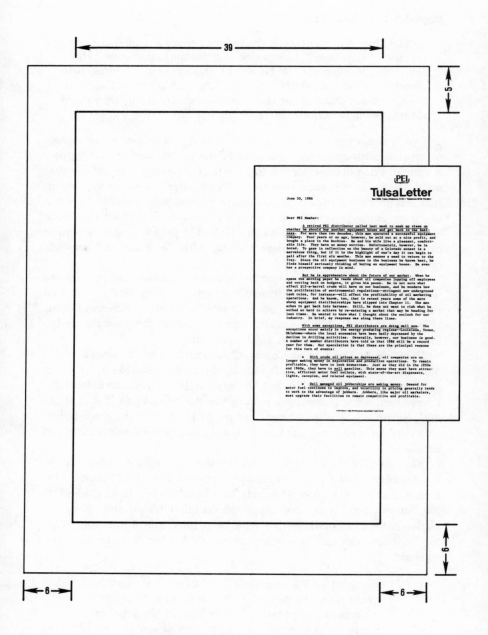

Figure 10
Full measure format.

Figure 11
Modified full measure format.

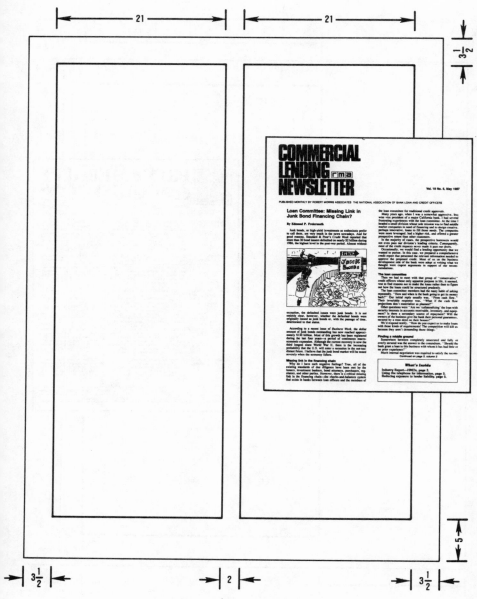

Figure 12
Two-column format.

Figure 13
Three-column format.

 **Investment Co.®** Publication

❊❊NoLOAD FUND❊X®

A Monitoring System for the Enterprising Investor

OUR 9TH YEAR, NUMBER 1. Includes 287 Funds. JANUARY 1984 ISSUE   ANNUAL TAX DEDUCTIBLE SUBSCRIPTION $87

REPORT

PAGE A

DECEMBER MARKETS: Both the Year-End and Santa Claus (4 days before Christmas) Rallies failed to materialize. Year-end tax selling did. (There's always an explanation.) But with equity indexes for the year ranging from the S&P 500's +17.3% to the AMEX's +30.9%, before dividends, it was a great year. (A glance down Column 5, Page 1, proves, however, that some "professional" money managers did, indeed, beat the odds and lost money.) After the market soared to record highs by mid-year, a correction finally set in, and minus signs dominate the 6, 3, 1 month periods, Columns 6-8. Interest rates drifted downward over the year, as fixed income investors weivered between fears of hopeless deficits rekindling more inflation, and hopes of a slow and healthy growth of the economy moderating credit demands. The outlook for 1984 is a 25% growth in corporate earnings (on top of 15% in 1983) and lower interest rates to mid-year. Our economy has incredible vigor, constantly overcoming government meddling. (Monopolies were outlawed because they were unfair. But what could be more unfair to consumers than breaking up the AT&T monopoly, the world's cheapest and most efficient telephone system?) Will the recovery be aborted before it runs its course? And in an election year? Not likely. ✦

acquisition approach. "We don't think much beyond this. The portfolio is full of dumpy little companies no one cares about."

Major holdings include Kimball Int'l, Gifford-Hill, Quaker Chemical, Geran Ind., Caro Corp., Western Pacific Ind., Ohio-Sealy Mattress, and La-Z-Boy Chair. F*X unsuccessfully tried to pin-down Mr. Ebright on his outlook for '84. "Value investors don't have outlooks. We're very dull. We are plotters, going from point to point, just like we did last time. We have no predictions and no opinions." Boring? Look at the record. During the charted period on Page B, **Penn Mutual** appreciated 366%. Questor Management also directs soon-to-be-added **Royce Value**, which will be a 12b-1 fund, paying 1% to brokers. (See 12b-1 discussion below.) No exchange options. 800/221-4268. For more **Penn Mutual**, see Chart and Footnote, Page B.

(It is true, as noted in the 1/5/84 Wall Street Journal, that the average stock fund underperformed the S&P 500 in '83. This shows clearly in the Star Box. Also note the percentage of Class 1, 2 and 3 funds that outperformed the S&P 500. Actually, 55 out of a total

---

❊❊ FOLLOWING THE STARS ❊❊

DOUBLE STAR PERFORMERS (❊❊ Left of Fund Name)

Months in Star Box		CLASS 1	Fund's Total	Port. %	Months in Star Box		CLASS 2	Fund's Total	Port. %	Months in Star Box		CLASS 3	Fund's Total	Port. %
Consec-utive	During Past Yr		Assets (Millions)	In Cash US Gov't	Consec-utive	During Past Yr		Assets (Millions)	In Cash US Gov't	Consec-utive	During Past Yr		Assets (Millions)	In Cash US Gov't
2	2	Fid S Fin Serv	30%	}	3	3	GT Pacific	$23	17%	1	4	Price Int'l	$129	10%
3	4	Penn Mutual	107	15 }	3	3	Mutual Qual Inc	58	8	1	3	Transatlantic	35	1
3	3	Safeco 6th	66	11 }	2	2	Fid Trend	636	6	3	3	Mutual Shares	251	9
{ 15	12	Fid S Tech	714	12 }	6	8	SteinRoe Specl	18	21	3	3	Scudder Int'l	133	5
3	3	Fid S Util	24	7 }	1	1	M/B Manhattan	76	6	1	2	Sequoia	339	16
1	1	Rainbow	2	15 }										
{ 1	4	Fid S Energy	81	18 }										
4	7	Bstn Specl 6th	26	23 }										
4	7	Quasar	47	6 }										

MONITORED FUNDS' PERFORMANCE RECORD 12/31/82 - 12/31/83 FROM THIS ISSUE

CLASS. AVERAGES - Year ending 12/31/83 (Column 5)

					BEST & WORST OF 287 FUNDS, Year ending 12/31/83 (Column 5)	
Class 1	+ 16.8%	Class 4	+ 17.9%		Class 1	Fidelity Select Technology	+ 52.6%
Class 2	+ 20.4%	Class 5, Corp & US	+ 8.4%		Class 1	Lexington Gold	- 7.5%
Class 3	+ 21.4%	Class 5, Tax Exempt	+ 7.2%				
S&P 500	+ 22.3%	Class 6	+ 0.2%		S&P 500	+ 22.3%

➤ Growth funds outperforming the S&P 500, Year ending 12/31/83 (Column 5): Class 1 - 27.5%, Class 2 - 48.8%, Class 3 - 46.2%

Note: Stars are assigned to the five (more if tied or if a load fund* is also starred) highest ranking (highest %) funds in Columns 3-9 on Pages 1 and 2 in each Class and Sub-Class. Over-all top performers in Classes 1, 2 and 3 are identified with stars left of fund name. These funds also appear in descending order of performance above. Ranking is an average of 12, 6, 3, and 1 month results, with credit given for stars in current time periods (Columns 5-8). Top performance is relative. During market declines, "top performer" means least loss, not biggest gain. There are no guarantees that past performance, good or bad, will continue.

    * Class 1 **Fidelity Select** funds went load 6/14/83 and are listed for the benefit of their prior noload owners.

FOLLOWING THE STARS: Erratic markets make erratic leadership. Class 3 Transatlantic Fund has joined Price and Scudder International and Class 2 G.T. Pacific in the Star Box. Overseas markets continue breaking records. Other new funds: Class 1 **Rainbow** and **Fidelity Select Energy**, Class 2 M/B Manhattan and Class 3 Transatlantic.

Class 1 **Pennsylvania Mutual**, no stranger to the Star Box, is a definite outperformer. Asked to explain Penn Mutual's starred performance, Portfolio Manager Thomas Ebright said, "We'd like to take credit, but it's discipline that does the work." The fund's small-company approach is what produced outstanding performance during the first six months of '83. While the portfolio is concentrated in issues of companies whose total outstanding stock is under $200 million, the weighted average market capitalization of the 120 current holdings is $103 million. In the second half of '83, when many small companies were getting killed, **Penn Mutual** was unaffected because it is value oriented. Many exciting high tech issues fell drastically, but **Penn Mutual** had unemotionally picked according to the bottom line. Management seeks companies whose stock sells for less than the business is worth on an ongoing basis. As illustration, Ebright described two approaches. The "Growth Investor" who is future-oriented, forecasts what might happen, projecting gleeful scenarios for some industries or companies, perhaps throwing in a bit of market-timing, generally having a good time analyzing. Then there is the boring "Value Investor", who cares about nothing except a possible valuation discrepancy between what a third party might pay for a company and what the market says it's worth. Pennsylvania Mutual follows this non-emotional course, which, Ebright says, is similar to the corporate

of 134 funds on Page 1 outperformed the S&P 500 in 1983. Followers of the Stars know you upgrade to stay with winners. Who needs average?)

F*X NEWS: Newly listed this month: Class 3 **Founders Mutual**, minimum initial investment $250/repeat $25, exchanges by telephone or letter with other Founders funds, 800/525-2440; Class 5 Tax-Exempt **Benham Calif. Tax Free Intermediate, Benham Calif. Tax Free Long Term**, minimum initial investment $1,000/repeat $100, exchange by telephone or letter with other Benham funds, 800/472-3389, in CA 800/982-6150; **Calvert Tax Free Long Term**, minimum initial investment $2,000/repeat $250, exchanges by telephone or letter with other Calvert funds, 800/368-2748; Class 5 Tax-Exempt MM **Benham Calif. Tax Free MM**, minimum initial investment $1,000/repeat $100, offers checkwriting privilege, 800/472-3389, in CA, 800/982-6150; Class 6 Government **Neuberger & Berman Government Money Fund**, $200/repeat $200, exchanges by telephone or letter with other Neuberger & Berman funds, 800/367-0776, in NY 800/367-0770. Name changes: Class 2 **Fidelity Asset Investment Trust** now **Fidelity Discoverer** and Class 3 **SteinRoe Balanced** now called **SteinRoe Total Return**.

DEFICIT PROBLEM SOLVED: On page one of the new 1983 1040 forms, Commissioner of Internal Revenue Roscoe L. Egger, Jr. tells us that last year the IRS received 3,500 voluntary contributions totaling $300,000 to reduce the public debt. (Make checks payable to the "Bureau of the Public Debt" and they will be deductible from your 1984 tax return.) At the 1983 rate, we can eliminate the entire $1.4 trillion debt in one year with just 16 billion more voluntary contributions of $85.71 each. (Unfortunately, there are only 5 billion men, women and children in the world.) ✦

DAL INVESTMENT CO.® IS REGISTERED WITH THE S.E.C. AS AN INVESTMENT ADVISOR. 235 MONTGOMERY ST., SAN FRANCISCO, CA 94104. 415/986-7979. (ISSN 0194-0104)

Figure 14

Other Design Possibilities   Once you have made the three major design decisions—logotype, column width, and color—there are other refinements you may want to introduce into your design. One involves the use of rules and borders. These are simply lines of varying thicknesses. You can draw a line completely around your body copy, either rounded at the corners or squared off. And there are numerous effects you can achieve by using either a hairline rule or a very heavy rule, or by alternating widths. Figure 19 (page 75) illustrates some rules and borders.

Sources for a wide selection of rules and borders, icons and generic symbols, spot illustrations, drawings, diagrams, and standing title elements can be found in readily available rub-on transfer sheets from your local art supply store. Clip-art subscription services provide camera-ready repro-quality black-and-white art and halftones for cut-and-paste or for computer scanning to integrate into text. One such clip-art service has been provided for years by Dynamic Graphics, Inc., Peoria, Illinois. Recently they introduced desktop clip art in software package form for certain computer systems.

A source guide for editors and designers covering the general production points I've mentioned relating to type- styles, color selection, printing processes, and technical terminology, and much more is *Graphics Master,* published by Dean Lem Associates, Los Angeles. It contains a wealth of type-style comparisons, color-selection charts, diagrams, and scales for measuring type, scaling photographs, and planning your camera-ready materials for the print production process.

For those nonsubscription newsletterers whose budgets cannot rise to catch the high winds of electronic newsletter production, *The Quick & Easy Newsletter Kit* offers

> Absolutely everything you will need to produce a show-stopping newsletter: nameplates, datelines, page numbers, story headlines, paste-up boards, guide sheets, boxes for stories, clip art, quotations, and an illustrated easy-to-follow user guide that takes you step-by-step from the planning stages to distribution.

Publisher and graphic designer Phyllis L. Stover says she designed the "just add typewriter" kit for schools, clubs, churches, organizations, and small businesses. Considering the ragged look of many giveaway newsletters, we recommend Stover's package as a simple method of giving even a low-budget internal publication the look of a tasteful subscription

Figure 15A

CPA administrative report

NOVEMBER 1986

This Month's Reports	File in Binder Section
Electronic Tax Services Supplement Looseleafs	2.7.5
Developing or Improving Your Image:	
Success Secrets of Winning Firms	2.11.19
Job Tracking Systems Come of Age	2.12.9

CPA/AR Triple Bonus: Photographs of our CPA Firm Image Contest winners in a special four-page Showcase supplement, and a ready-to-use image checklist to help make your firm a winner. **Plus,** highlights of the recent Missouri MAP Conference.

CPA/AR salutes CPA firms with winning images

Our judges had a most difficult task choosing the four best image packages from the many outstanding entries in our recent CPA Firm Image Contest. Congratulations to the winners—see samples of their winning image programs in the Showcase supplement and at AICPA's Firm Administrators' Conference, 11/17-18 at the Vista International Hotel in New York City.

Practice Image Excellence Award: Dorrough, Parks & Co., CPAs, Knoxville, TN. **Special Merit Award:** Garcia & Ortiz, PA, CPAs, St. Petersburg, FL. **Achievement Award:** Gray, Gray & Gray, CPAs, Boston, MA. **Honorable Mention:** Barrett & Smith, CPAs, Las Vegas, NV.

Financial management workshops for CPA administrators slated

The Association of Accounting Administrators (AAA) hosts two regional fall conferences on CPA firm financial controls: 10/24 at Philadelphia's Four Seasons Hotel and 11/21 at the Nugget Hotel in Reno, NV. Discussion leader for "Financial & Productivity Controls for CPA Firm Management" is CPA Joseph Derba, Jr., president of Derba & Co., PC, Lexington, MA. Each day-long program will focus on preparing an annual budget and using it as a working tool, along with management reporting and long-range financial planning.

These workshops promise to be an excellent opportunity for administrators who want to learn more about internal financial controls. We've heard Derba speak on this topic previously—he knows his stuff and presents it well. **Registration fee:** $175 for AAA members; $195 for nonmembers; $150 for additional participants from same firm. For further information, contact Clifford M. Brownstein, Executive Director, AAA, P.O. Box 11000, Washington, DC 20008. (202) 537-1220.

Art gallery in DH&S office reflects firm image

Works by 18th century artists, African and Haitian art, contemporary tapestries and potteries are among the museum-quality art objects displayed in Deloitte, Haskins & Sells' Milwaukee office. Using an art collection was conceived by an office designer who planned the firm's new Milwaukee quarters.

The Resource Successful CPA Firms Use in Firm Administration

Figure 15B

MPR Materials and Processing Report

Vol. 2 No. 1 April 1987 ISSN 0887-9249

THE LEADING EDGE OF TECHNOLOGY WORLDWIDE

Superconductive Ceramics 1	Confocal Microscopy 2
NMR for Composite NDE 4	CT Scanning of Ceramics 3
New Materials Economics 6	Fluorescence Spectroscopy 5
Calendar 10	MMC Welding Breakthrough 6
	Noteworthy 8
	Patent Report 9

■ **High Temperature Superconductivity Reported in Oxide Ceramics** Superconductivity above 100 Kelvin (−173°C, −280°F) has been confirmed in a new class of superconducting materials, alkaline earth metal oxides. This revolutionary development was reported at an extraordinary nightlong special session, attended by thousands of scientists from all over the world, at the Annual Meeting of The American Physical Society on March 18 in New York City. As noted by the chairman, Neil Ashcroft, materials science has been a key contributor to this breakthrough.

It was only last November that K. A. Müller and J. G. Bednorz at IBM's Zürich Research Laboratory published their discovery that a novel material containing lanthanum, barium, copper, and oxygen, $La_{2-x}Ba_xCuO_4$, becomes superconductive at 30 K. Once their results, which were initially treated with skepticism, were verified at Tokyo University by S. Tanaka's group, the race of progress toward materials with higher and higher superconductive transition temperatures was unprecedented.

By substituting strontium for lanthanum, Paul C. W. Chu and coworkers at the Universities of Houston and Alabama raised the superconductivity onset temperature to 40 K before the end of 1986. At about the same time, working independently, Zhongxian Zhao's group at Beijing University reached a temperature of 46 K. Then on January 28 the Houston group announced a remarkable achievement, an yttrium-containing material, $Y_{1-x}Ba_xCuO_2$, that becomes a superconductor at 90 K (above the boiling point of liquid nitrogen, 77 K, −196°C, −319°F) and thus can be maintained in a liquid nitrogen Dewar flask at ambient pressure. For the past 75 years, until the discovery of these high temperature superconductors, metals like Pb, Hg, and Nb and intermetallic compounds like Nb_3Sn, Nb_3Ge, and $NbTi$ have been the only type of materials that, when sufficiently cooled (below 23 K, −253°C, −426°F), lose all their electrical resistance and expel all magnetic fields in their interior—the two main criteria for superconductors.

The new ceramic superconductors are actually neither very exotic materials nor difficult to make. They belong to a familiar class of ceramics known as perovskites, characterized by having three oxygen atoms for every two metal atoms in their crystal structure. However, there is something different about the superconducting perovskites—they are oxygen deficient. In effect, their crystal structure is missing about one in every three oxygen atoms. Figure 1 is an idealized depiction of the position of the individual atoms that comprise the smallest fundamental unit of a superconducting material, as verified by researchers at IBM's T. J. Watson Research Center.

The superconductors produced by Chu and others were found to be mixtures of at least two phases. It was further found that only those materials containing a layered structure of black crystalline material as the main phase have the highest superconductivity transition temperatures. As a consequence of

Fig. 1 $YBa_2Cu_3O_x$
□ = O, vacancy; ● = Cu

Figure 15C

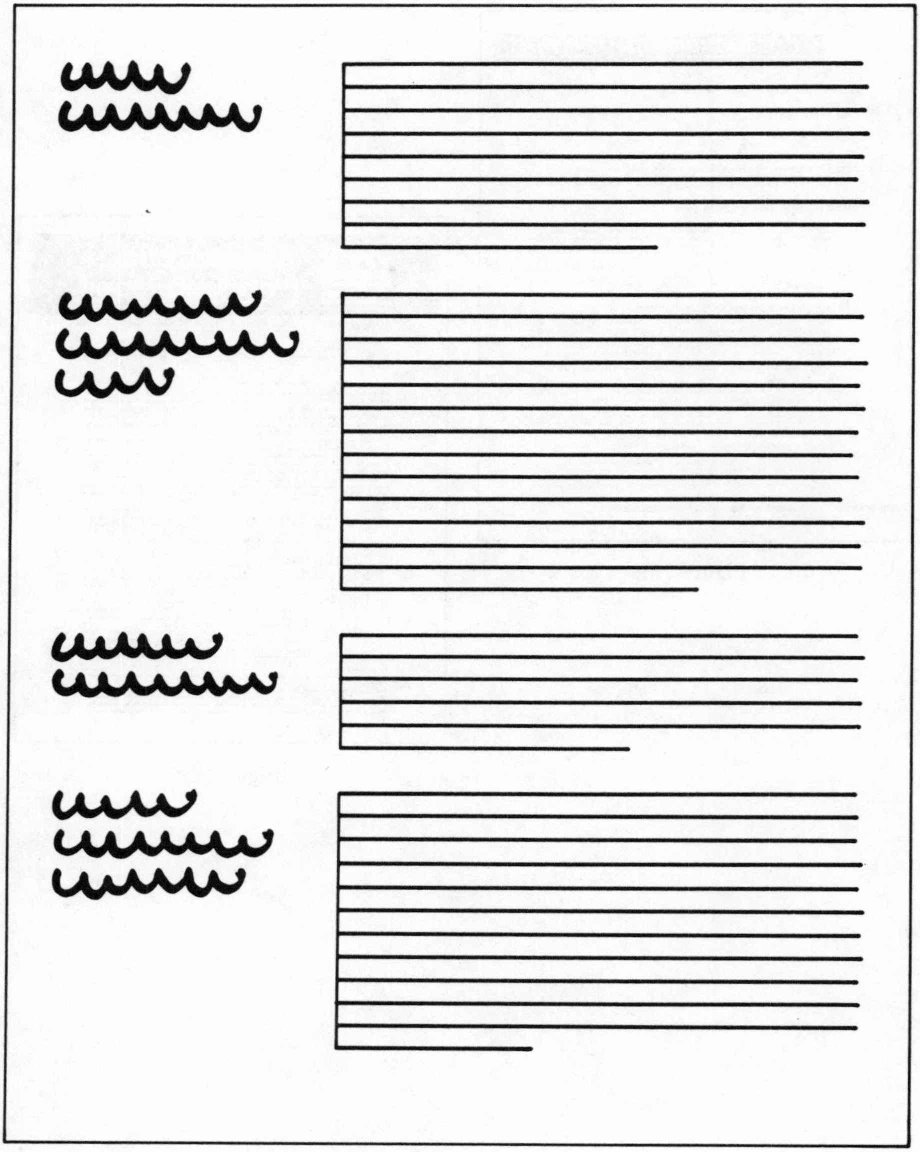

Figure 16A

The Executive Letter

March 30, 1987   Vol. 39 No. 13

NEW TORT POLICY REPORT ISSUED

The Reagan Administration last week gave strong support to tort reform efforts and offered a weak defense of the McCarran-Ferguson Act. The Interagency Tort Policy Working Group issued a new report, saying that the liability crisis persists, with prices too high for some and coverage not available for others. Blame was placed squarely on the civil justice system, with an accompanying analysis from the Justice Department's Antitrust Division saying that there is no evidence to support charges that the insurance industry has acted improperly. (See the Special Report in this issue.) Asked for his position on the proposed repeal of the McCarran-Ferguson Act, Assistant Attorney General Richard Willard told reporters he sees no need to change that law in order to address insurance availability/affordability problems.

SENATOR SIMON SAYS: CHANGE ANTITRUST LAW

Sen. Paul Simon (D-Ill.) last week broadened the debate over the McCarran-Ferguson Act by introducing legislation that would end the insurance industry's limited federal antitrust exemption but would specifically sanction certain joint activities such as risk pools and data collection. Many observers believe the Simon bill (S464) will be viewed as the moderate alternative to Sen. Howard Metzenbaum's (D-Ohio) proposal (S89) for total repeal of McCarran. In introducing his bill, Simon said, "I believe that the exemption is clearly overbroad and should be narrowed on general antitrust policy grounds, irrespective of any preventative effects such changes might have on future liability crisis."

SELF-INSPECTION FOR MOTOR CARRIERS STUDIED

The Federal Highway Administration (FHWA) has proposed allowing motor carriers to perform self-inspections in order to comply with the safety requirements of the Motor Carrier Safety Act of 1984. The Insurance Institute for Highway Safety has criticized the proposal, saying it is not "the answer to the current problem" of defective trucks on the nation's highways. The FHWA would also require carriers domiciled in states with existing annual safety checks to comply with the state's program. Permission to self-inspect would not be granted to carriers with fewer than five trucks, however. Such carriers would have to contract out

Figure 16B

TOM PETERS On Achieving Excellence

THE MONTHLY NEWSLETTER THAT DARES MANAGERS TO TAKE INSTANT ACTION

JANUARY 1987
VOL 2 NO 1

INSIDE

Golden Needles' Rules of Thumb

How to Cultivate Innovation

Since You Asked ... Q&A

Rescuing the Red Cross

Pockets: May the Force Be With You; Running Interference; Extra, Extra

LEADING EDGE

Innovate Or Die

"It takes five years to develop a car in this country. Heck, we won World War II in four years," contends H. Ross Perot, the recently deposed General Motors board member. But it doesn't have to be that way. GM's product-development cycle today is about twice as long as Toyota's and Honda's.

Companies in other industries are learning to speed up innovation — by getting closer to the action. Campbell Soup reorganized about 48 months ago from a vertical, functional monolith into more than 50 smallish business units. One result: quadruple the speed of new-product development in a fiercely competitive market.

Procter & Gamble has undertaken a major reorganization toward multi-function, team-based product development to slash product-development time. IBM introduced over a dozen independent Business Units that accomplished the same end. Milliken & Co., the textile firm, underwent a radical late-1985 reorganization aimed at almost order-of-magnitude cuts in new product sample delivery time, and results are exceeding expectations.

The list goes on. New competitors pop up daily — big and small, foreign and domestic — in every market sector. Health care and financial services are at least as volatile as semiconductors and biotechnology. In retailing, Penney and Sears feel the heat from The Limited, which can move about 33 percent faster to stock their shelves with newly discovered items.

Learning to innovate faster — to try more, test more, start more, cut off failures faster — is essential for survival. Anyone whose five objectives doesn't include a vow to slash product development cycle time by a factor of two to ten in the next two years may be doomed to irrelevance or outright failure.

Tools include structural change (flattening the organization and getting all staff closer to the market) to attitudinal change (getting innovation in the air and reducing fear of failure).

The main stumbling blocks are organization and management principles designed, often decades ago, to cope with a stable world. Somewhat crazy champions are ignored or fired. We must learn to love them — and their disruptions — or perish.

Reorganizations are gut-wrenching traumas, even in smaller firms. IBM, in an effort to master its new uncertainties, has reorganized, from top to bottom, three times since 1981. I frankly feel that any firm not reorganizing once every nine months or so is probably missing the boat.

We must learn to love change and welcome it as intensely as we have hated it and avoided it in the past.

On Achieving Excellence™ is published monthly.

Publishing Offices:
425 Brannan Street, Suite 200
San Francisco, California 94107
1-800-821-0851, ext. 307

Publisher
Tom Peters
Editor
Jayne A. Pearl
Assistant Editor
Kathy Dalle-Molle
Management Services
InterCon Group

Subscription Fees:
One year, 12 issues $197
Two years, 24 issues $343
Add $25 for subscribers from Canada and Mexico. Other foreign orders, add $30.

©1986 TPG Communications
ISBN: 0887-5502

Figure 16C

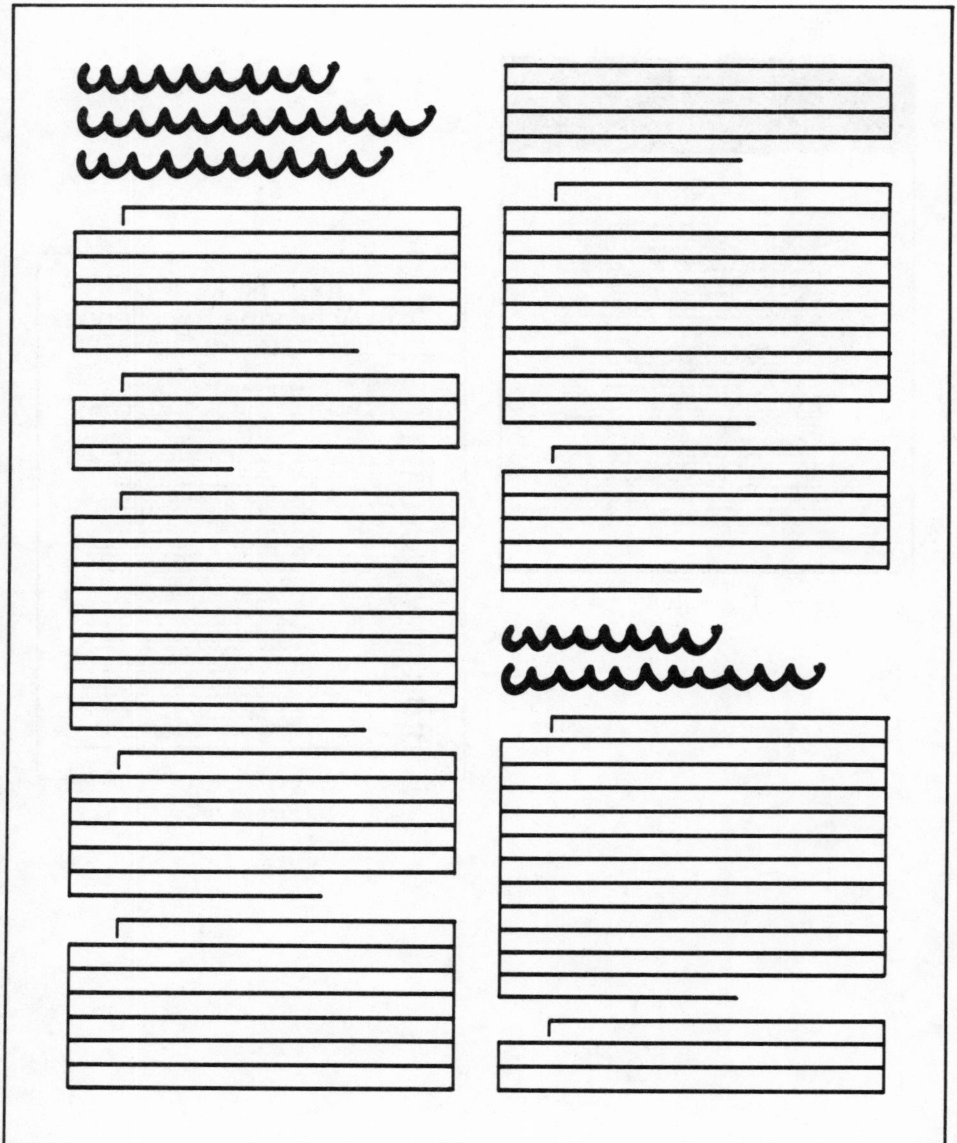

Figure 17A

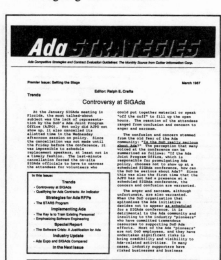

Figure 17B

Figure 17C

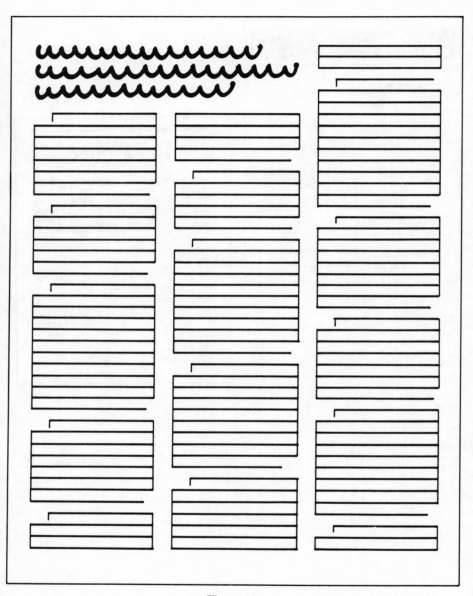

Figure 18A

Figure 18B

Figure 18C

letter. Figures 20A and 20B (pages 76 and 77) shows samples from the fifty-five pages of pasteups and supplies.

Standing Elements   Here is a checklist of other standing elements of the newsletter that will have to fit into your design.

Address   You can put this on the front or the back or both. I favor the front because that's where people look first. If you use a post office box as an address, also include a street address. People are often suspicious of post office boxes when dealing by mail. I realize that if you are a moonlighter and don't want to be bothered at your home you may have no choice but to hire a post office box. In larger areas you can rent an address from an answering service. Your mail will be delivered to the box, but people will also have a physical location. A practical reason is that more and more deliveries are being made by United Parcel Service (UPS), and they will not deliver to a post office box.

Descriptive Phrase   A descriptive phrase after the name of your newsletter can be helpful—for example, "Covering the wallpaper industry," "The accountant's authoritative guide," and so on. This can be worked into the logo design, and it can also appear in your masthead (see Fig. 15C, page 67).

Notice of Copyright   All that is needed is the copyright symbol, date, and name of publication. Some publishers also add stern language, such as "Reproduction of contents strictly forbidden without permission of publisher." This provides you no additional legal support, but some publishers feel there is a psychological advantage in this warning to would-be violators. You need put the notice of copyright in only one place, usually the front page or masthead.

Page Numbers   These should be used even in a four-page newsletter. People are easily confused. Make it easy. From a design point of view, consider alternatives to the usual bottom of the page. Pick a typeface that is part of your design style. If you use a second color, it can be picked up on the page numbers. Another reason for page numbers is your cumulative index. (This is discussed under "Selling Subscriptions to Libraries," pages 122–23.)

Masthead   This is where you put basic information about the newsletter. List the name, address, phone number, date of issue, volume and issue numbers, and copyright notice. You may want to include a descriptive phrase or even a paragraph about the newsletter. You should also list the editor, publisher, and any other editorial staff with titles. This is the place for subscription prices and subscription office address, if different. Note that there is no legal requirement to list your subscription price. Some publishers prefer to invite people to write for full information

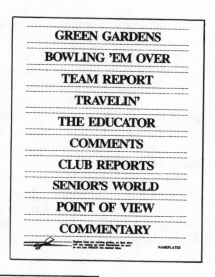

NAMEPLATES

QUOTATIONS FOR 2 COLUMN FORMAT

Figure 19

instead. All of this can be put in very small but legible type. It should be set in type even though the newsletter is typewritten. It then becomes part of your design and takes less space (Fig. 21; pages 78–79).

Date and Volume Number Even though this is in the masthead, give consideration to placing it on the first page right under the nameplate or logo. Volume numbers are important for reference and also as indications of the age of the newsletter. A volume usually covers one calendar year.

ISSN   The International Standard Serial Number (described in Chapter 7) can be placed either on the first page or in the masthead.

Table of Contents   You may want to consider this optional design element, especially if your newsletter is more than four pages. It should be positioned on the left column or at the bottom of the first page. Since the contents will take away valuable editorial space, make sure its presence is essential to the reader.

Paper   What kind of sheet of paper? Designers and printers refer to paper as stock. It comes in hundreds of sizes, weights, finishes, and textures. Incidentally, all of these characteristics will affect the cost of the paper you choose. Importantly, narrow your selection early on and obtain some price comparisons for preparing your budget. This first

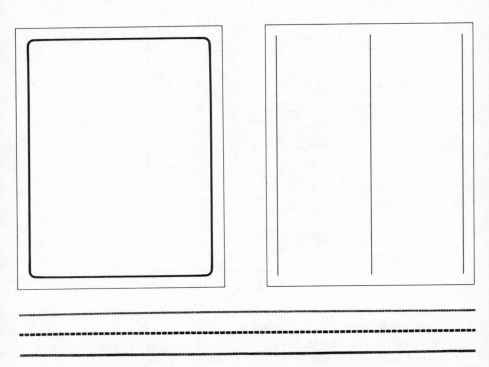

Figure 20A

hurdle in basic design can be overcome by requesting manufacturer's swatch books or samples from a printer. Generally, a sixty-pound offset stock offers sufficient opacity for good ink coverage as well as adequate weight for low postage-rate considerations. For most newsletters, coated or glossy stock is not suggested—unless photographic content requires extra-fine reproduction quality.

Screens   Also known as benday tints. You may choose to highlight your banner, masthead, table of contents, or certain copy areas without the use of extra rules or borders. Screen blocks in graded tones from 10 percent to 30 percent value in either color or black will give an extra dimensional effect without detracting from the words printed over them.

Halftones   Printers use this conversion process for printing continuous tone photographs. Halftones are reproduced in one color; duotones require one color plus black. These are the most common variations of picture reproduction in newsletters when photos are required. Special

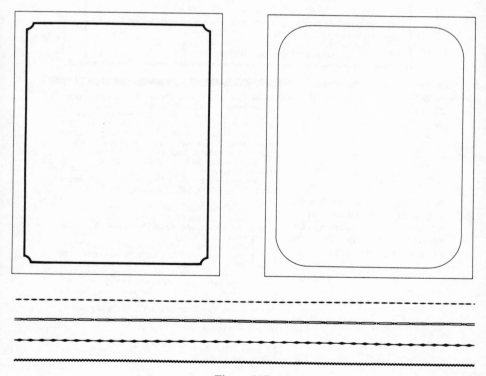

Figure 20B

Figure 21

The masthead is commonly placed on page 2 of a newsletter. However, there is no common design treatment, since masthead designs usually follow the main layout flow of the whole publication.

EDITORIAL EYE ETE / EEI

Published 12 times a year by Editorial Experts, Inc.
85 S. Bragg St., Alexandria, VA 22312 (703) 642-3040

Founding Publisher: Laura Horowitz

Publisher: Daniel J. Horowitz; Editor: Bruce Boston
Managing Editor: Eleanor Johnson
Production Manager: Diana Clayton
Contributing Editor: Priscilla Taylor
Production: EEI Word Processing Center, Betsy Colgan
EEI Production/Graphics Manager: Pat Gerkin
EEI Publications Manager: Eleanor Johnson

Circulation Manager: Page Anderson
Subscriptions: 12 issues, $49/ 8 issues, $33
Canadians, add $5 per year. Overseas $62 per year.
Single copies—$4; Multiple subscription rate available.

Subscribers may reprint up to 300 words of our original material if they send us a copy and give credit as follows:
The Editorial Eye, 85 S. Bragg St., Alexandria, VA 22312.
Written permission needed to reprint more than 300 words.

a. (above) This masthead re-creates the nameplate of the newsletter. Note permission phrase.

Natural Living Newsletter is published 12 times a year by NLN Publications Inc. Editorial and subscription address: P.O. Box 849, Madison Square Station, New York, NY 10159. Subscriptions: 12 issues, one year, $28. For change of address, please enclose a mailing label from a recent issue. **Please notify us six weeks in advance if you intend to move.** Back issues are $3.00 each. Inquire for quantity discounts. © 1986 by NLN Publications Inc.

Correspondence to **Gary Null** should be addressed to Gary Null, c/o WBAI, 505 8th Avenue, New York, NY 10018.

Natural Living Newsletter sometimes makes its mailing list avaulable to others. If you do not wish your name to be made availabe, please let us know. You must include a mailing lable.

Information contained in Natural Living Newsletter has been carefully gathered from sources we believe to be reliable, but we cannot guarantee the accuracy of all information. Some issues of Natural Living Newsletter deal with medical subjects. Natural Living Newsletter does not diagnose, prescribe, or treat any illness. Nor does it recommend one course of treatment over another. Natural Living Newsletter is meant to be one of many sources of information to help people take responsibility for their own health.

Publisher: **Gary Null**
Editor: **John Lobell**

b. (right) This masthead was output by laser printing, as was the entire newsletter. The editor uses this space for disclaimer notices also.

The Main Menu ▶▶▶▶▶▶▶▶▶▶▶▶▶▶▶▶▶▶

Deborah de Peyster, *Editor*

Steve High, *Contributing Editor*

Kelly Stirn, *Contributing Editor*

Paul Statt, *Contributing Editor*

Eileen Terrill, *Managing Editor*

Kelly Stirn is the AppleWorks engineering product manager for Apple Computer Inc. Steve High was a member of the AppleWorks development team and now owns Steve High Public Relations. One of his clients is Applied Engineering Inc.

The Main Menu (ISSN 0890-2585) is published monthly by CW Communications/Peterborough, Inc. 80 Elm Street, Peterborough, NH 03458. U.S. subscription rates $49.97, one year. Application to mail at second class postage rates is pending at Peterborough, NH, and additional mailing offices. Entire contents copyright 1986 by CW Communications/Peterborough, Inc. No part of this publication may be printed or otherwise reproduced without written permission from the publisher. POSTMASTER: send address changes to The Main Menu, 80 Elm Street, Peterborough, NH 03458.

c. (above) *This masthead takes two-column width but is clean and informative.*

d. (right) *This masthead occupies the entire left-hand space of a full-length page. It contains all vital information, however.*

Defense + Foreign Affairs

Defense & Foreign Affairs Daily and the monthly *Defense & Foreign Affairs* are successors to *Defense Newsletter* and are published by The Perth Corporation.

Editorial and publishing coordinating office: 1777 T St NW, Washington DC, 20009. Telephone: (202) 223-4934. Telex: 64161.

UK Office: Unit 5, South Thames Studios, 5-11 Lavington Street, London SE1. Tel. (01) 928-9266. Telex: 933640 SOUTH.

Editor-in-Chief & Chairman: Gregory R. Copley *Associate Editor-in-Chief:* Dr Stefan T. Possony *Publisher:* Martin Shaw.

Editor: Dr Michael Collins Dunn *Deputy Editor:* Julia Ackerman *Staff Writer:* Martin Cohen *United Kingdom Bureau Chief:* Ian Curtis. *South Asia Bureau:* Asian Films/ Sanjiv Prakash

Contributing Editors: Ross S. Kelly (Special Operations); Clare Hollingworth OBE (Hong Kong); Frederic Smith (East Bloc Affairs); Donald Walsh, Jr. (Small Arms).

Reporters: Kathryne Bomberger, Scott D. Dean, Steven Dierckx, David Lewis, Ricardo Marcos.

Subscription Rate: $697 per annum, including *Defense & Foreign Affairs Daily* (5 days a week, 50 weeks a year), and *Defense & Foreign Affairs* (monthly magazine).

Controller and Circulation Manager: David G. Desormeaux **Circulation Coordinator:** Meriel Brooks. **Circulation Enquiries:** (202) 223-4934. **Associated Publications:** *Defense & Foreign Affairs Weekly,* *Defense & Foreign Affairs* (monthly magazine), *Defense & Foreign Affairs Handbook* (annual).

ISSN: 0193-4643. Copyright © The Perth Corporation, 1987.

textured halftones may have a place in your layout depending on the photo subject and image desired. Your designer can help you determine which technique is best for your newsletter.

Promotional Material Your next design decision should be to take many of the decisions you have made in your newsletter layout (particularly the logotype, logo, and tag line) and adapt them to every piece of your promotion package and letterhead. A sound design concept gains synergy with repetition. You've worked hard to create the best possible image. Now use it every chance you can.

Selecting a Typeface Your final step is selecting a typeface for the body of the newsletter (*body* type). Start a "swipe file," your own collection of various newsletters. Look them over and also study the pages reproduced in the Editing section of *The Newsletter on Newsletters.* These will help you recognize the opportunities and perils in newsletter formats.

Size of Typeface Type sizes are measured in points. No need to understand the technicalities. Just remember that for readability, the smallest type is nine point; the largest, twelve point. Caution: Various suppliers of typefaces have their own versions. A nine-point face from one company may be larger or smaller than that of another. Make your own decision on what seems most readable.

Serif versus Sans Serif All typefaces are one or the other. *Serif* has a small line at the top and bottom of the line strokes, as you can see in the body type of this book. These additional lines seem to serve as "hooks" for the eye, making the lines easier to read. Times Roman is the best-known typeface in the serif style and no one can go wrong using it. *Sans serif* has no "hooks." It is attractive in headlines, but as a body type it just doesn't work. This has been demonstrated so many times that there is no argument. Yet some people persist in using sans serif, principally Helvetica. *Board Report for Graphic Artists,* Drew Allen Miller, publisher, ran the results of a survey of 306 readers of specialized magazines and 81 art directors on their preferences for body-copy typefaces. Readers, however, ranked Helvetica first, while art directors gave the nod to Century.

Both groups also gave high marks to Garamond, Melior, and Times Roman. To that list, I would also add the following typefaces most appropriate for newsletter body text: Baskerville, Fairfield, Optima, Palatino, and Stymie Light.

To counter those lists, I've assembled what I consider the ugliest fonts, many of which are unfortunately being used for text today: Avant Garde Extra Light, Cheltenham Old Style, Futura Light, News Gothic

Condensed, Serif Gothic, and Souvenir Light. I remain firmly opposed to using sans serif typefaces for text, and four on the bad list are sans serif—a style originally designed for advertising copy and headlines and still appropriate for those uses.

Spacing Typefaces also vary in the space occupied by the characters. Some are quite open—*expanded*—others are tight—*condensed*. A condensed typeface provides more characters per line but may be harder to read. The weight of type lends to readability as headline or body type. Bold, Extrabold, and Ultra Heavy versions of most fonts make good headline type. Light, Medium, and Book versions make good body type. Typesetting allows other spacing modifications for optimum readability: *letterspacing*—adding white space between characters or wider spaces between words or groups of words. If not done with the greatest of care, letterspacing can lead to disastrously poor typography. Also, too much letterspacing in successive lines slows the reading and comprehension rate of the reader. *Kerning*—the opposite of letterspacing. Minute increments of space can be subtracted from between certain character pairs in order to fit better and therefore become more appealing to the reader. Although these techniques are not available on typewriter and word processor output, they can be accomplished on certain desktop systems and on professional typographic equipment. Spacing between lines—called *leading* (pronounced ledding)—is also a factor in readability. The specification *nine on eleven* means nine point type with two extra points of space between lines.

Justified versus Ragged Right If you use typewriter type, the right-hand lines will be uneven in length, or ragged. You can use a Veri-type typewriter or a word processor (see Chapter 6) to get an even right-hand line, but each page must be typed twice. In typesetting, you can justify each line so that the right-hand side is perfectly even. Many people use typesetting for this reason. Perversely, some art designers specify typesetting rather than typewriter and then have it set ragged right.

Typewriter Type Richard L. Clement's *Form Book for IBM Selectric and Remington SR-101 Typewriters* has illustrations of the various faces available, as does your typewriter or word-processor supplier. You can get both serif and sans serif type. Courier, a serif, is one of the most popular. Typewriter type is usually elite (twelve characters to the inch) or pica (ten characters to the inch). You also have a choice in spacing between characters, in this case described in terms of *pitch*. A twelve-pitch type element has twelve characters to the inch; a ten-pitch type element has ten characters to the inch, and hence is more open.

Electronic Word Processing Michael Kleper's book *The Illustrated*

Handbook of Desktop Publishing and Typesetting goes into much detail on the history and comparisons of composition methods from typewriter, electronic word processing, and desktop typesetting to regular typography. It is probably the single most authoritative reference book on this subject that you can put in your library. The important thing to remember about electronic word processing and desktop typesetting is the quality of the final output. Dot matrix, letter quality, and laser type all produce printed words, but it is the quality of the reproduction that has such a critical impact on content and design (Fig. 22). Each form has its application and when used appropriately can be extremely effective. The interesting thing to note is that one of the goals of the dot-matrix and letter-quality generation of printers has always been to *imitate standard typewriter output.*

Regular Type   Mark Beach's book *Editing Your Newsletter: A Guide to Writing, Design, and Production* has illustrations of many typefaces, as does, of course, your printer or art designer. If you decide to use regular type, I hope it will be because you honestly believe it will look better, not that it will serve as a device to crowd in more words. It's true that you can get more characters per line than from typewriter type. But more is not necessarily better. All good art is measured against the limitations imposed. The art of newsletters, as developed by Kiplinger and followed by many others, is to provide the readers with useful information within four typewritten pages, without changing margins or typefaces to crowd in more. In this connection, I recall an issue of the weekly newsletter put out by the Bank of America to inform employees of actions by the bank that affected them. The issue ended in the middle of the second page. I learned that this was deliberate—that was all that was important that week and the editor refused to pad with irrelevant material to meet the customary journalistic dictum that there must be no "holes."

Design Readability   The Cahners Publishing Company did a survey on design readability and came to these conclusions:

- Black-on-white type reads 11.7 percent faster than reverse type (white type on a dark background).
- Type set in upper- and lowercase reads 13.4 percent faster than type set in all capitals. (Uppercase means capital letters, lowercase means noncapital letters.) It follows from this that in a typeset newsletter with many heads you should use upper- and lowercase. Some designers now recommend "upper declining," with the first word having an initial cap and the balance of the line in lowercase.

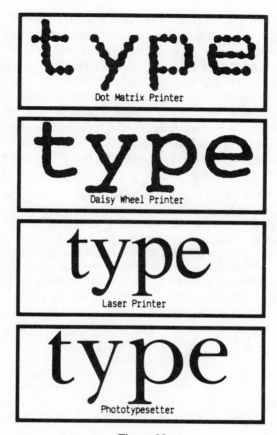

Figure 22

Enlarged characters from a dot-matrix printer, a daisy-wheel printer, a laser printer, and a phototypesetter: reproduction quality from each output source.

- Bar charts illustrate quantity comparisons better than line graphs.
- Bars labeled with numbers or symbols are easier to read than bars keyed by color or shading.
- Ragged-right columns do not affect readability for good readers. For poor readers, ragged-right columns provide easier readability than justified right, although careful spacing can eliminate the difference.
- Showing a product in place or in use rated higher readership than showing the product with people. Showing the product alone rated the lowest.

Grids When you begin to lay out your two- or three-column typeset newsletter, you will find a bewildering number of variations. A way to keep things under control is to use the grid system, which has certain patterns you can adapt in placing stories and photos. You can learn the use of grids by practice or turn to a designer who understands them. As a start, I recommend *18 ready-to-use grids for the 8½" × 11" page* by Jan White, available through the *Ragan Report*. White, the author of *Editing by Design,* is one art designer who recognizes that the editor, in the long run, must control the design.

Design Is for the Editor A statement by Jan White seems an appropriate close to this chapter.

Design is NOT a bunch of secrets only revealed to some wild-eyed practitioners. It is, instead, a working tool for the working editor. When design is done for its own sake, then it is indeed a scary monster (depending, as it does, on subjective "liking"—something nobody can argue about). But when you see design as just a means of calling the readers' attention to that which you, as editor, consider the important element, then design is no longer art for art's sake. It becomes a technique for communication's sake.

6

Producing and Printing Your Newsletter

Saving Time and Money Is Your Major Objective As a publisher, it's your job to get your newsletter printed as inexpensively as possible, consistent with the quality standards you have established, and to spend as little time as possible in the process. As an editor, it's your job to devote a maximum of your time to developing stories, writing stories, getting others to write stories—and as little time as possible to the composition and printing of the newsletter. This is true whether you are a volunteer for the local chamber of commerce newsletter, a lone entrepreneur working at home, or a professional editor supervising other editors.

There are consultants to the field who write books and conduct seminars on production methods, including layouts, pasteups, rub-on type for heads, and all the other techniques used by art directors. There is nothing wrong with their advice and much of their teaching is effective. In my opinion, however, they are diverting editors from their primary job, which is to write and edit.

An old story reveals my bias. It is said that an army colonel developed a simple test to determine whether some second lieutenants had the leadership qualities needed for advancement to higher rank. He gathered the candidates together and posed this situation: "You are advancing through rough terrain and your vehicles are blocked by a large tree. How do you get the tree out of the way?" Some of the candidates talked about saws, axes, demolition, and how to get the tree to fall in the right direction. Only one candidate had the correct answer. He said, "I would call for the top sergeant and say, 'Sergeant, remove that tree.' " This is how I feel about printing and production. Get someone else to do it.

Of course there are some basics you must know, but merely to understand how to deal with artists and printers, not to do the work yourself.

You wouldn't want your printer to write your newsletter. Why should you move in on his turf?

The following is a discussion of the basics you must understand and some examples of how various newsletters are produced.

Many people think that setting type and printing are the same. They are not, and the distinction is important. It is unlikely that you will be engaged in the printing process, other than, say, operating a photocopier. But it could well be that you will be involved in what is called type composition, for this is part of the editorial function.

Composition is preparing the newsletter for printing. *Printing* is reproducing the newsletter in quantity.

Composition   Here you have important decisions to make. The choices are:

- Typewriter or similar electronic strike-on equipment
- Word processor (PC system) using dot-matrix or daisy-wheel printer
- Desktop typeset using laser printer
- Regular typeset composition using phototypesetting or digital typography

Typewriter Composition   As we discussed earlier, typewriter composition is by far the easiest method (see Fig. 23 for a good example). It is essential to use an electric typewriter (because the touch of the keys is even) and a carbon ribbon. Type the newsletter just as you want it reproduced (use a backup sheet for sharper impression), and it will be camera-ready. I am assuming here that your headlines will also be typewritten, although perhaps in a different type style, which you can get with an interchangeable element machine.

Too few people, by the way, understand the versatility of such a machine. In Richard L. Clement's *Form Book for IBM Selectric and Remington SR-101 Typewriters,* each chapter represents a different typeface, variations in spacing, different type sizes, and different combinations. It will tell you all you need to know about typewriter composition.

There is one variation you should know about. If your typewriter face is unusually large, you can type your copy on large sheets, then have the printer reduce them to 8½" × 11".

When the copy has been typed in camera-ready form, you may still find some typographical errors. You can indicate them in the margin with a blue nonreproducing pencil. These marks will not be picked up by the camera. If it is a matter of correcting one or two letters, they can be whited out with correction fluid and the correct letters typed over. If the correction requires redoing one or more lines, you can cover the lines

ISSN 0028-9507

THE NEWSLETTER ON NEWSLETTERS

FOR THE NEWSLETTER PROFESSIONAL: Reporting on the newsletter world—editing, graphics, management, promotion, newsletter reviews, and surveys.

Vol. 24, No. 17   (Including Services Directory)   September 1, 1987

NO END IN SIGHT TO DESKTOP PUBLISHING'S INFLUENCE ON NEWSLETTER BUSINESS

In 1873 E. Remington & Sons of Ilion, NY, manufactured the first typewriter with practical application, and two years later Thomas Edison invented the mimeograph (which he sold to A.B. Dick). Rarely in such a short period of time have innovations so dramatically changed the face of the production and dissemination of business information--but we're now witnessing it again with desktop publishing.

NLers are prime beneficiaries--both as users of computer-aided, in-house publishing systems and as major providers of information on the subject. Almost a dozen successful newsletters address desktop publishing, and every day thousands of desktoppers are learning the newsletter medium.

The following articles (including our regular feature, Follow-Up) present some of the latest developments--from a NLer's point of view--in the desktop revolution.

CORPORATE PUBLISHING NL NOW PUBLISHED SIMULTANEOUSLY IN GERMANY

InterConsult's Corporate Publishing, "The Newsletter of Electronic Products and Management," signed an agreement with MACup Verlag, Hamburg, West Germany, that now brings the newsletter out every Monday morning in both English and German in both America and Europe. Cambridge, MA-based InterConsult president David H. Goodstein says:

"The purpose of this joint endeavor is to both export information about the American publishing industry to Europe, and to update the American reader about trends and news from the European market. InterConsult will continue to respond to the growing needs of the international market on electronic publishing by similar agreements in other countries."

MACup Verlag president Thomas Rehder, publisher of the German magazine Page on desktop publishing, cites the success of this June's European Corporate Electronic Publishing Exhibition--co-sponsored by InterConsult--as evidence for high interest on the part of both American and European firms to exchange information.

Figure 23

with self-adhesive correction tape, which comes in various widths, then retype. Most stationery stores stock these items.

The electronic memory typewriter automates certain functions and ranks between the electric typewriter and the personal computer in both cost and efficiency. Such attributes as full-page storage capacity and self-correcting dictionary make editing articles, proofreading, and page makeup much more efficient than having to retype material over and over because of errors, deletions, or sequence changes. Hard copies can be run off, corrected, and revised on subsequent printouts without rekeying entire pages.

The basic steps necessary for preparing camera-ready copy from typewriter composition are diagramed in Figure 24.

Word Processing   Basically a word processor is a typewriter with a memory. This memory makes corrections much easier, and your copy can be stored for future use, then played out automatically at high speed.

The electric typewriter was the first big step toward word processing. It uses what is termed hard copy—really just pieces of paper. With a typewriter, you store copy for future use by filing it. When you need it, you take it out of the file and type from it for camera-ready copy. With memory systems, you can store copies magnetically on cards, tapes, or disks, depending on the equipment. If you want to add material, you can play out the copy, stop, add the new material manually, then continue to play out. You can repeat this process until your final copies are ready for the camera.

There is a variation possible if you want regular type—the optical scanner. Rather than having a compositor rekeyboard from your manuscript, your typographer can use an optical scanner to generate signals that operate a phototypesetting machine. The advantage is that since the setting is done electronically, there is no human error and no need to reproofread. This process has an advantage over regular type composition: once you have perfected your copy, it can be transformed into a designated typeface of any width you desire.

There are other technical developments that are constantly being improved upon. Paper itself is no longer necessary. Text editors are typewriters that display your words on a tube like a TV picture tube, rather than producing them on paper. This tube is called a CRT (cathode ray tube). When your copy is displayed, you can make changes just as you would do by hand on paper. The text editor allows you to continue making corrections until you are satisfied. You can adjust the widths of the line and type sizes. When you are through, just push a key command and get your printout.

TYPEWRITER COMPOSITION

EDITORIAL

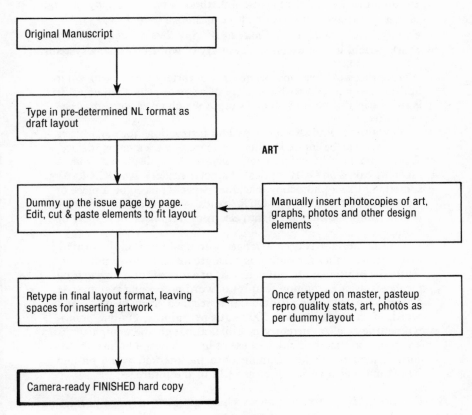

Figure 24
Typewriter composition flow to camera-ready copy.

No longer are you limited to receiving typewriter composition. The copy can be transmitted, as I mentioned earlier, to a phototypesetter and emerge camera-ready. It can even be transmitted to a photocopier if you want only a few copies. (Of course, you can do this manually with a typewritten printout.) There is also a method to put your copy through a scanner to produce stencils or offset masters.

Editing Your Newsletter: A Guide to Writing, Design, and Production, by Mark Beach, has an excellent summary of word-processing systems.

Word processing systems begin with a variety of ways to enter information and end with a variety of ways to print final copy. It is this variety of both input and output which gives word processing its flexibility.

You already know rough copy and instructions for corrections and format can be entered from a keyboard or via a memory device. Words can also be entered into memory and displayed from a machine called an OCR (optical character reader). An OCR looks something like a photocopy machine: paper is placed on a piece of glass or fed into a slot. The OCR "reads" what is on the paper by transforming the characters into electronic impulses for display or storage. . . .

Once material has been arranged into final form on the display medium, flexibility for output is even greater than for input. Currently the printing units, either as part of a text editor or as separate mechanisms, are common features of word processing systems. At a push of a few keys all material is recalled from memory and typed, often at speeds over 500 words per minute. On-line photo-typesetting is also currently possible, although the equipment is less common than printers because of its high cost. On-line photo-copy machines are just coming onto the market, while on-line stencil and negative scanners are still in the future.

Dr. Beach also furnishes an excellent glossary of word-processing terms. Here is a partial sampling.

Daisy wheels are about three inches across and look like a daisy or sunburst. They hold letters and symbols in printers and allow for very high-speed printing.

Floppy disks look something like old 45-rpm records and are the most popular storage medium in word processing.

A *font* is the carrying mechanism for letters and other symbols used to type or print. A daisy wheel is a font. So is a type element (ball) and a film strip in a phototypesetter.

The *hot zone* on a text editor is the last six or eight spaces in a line of type. When the machine hits the hot zone, it will stop its automatic printing to allow the operator to hyphenate words by hand.

Machines *interface* one another when they have been built to work together. For example, an OCR might interface with a CRT text editor but not with an older LED memory typewriter.

A *mag (magnetic) card* is the same size and shape as the common IBM computer punch card and is another common memory system.

The *menu* is the set of instructions entered into the machine from a memory system. The operator selects a specific instruction from the menu and presses the right keys, ordering the machine to carry out the function.

A piece of equipment is *off-line* when it can receive input only from a piece of hard or soft copy.

On-line equipment is wired together so one machine will feed directly into another.

Standalone systems will perform all desired functions from within themselves and their memory software. If they are set up to receive outside help, for example from a computer, they are called *time shared.*

Examples of Preparing Your Newsletter for Printing   When I started in the newsletter business, I used an electric typewriter. Even when first outlining a story, I found myself thinking in terms of the final product. Most newspaper and magazine reporters don't think that way. They know how to type out even lines to get an accurate word count. But the actual space needed for the printing is someone else's decision. When you are writing your own newsletter, you quickly realize that you can save yourself time by thinking of the end result right away.

Character Counting Is Where You Start   Determine how long you want your lines of type to be. Let's say that you decide on seven inches. Look at the scale on your typewriter and you will see that seven inches equals eighty-four characters or spaces. (This will vary with typewriters.) Set your left and right margins for eighty-four characters, and start composing your stories in this length. Make corrections, retype if necessary, but don't make anything definite. When your stories are written, decide on an order for them, cut them apart, and paste them on sheets of paper on a back issue of your newsletter. At this stage, if you have a supervisor or client who approves the final product, show him or her this pasteup. Any changes can be made easily. When okayed, the entire newsletter can be retyped. But remember, you'll have to proofread again for typos and, most annoying, missing lines. Then your newsletter is ready for the camera.

If you have a word processor, you can improve on the process just described. Here's the way I do *The Newsletter on Newsletters.* Stories are written double-spaced to the correct character count in order to estimate their length. The story is then typed on an IBM Mag Card II typewriter, and the story is recorded on a magnetic card, which is identified by a number. It is proofread and corrections are made on the copy. The card is also corrected. The identifying number is written at the top of the story, and the number of lines is written on the bottom. The story is now filed.

When the day comes to put together the newsletter, I have a file folder full of stories that have been approved and proofed. I write the numbers of the four pages on a sheet of paper, noting that page one takes forty-five lines (Fig. 25) and the inner pages take fifty-eight lines. It now becomes a process of deciding the order of the stories, noting the number of lines for each one and its identifying number, and adding one line for each space between stories.

It doesn't always work the first time. Suppose at the end of a page you have two lines left. If you start a new story you will have to use one line for the head and one line for the space, with nothing left to start the story. So you must adjust the story above, either adding, subtracting, or substituting. Now give the sheet of numbers to a typist, who pulls out the

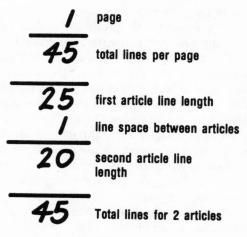

$$\frac{1}{45}$$ page

total lines per page

$$\frac{25}{1}$$ first article line length

line space between articles

$$\frac{20}{45}$$ second article line length

Total lines for 2 articles

Figure 25

appropriate cards, puts paper in the typewriter, and pushes a button. The entire page is printed out perfectly. It takes very little time and I can't think of any reason to make it more complicated.

Publishers with a number of newsletters are converting to word processors with CRT units, in which the typed material is displayed on a video terminal, corrections and adjustments are made, and the completed story is stored in the system's memory. Each editor has a terminal. When it comes time to produce the newsletter, the editor in charge calls up all of the stories from the memory and arranges them in proper order. Camera-ready copy is produced in a matter of minutes.

You can follow the same procedure for a two-column format. This does introduce some complications in layout. If you want to start a long story far down in the first column and continue to the second column, you may want an identifying head at the top of the second column. Some two-column newsletters divide their columns into regular departments, then confine stories to the space allotted. The basic steps necessary for preparing camera-ready copy from word-processor composition are diagramed in Figure 26 (page 94).

Desktop Publishing This option is really a complex series of options. At the outset, I strongly recommend you enlist the advice of your local computer store owner or a qualified hardware-software computer consultant to match your needs with an appropriate personal computer system.

Desktop publishing is an application of personal computers that lets you combine all the functions of newsletter publishing into a series of automated steps. These basic functions are writing and editing, layout and design, page makeup, and typeset composition.

You can bring text and graphics from various sources (via OCR, soft and hard disks, telecommunications interface) into the computer and onto an electronic page—your video screen—where the elements can be moved and edited to your satisfaction before you print a completed page on a dot-matrix printer, laser printer, or phototypesetter. Figure 27 (page 95) shows the flow of these functions from manuscript copy to finished, camera-ready pages.

This kind of system seems like the best of all worlds. Combining the simplicity of typewriter composition, the technology of word processing, the quality and feel of typeset composition with a generous mix of new high-tech hardware and software features, a new breed is created: desktop publishing.

For the purpose of producing your newsletter, the most prolific category of desktop publishing products, with the widest range of capabili-

WORD PROCESSOR COMPOSITION

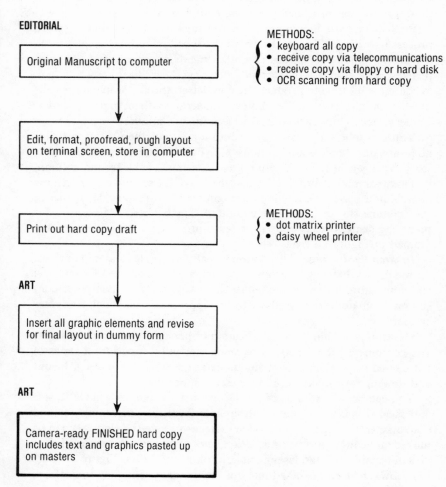

EDITORIAL

Original Manuscript to computer

METHODS:
- keyboard all copy
- receive copy via telecommunications
- receive copy via floppy or hard disk
- OCR scanning from hard copy

Edit, format, proofread, rough layout on terminal screen, store in computer

Print out hard copy draft

METHODS:
- dot matrix printer
- daisy wheel printer

ART

Insert all graphic elements and revise for final layout in dummy form

ART

Camera-ready FINISHED hard copy includes text and graphics pasted up on masters

Figure 26
Word-processor composition flow to camera-ready copy.

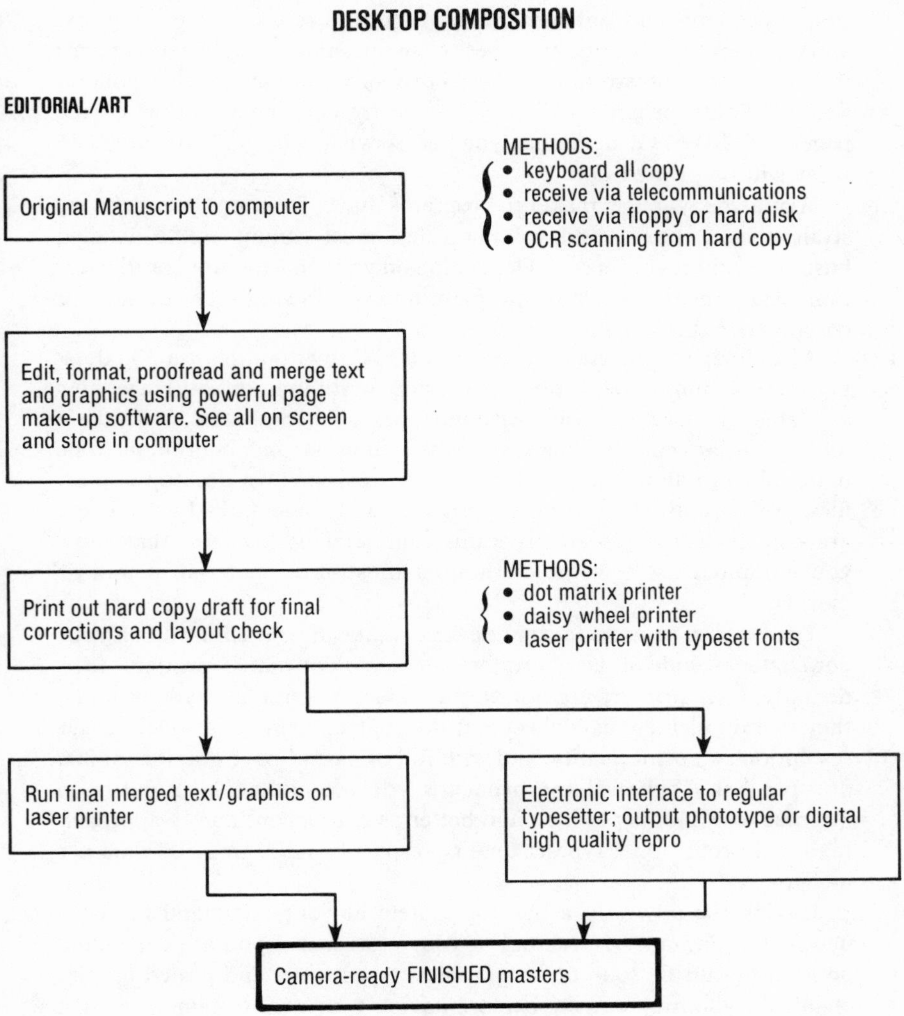

DESKTOP COMPOSITION

EDITORIAL/ART

Original Manuscript to computer

METHODS:
- keyboard all copy
- receive via telecommunications
- receive via floppy or hard disk
- OCR scanning from hard copy

Edit, format, proofread and merge text and graphics using powerful page make-up software. See all on screen and store in computer

Print out hard copy draft for final corrections and layout check

METHODS:
- dot matrix printer
- daisy wheel printer
- laser printer with typeset fonts

Run final merged text/graphics on laser printer

Electronic interface to regular typesetter; output phototype or digital high quality repro

Camera-ready FINISHED masters

Figure 27
Desktop composition flow to camera-ready copy.

ties, is page makeup software. Such programs are used for placing text and graphics on a page, editing these elements, and seeing "what happens if I move this illustration, enlarge this box, or change this column width." Some programs display an electronic representation of the page—WYSIWYG, or "what you see is what you get"—identical to what will be printed out.

While many page makeup programs have functions for drawing straight lines, boxes, and column rules, most cannot create detailed business graphics or images. Depending on your chart, graph, or illustration requirements, you may add painting and drawing software to your computer tool arsenal.

Also, image digitizers and scanners (OCRs) with at least a 300 dots-per-inch scanning resolution (suggested minimum quality) are now available and are compatible with most personal computers. With these tools you can convert black-and-white line art and continuous-tone material from almost any source to prepare your own desktop clip-art files. (Be careful when using copyrighted and trademarked art.) There are also electronic clip-art programs commercially available that allow you unlimited use of some of the best illustration material in today's market.

The types of printers (output devices) that can be used to run off your newsletter include all laser printers and some dot-matrix printers. Incidentally, laser printers are not only capable of emulating typeset fonts, they can duplicate daisy-wheel and dot-matrix printers at much better resolution and print quality, and with full or partial-page graphics at 300 dots per inch. Technical improvements will soon allow this resolution to increase to 600 dots per inch and better as efforts continue to approach high-end professional typeset quality (typically 1,200 to 2,500 dots per inch).

Having the power of a desktop system at your command for your newsletter may not be essential in your case. But if you are depending on a lot of outside sources for graphics, typesetting, and pasted-up mechanicals, you may want to explore having your own system or using a desktop service to handle some of these functions. Depending on your location, many variations on this theme are possible.

Regular Type   Your last option is type. Books, magazines, and newspapers are set in type. Years ago, all type was cast into metal, called hot type. It was locked into forms, ink and paper were introduced, and the printing was made directly from the metal type. This process is called letterpress. Even if you can locate an old-fashioned printer who uses the method, it would be far too slow and expensive for a short-run (that is, small-quantity) newsletter. You may, however, still encounter a linotype machine that casts hot type. A high-quality proof, called a reproduction proof, can be obtained from the type and then printed by the photo offset method. But this would probably be a costly process for a small newsletter.

Cold-type composition machines (used or reconditioned), such as the IBM composer or the AM Varityper, can be found that are inexpensive and simple to operate. Similar to an electric typewriter, these strike-on machines have interchangeable type-font elements in a wide variety of sizes and styles. You may want to operate one in your office, just as you do a typewriter. There is an important difference between cold-type composition and the typewriter method. In typewriter composition, you write the stories and then type them in the order you want for your newsletter, thus making them ready for the camera. In cold-type composition, you don't know as readily how your stories will fit. They will come out a different length from your original copy because each alphabet character has its own width, similar to proportional spacing. Also, because the type fonts vary in size from typewriter manuscript, you have to make a dummy to determine how it will all fit into your newsletter.

The first step is to make a photocopy, so that you can cut and rearrange it in a rough pasteup. Next you must read the proof for errors and have corrected galleys run off. And then in order to get the newsletter in the form you want, you must mount the type on illustration boards, available from art supply stores. If you have the skills, you can do this yourself, or you can hire an artist. The result is a camera-ready mechanical.

You will probably have to go through at least some of these same steps if you have your type set by a professional typesetter or if you have similar service provided by your printer. Most composition equipment today is electronic phototypesetting or digital typesetting and too expensive to be owned by the single-newsletter publisher. Even though the basic operation and end result are similar from machine to machine, the computerized composition equipment available professionally has as many options as desktop publishing systems. Some equipment can scan or digitize original manuscript, read codes from preformatted disks, and interface by cable or telecommunications with personal computers. It is best to explore the services available near your location and determine the best mix of resources to get your newsletter out on a consistent and regular deadline basis.

With any of the forms of typography I've discussed, you have added two steps and additional cost for the privilege of setting your newsletter in a regular typeface. I urge you to consider carefully which form of composition most suits your purposes.

Another production consideration is the complexity of your layout—whether it will be full measure, two column, or three column. The more complex, the more time consuming.

Laying Out the Newsletter   Regardless of the composition method you decide to use, at one time or another during any of these processes a dummy layout may have to be prepared, revised, or created manually. This job could fall to you as editor or artist. Quite commonly it is a joint effort between editor, artist, and typesetter. Even though you may not do the job personally, you should know about the procedure for planning and scheduling purposes and for preparing cost estimates.

This process is the same as for newspapers and magazines. Step one is to select the articles or stories that are in galley type (Fig. 29A; page 100). Next, cut apart the galleys so you have strips of type (Fig. 29B). Step three, gather other elements such as illustrations, special headlines or department heads, graphs, and so forth (Fig. 29C). Next, take a dummy sheet that is ruled to show space for columns and tape or paste the galley type and copies of illustrations in place (Fig. 29D). Step five, after this rough layout has been approved and corrected as needed, prepare pasteup mechanical boards of each page using the final repro-quality galley type from your hard-copy output source. At this time you pasteup your line art illustrations, graphs, and other art elements and keyline, scale, and crop any photographic material to be included (Fig. 29E). This final step in manually preparing camera-ready art must be done with precision drafting tools, and pasteup boards must be kept straight, neat, and clean for best printing reproduction. Art wax is used to hold all the repro materials in place. Another material commonly employed in studios is rubber cement (Fig. 29F).

Using Photos and Other Illustrations   Most informational newsletters don't use photos, although investment letters often have charts and graphs. Include a photo only when it enhances the editorial message. For example, when *The Geyser*—which covers the field of geothermal energy—reported on the installation of a vast $8 million geothermal facility in the Imperial Valley, a few dramatic photos quickly conveyed its scope and size. *The Old-House Newsletter* tells its readers about the architecture and the interior structure of old houses. Its value is obviously increased by photos and sketches. The same is true of *Kovels on Antiques and Collectibles*, in which a drawing or photo of an item conveys more than a page of description.

REGULAR TYPESET COMPOSITION

EDITORIAL/ART SOURCES

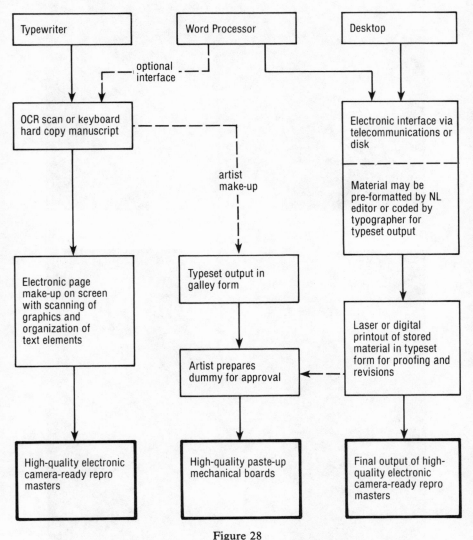

Figure 28
Regular typeset composition flow to camera-ready copy (with variations).

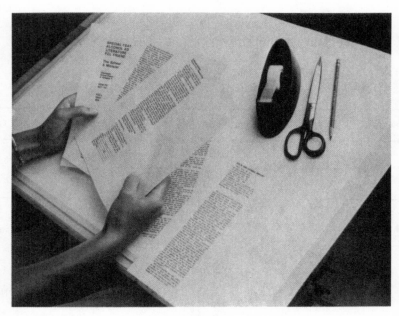

Figure 29A

Figure 29B

Figure 29C

Figure 29D

Figure 29E

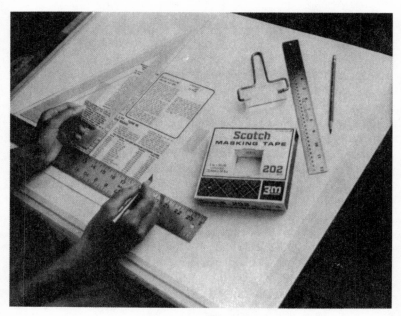

Figure 29F

The farther down you move on the pyramid (see Chapter 2), the more newsletters there are that can make effective use of photos and cartoons. Employee and community newsletters need to feature people, and what better way than to run their photos? Because of the improvements in offset printing, you no longer need professional photos, desirable though they may be. Even Polaroid film will suffice many times. Keep in mind, though, that photos add to the production costs.

Sizing Photos Professional photos are usually 5" × 7" or larger. This is because editors require varying sizes to fit their space requirements and it is easier to reduce a photo than to blow it up. Reducing also improves printing quality; blowups distort it. (A reason why most amateur photos are less desirable, aside from lower quality, is that they are printed in smaller sizes, hence difficult to reduce.)

The process of obtaining the desired size of a photo for reproduction is called scaling. Simple scaling devices are available from photographic stores or a printer, but I find the diagonal line method the simplest (Fig. 30). Put a piece of tissue (onionskin paper used for carbon copies of letters will do) over the photo. Place a ruler at the bottom left of the photo to the top right corner and draw a diagonal line. Then place the ruler along the bottom of the photo and measure the desired width— three inches, for instance. At the three-inch point, draw a perpendicular line until it intersects with the diagonal line. Measure the length of the perpendicular and you will have the height of your picture.

Cropping A photo may have background that attracts attention away from the subject. To eliminate the background, place a tissue over the photo and draw the photo as you want it to reproduce, with the other elements of the photo blocked out. Now measure this area, apply the diagonal line method, and you have the correct size. Be careful, however, in doing this to the sides of a horizontal photo without cropping top and bottom also. If you do only the sides, you will change the whole proportion of the photo, and it may take more vertical space than you desire.

A Tip That Will Save You Lots of Time and Headaches, If Not Money This is so simple and so obvious that you won't believe it is being ignored in sophisticated publishing offices around the nation. When a photo comes to you that you may want to use in a future issue, make sure that the name of the person or place or thing is on the back. You'd be amazed how quickly you'll forget otherwise. One caution: Don't write on the back with heavy ink or a sharp point. You could damage the photo. The best technique is to write or type identification on a gummed label and affix it to the back. The photo credit, if any, should also be included.

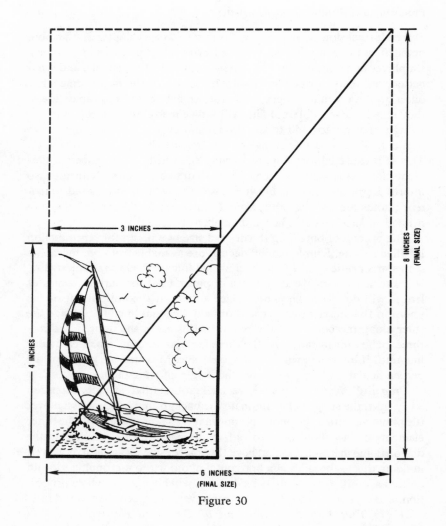

Figure 30

Tools of Your Trade A newsletter editor needs very little equipment, aside from a typewriter or word processor, but a pica ruler is basic (Fig. 31). Printers measure in picas, not inches. The pica ruler has picas on one side, inches on the other. Six picas equal an inch. It's easier to measure in picas because you avoid awkward lengths like one and five-sixteenth inch, for instance, which is simply eight picas. The pica ruler also has a perpendicular piece, so that you can anchor the ruler against the side of your paper and make sure that your typewritten lines are level.

It is similar in principle to the T square that artists use for drawing straight lines.

You also need editing scissors that are long and pointed. They save time when trimming galley proofs, the long repro sheets that typographers furnish for pasteup. A paper cutter would do the trimming even faster, but it is costlier and more cumbersome.

Additional useful items are paper clips and a stapler (use both sparingly) and a tape dispenser. Anything beyond this moves you into the realm of the commercial artist.

If You Insist on Doing Everything Yourself As I said earlier, one reason I oppose editors' doubling as artists is that I think an editor has enough to do to write a literate newsletter; another is that newsletters do not require elaborate graphics. Remember, all that needs to be done is within the capability of a typewriter with interchangeable elements. If you read Richard Clement's book on typewriters, mentioned earlier, you will come up with an amazing number of variations to please most tastes. Also you'll produce camera-ready material and not need to do a pasteup on illustration board.

A volunteer newsletter or one with a very low budget should try to obtain the services of a volunteer with a talent for artwork—someone who can work in tandem with the editor. This person can learn the art side and the editor can go back to his or her typewriter.

There will always be people who like to do the whole thing themselves in spite of all warnings. And I concede that there are, indeed, production areas where a little knowledge of graphics production can save time and money.

Take headlines. Mark Beach points out that there are five ways (other than typing) to make heads.

- Hand lettering. This requires a good artist and the work is slow. But if you have some departments in your newsletter with standing heads, this is a good way to get something distinctive.
- Words from other publications. Cut them out of magazines and catalogs.

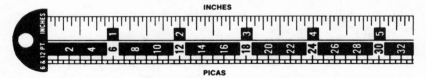

Figure 31

- Transfer lettering. Lettering sheets can be obtained from art stores. They're easy to use, but they become stale over time. They are hard to set evenly. A light table—with a glass top and a diffused light underneath—helps. (These sheets often contain standard symbols as well.)
- Typesetter. Use this method only if you have your copy set in type.
- Headline-making machines. These are fast, easy, and range in price from $395 to $695.

If you want to paste up a finished mechanical, Dr. Beach's book tells you how to do it. He even describes how you can build your own light table.

There are several other publications of use to the inexperienced newsletter editor at the do-it-yourself level, and some are included in the Bibliography.

Printing You have three choices of printing processes: mimeograph, photocopy, or photo offset.

Mimeographing is by far the cheapest process. The basic mimeograph reproduces from a thin paper stencil. You type directly onto the stencil, use correction fluid for changes, then place the stencil on a drum, and either crank or push the button. For short runs, this process is fast and simple if you operate it properly. It also produces the poorest quality of the three methods.

Mimeographing has been upgraded in recent years. Stencils can now be made electronically, and you can put any kind of camera-ready composition—type or typewriter, artwork, photos—on them. You can also use color. If you want to buy a machine rather than use a commercial printer, the mimeograph is less expensive than other printing machines. However, when you finish, you will have a set of 8½" × 11" sheets, rather than the typical folders made from 11" × 17" sheets that we associate with newsletters.

Photocopying produces higher quality at more expense. An ordinary model also limits you to single 8½" × 11" sheets as in mimeographing. However, in large cities there are photocopying printshops with more sophisticated equipment that will print on both sides, collate, and fold. You will pay more for this, but for a few hundred copies it may be worth it.

Photo offset produces the best quality and is not necessarily expensive in quantity. Most printing plants use the photo offset process. Whatever is to be printed is photographed. From the negatives, plates are made that can be put on a press; ink is added; and the press reproduces the image of the plate on paper. Whether this press is sheet fed, web fed, or the like is immaterial to you as an editor. It will be important to you, briefly, only when you begin to buy printing. Then you will have to learn what size presses are best for the quantity you are going to run. Otherwise, as an editor, your concern is that the printing process turns out sharp and clear copies that aren't smudged or crooked. There are suggestions in the Bibliography for materials that explain the printing process. And I recommend spending an afternoon in a printshop. There is much competition among printing plants and a tremendous spread in prices for the same work. It really pays to shop around. Offset printing with type composition will produce the best quality available (Fig. 32; page 108).

As I have stressed, even if you can afford it, don't make your decision to use type rather than typewriter composition on the basis of printing appearance. You will be taking a big step away from the traditional newsletter format, which has proven so successful for subscription letters. Many in the field, such as Kiplinger, believe that typewriter composition is an asset, a hallmark of the professional newsletter publisher. In my years of newsletter watching, I've noted that often the most expensive newsletters in printing quality are put out by nonprofit groups or sell for $5 a year, while the $300 and up subscription letters are typewriter composition. Whatever the sponsorship of the newsletter, it's the content that comes first.

Selecting a Printer Despite the competition, not all printers want to print newsletters. Many will accept the job without being truly dedicated to it, and you will suffer. Printers often accept the job because they hope you will give them some other kind of work that they would really rather do. Or they will accept it because they are afraid you will go to the fellow across the street and *he* might end up with your more desirable printing.

To understand why this is so, you must know a few things about the printing industry. It is an extremely complicated business. It sells volume. Each set of one hundred pieces of paper that rolls off the press costs less than the set before but the higher the total of sets the more the printer makes. Printing presses are designed to do specific jobs. The press that easily accommodates the newsletter size and quickly runs off a few thousand copies is a dwarf compared with the presses designed for magazines, brochures, and newspapers. This simpler press costs the printer considerably less to purchase. Printers wallow in equipment that

PRINTING PRODUCTION SEQUENCE

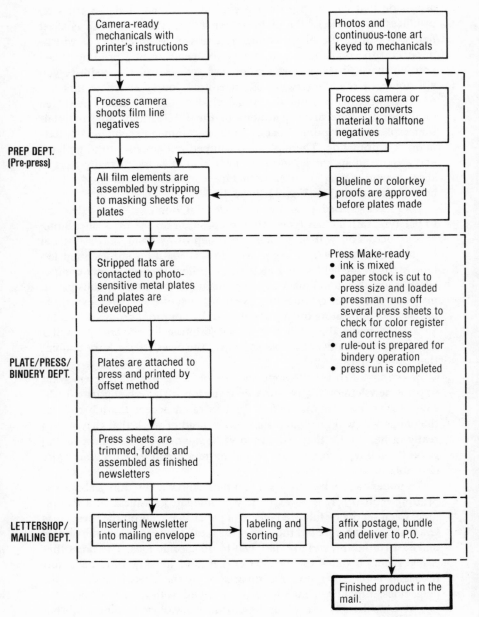

Figure 32
Production sequence for printing and mailing a newsletter.

costs them lots of money and may be subject to replacement because of new technology. Each press has a price tag, an estimate of how much money it should generate each hour. If a printer with large equipment accepts your job and puts it on a press that is designed for large quantity and speed, he has to charge you more. It's that simple. So spend time finding the right printer. Be specific on what you expect, both in quality and time.

Costs Because the cost of even the most expensive printing job on a newsletter is tiny compared with the cost of other forms of printing, some publishers are deceived by prices. Several years ago I priced a four-page newsletter, a thousand copies, at several printers in New York. I got estimates ranging from $95 to $180. Another price factor is time. If you have a monthly newsletter, you can accommodate a five-day printing production schedule and get a low price. But if you have a weekly newsletter, and you want to mail on Saturday and keep your news columns open until Friday afternoon, you're going to pay a premium.

Paper is a continuing problem because of rising prices. Your printer's bid will probably be based on a standard paper that is in stock or is easily obtainable. If you require something special, you will pay more. You may find that you will pay less by selecting a cheaper stock and buying a large quantity in advance. Usually a sixty-pound offset stock is sufficient, providing enough opacity so that the type will not show through on the back side. Coated stock is not used by most newsletters.

If you have decided to produce your newsletter in more than one color, you can implement an additional step at this stage. You can design your extra color to be used for standing matter that doesn't change from issue to issue and preprint this information. There are three benefits to this type of planning.

1. You are buying the paper needed (I suggest a year's supply) in advance at the best price because paper costs are bound to increase within that period.
2. You are assuring that the stock will match from issue to issue for at least the first volume. Some papers have been known to be discontinued or replaced by the manufacturer. Since no two papers are exactly alike (even in plain white offset, look closely!), having your stock stored avoids this problem.
3. You are buying time for your routine press run by having the second color preprinted in advance. This is especially important if your newsletter has a tight production schedule with quick turn-around requirements. For example, on a weekly, biweekly, or monthly

newsletter, the number of actual print production days available to shoot, plate, print, and mail can be reduced to as few as three working days. By having the stock available with one color already in place, the printer has only to deal with imprinting the black master copy for that particular issue. Print drying and press time are cut to the minimum.

There are a couple of warnings about preprinting your newsletter. You should be certain of the design and material contained in the second color. If a change is required in midyear, you'd have to scrap the balance of preprinted stock and start over. Printing too far in advance may cause problems with the printer's ability to store the larger quantities of preprinted stock at his facilities. Also, depending on the climatic conditions of his shop, paper stored over too long a period may warp or curl and cause difficult problems in being fed back through the press for the second color. It is always advisable to discuss the preprinting approach with your printer directly and learn the pros and cons as they apply to your exact situation.

Envelopes are something that many newsletters often overlook. Some newsletters use self-mailers, which I'll discuss later, but most newsletters are sent in envelopes. Your printer may keep a supply of standard number 10 envelopes in stock, which he can quickly print with your corner card (your name and address, printed in the upper-left corner) whenever you need them. He may charge you $60 per thousand. That's not much if that's your mailing quantity, but if you have a monthly, you'll need twelve thousand envelopes a year—at $48 per thousand, or $576. Twice monthly, you'll use twenty-four thousand at $36 per thousand, or $864. And weekly, fifty-two thousand at $24 per thousand, or $1,248. (These figures are 1987 quotes.) Now suppose you ask your printer to supply a year's worth. The price will come down. Suppose also that you go to an envelope manufacturer—you may get fifty thousand for $19 per thousand. In that case, you must find out whether your printer will charge you for storage. If stored too long, the envelopes may stick together. All these variables must be considered. As you can see, learning to save money at the start adds to your income in the long run.

Should You Do Your Printing In-House?   Some publishers do and they swear by it. Others do and they swear at it. As I wrote earlier, I'm constitutionally opposed to learning someone else's trade because it will interfere with what I want to do and what I can do best. At the least, I'd recommend that you start with an outside printer and add up the pros and cons before you even consider doing it yourself.

If you're operating on a shoestring, the idea of you and your spouse happily running off a newsletter in your basement may sound appealing. But, as noted above, printing requires equipment that must be kept up-to-date. You should first investigate the costs.

I have known Peter S. Nagan, of Washington, D.C., for many years. After several years of editing and publishing newsletters, he decided to set up an in-house printing plant, thinking that it would offer, first, convenience and, second, independence. But when he examined the figures he found that he would not be able to keep his plant fully occupied with his own newsletters and would have fixed expenses that would eat up his savings. Since Washington is replete with newsletters, he decided to form a printing company that would specialize in them. Now he has several hundred outside clients and two profitable businesses instead of one. Here are his 1987 estimated costs for setting up an in-house printing plant.

Starting Equipment for an In-House Printing Shop

The items below are what a newsletter publisher would need for a fairly self-contained in-house printing shop.

A. B. Dick or Multilith capable of handling an 11″ × 17″ sheet—one color—with accessories	$20,000*
Small camera, plus plate burner	4,700
Darkroom equipment and plumbing	3,000
Baumfolder—14″ × 20″ tabletop, friction-feed	2,500
Small, automatic-feed postage meter	3,300
Tier	1,500
Assorted light tables, worktables, cabinets, etc.	2,000
TOTAL INVESTMENT	$37,000

Costs of Operating an In-House Print Shop

Fixed Costs (or Overhead)

Depreciation of $37,000 in equipment over 5 years using straight-line method	$7,400 a year
Rent—500 square feet @ $15 a foot	7,500
	$14,900

You could reduce the commitment by having certain steps handled outside—buying your negatives and plates or getting several sets of envelopes addressed at a time. But if time is a factor, buying negatives and plates from another source creates very nervous situations as dead-

*Figures a supplier would quote you may vary with the particular model, its accessories, and the effects of even mild inflation.

lines approach. What's more, if you contract out too much of the job, you lose much of the control and economics of your own shop.

Nagan notes that he has not included the cost of an inserter, which could run from $2,000 to $10,000 or more; it would yield great savings in time, but it is one step that could be done by hand. Nor is there an item for a drill for punching holes; such frills could boost the total further.

Incidentally, Nagan has found that buying used equipment is only asking for trouble; so all prices are for new machines.

Variable Costs

Labor at 45% to 50% of your present printing and mailing bill, depending on your press runs. (Nagan's full-time operation rarely gets below 35%.)

Paper and ink at 15% to 20% of your present printing bill.

Printing supplies at 3% to 5%.

Maintenance and repair of equipment at 2% to 3%.

Outside addressing at 7½%.

Miscellaneous (insurance on equipment, deliveries, etc.) at 1% to 2%.

Others might offer different operation percentages. But based on our experience, we would draw the following conclusions from the figures: Your variable costs would run 75 percent to 90 percent of present printing and mailing bills, depending on volume. If 75 percent, then you would need to be doing a volume of about $60,000 a year to break even (75% of $60,000 = $45,000 plus $15,100 in fixed costs). If variable costs were 90 percent, then you would need to do $127,000 a year to break even (90% × $127,000 = $114,300 plus $15,100 in fixed costs). The break-even levels could be significantly lower if you operated with used equipment and other short cuts, but over time the breakdowns would be correspondingly more costly.

Other large publishers who have investigated have found that they also need outside business to justify an in-house operation. If you're in an area where there are many newsletters, it might be a profitable business. But if you're the only newsletter in town, it's a different matter.

A Word About (Against) Staples   Most newsletters are printed on an 11″ × 17″ sheet, folded to 8½″ × 11″, then folded in three like a letter and inserted in an envelope for delivery. Certain smaller presses do not accommodate this size and the newsletter is printed directly on both sides of 8½″ × 11″ sheets, collated, and folded in three. Some publishers staple the sheets in the top left-hand corner, as one would with a multi-page letter.

I think the stapling is a mistake. It's okay for a letter, which is typed on one side only. But when material is on both sides, the reader is inclined to give short shrift to the back side just because it's awkward to hold and to read. It's much easier for the reader if you forgo the staples—and it saves you time and expense as well. As long as each page is numbered, the reader will not lose his or her way.

I am even more adamant about stapled self-mailers. Few of us have a staple remover handy. The tendency is to rip open the newsletter, destroying parts of the interior and leaving readers with a mess they're inclined to throw into the wastebasket. The truth is that the self-mailer will travel safely through the mail without staples or tape, since a newsletter folded by machine has a fold strong enough to keep it closed. Professional newsletters are done this way all the time.

Whether your newsletter is folded or in single sheets, you may want to three-hole punch it (printers call this drilling) for ease in filing in a three-ring binder—particularly if you are giving or selling binders to your readers. This can also be effective in conveying the idea that your newsletter is worth keeping as a reference. An alternative is to have the printer reproduce three circles in the places where the holes would be, thus saving a few dollars, but making the same point.

7 How to Obtain Subscriptions

The major expenditure for a subscription newsletter is the subscription promotion budget. As you have seen, the editorial and production costs of a newsletter are relatively small. But it takes money to get money back from subscriptions.

Added to the sheer expense of promotion is the fact that most newsletter publishers come into the business from the editorial side. Few are experienced in marketing. Lee Euler, *Tax Avoidance Digest,* reports that marketing skills are harder to find than editorial, that marketing is usually the weakest link in newsletter operations. He advocates one marketing employee for every two newsletters, contending that a good marketing person should increase sales by five times his or her salary. Euler himself spends 40 percent of his gross on marketing.

There are four kinds of advertising available: space advertising, radio and TV, telephone, and direct mail. Supplementing these are publicity and subscription agencies, which I'll discuss later in the chapter.

Space Advertising This simply means buying space in newspapers and magazines. I use the term to differentiate from small classified ads and from advertising through the mail, radio and TV, and telephone. The secret of all advertising is to target your message to your designated audience. Newspapers and magazines have become adept at analyzing their readerships by demographics—their geographical locations, age groups, marital status, occupations, income. For huge circulations, the cost per reader for this information is only pennies, but the total expenditure can be in the hundreds of thousands of dollars. To the advertiser who is expecting hundreds of thousands in return, it is worth it. But to the newsletter publisher, this is a shotgun approach. He or she is looking for prospects only in his or her narrow field of interest. In fact, for the average business newsletter, even a free, full-page ad in the *New York Times* would do little good.

Let's take a look at where newspaper and magazine ads are most effective to see why they usually aren't suited for newsletters. If you are Sears or Ward's, your readers know where to find you. All you are doing is telling them about some special items that are available at a special price. If you are a national advertiser, such as an automobile or cosmetics company, you are calling attention to the product and readers will know where to find it. But when you are a small, specialized service, used by only a few people, you have to tell your readership where to reach you. This will require almost immediate action on their part—reaching for the phone or filling in a coupon and mailing it.

Coupons, then, are the best bet for newsletters trying space ads. Adding an 800 number is better, but you are also increasing your costs. Use an attention-getting headline, describe the benefits of your newsletter, and include a coupon the reader can fill in and return to you. For maximum response, offer a free sample or a free report. When sending the free item to the responder, enclose a sales letter asking for a subscription order. Keep track of the number who take out subscriptions to find out how well your ad pulled.

A variation is "qualifying" your respondents. Instead of a free offer, charge $1 to $5 for one or more copies of your newsletter. Fewer will respond, but they will have qualified themselves as stronger prospects by paying something, hence showing some interest in your product.

Investment letters, which advertise in the business sections or in investment magazines, seem to do best with coupon ads. This is because a large proportion of readers are interested in financial matters. Other newsletters aimed at smaller, more specialized segments are not likely to do as well. However, it's well worth testing a coupon space ad to see whether this approach will work for you.

Radio and TV   Radio and TV have some of the same characteristics of space advertising because the audiences are large. TV is dominated by national advertising; local advertising is usually for stores. Occasionally you will see a special product advertised, such as a cooking utensil, which you can purchase by calling a toll-free number. In this case the advertiser is seeking a direct response—action now—but he or she must have a product that has great universal appeal and it must be cheap.

Many radio stations are more specialized, gaining certain audiences—youth, classical music lovers, sports fans. But even these narrower audiences are often too broad for your special message. And since many people listen to the radio in their automobiles, it is difficult for listeners to remember a telephone number if they want to respond.

The *Kiplinger Washington Letter* and a few other newsletters with broad appeal can use this medium successfully. It is too costly per return for the rest.

Telephone   Some newsletters have found telephone selling effective. But it is costly, requires skilled salespeople (there are several companies that specialize in this kind of selling), and sometimes has strong negative effects. Because it is an interruption, many people, at home or at work, are highly irritated by telephone solicitation. This seems to be particularly true of professional people, many of whom are newsletter prospects. However, what counts is how well this medium works for you. By all means test it.

Using the telephone for subscription renewals is quite a different matter. Many newsletters have found that after a renewal series by mail has run its course, a number of the holdouts can be reached by phone and brought back in. If your list is small, it is quite possible to telephone them yourself, or have a staff member do it. Some people tell me that such calls not only work but are often the beginning of firm friendships.

Direct Mail   This is a complicated and costly way of doing business, but it is the only advertising medium that works for the majority of newsletters. While direct mail irritates some people, the irritation is not as immediate and personal as with the telephone. All they have to do is throw away your mailing.

Direct mail is so called because it has the element of direct response—which is the one requirement in selling subscriptions. (In the years ahead, many of the direct response strengths of direct mail may be assumed by electronics; but until that day comes, you must concentrate on direct mail.)

If you have never been involved in direct mail, you will find it a fascinating field—calling for lots of creativity, yet having the capacity for measurable results. It can prove whether or not a technique works, tell you your costs, and—within certain boundaries—predict dollar return. It is a pragmatic field. Either it works or it doesn't. The rules for successful direct mail are deceptively simple. Locate your target audience, mail to it, and measure results—if it works, mail again. It is similar to poker in that you can learn the rules in five minutes, but it takes a lifetime to play well because there are infinite variations and combinations to be studied and mastered.

Mailing Lists   In the chapter on marketing, I explained that you must have names and addresses before you have a market. Your job is to inform these people about your service and to persuade them that they should subscribe. The selection of the right lists is the single most important effort in direct mail advertising. The most amateurish sales letter to the right list will do better than a beautiful presentation to the wrong list. Naturally, you want to be expert in all aspects of direct mail—the list, the offer, and the direct mail package. But the list is where you start.

There are three general categories of mailing lists: house or customer lists, mail response lists, and compiled lists.

House Lists. These are lists you have put together of your customers— people who have subscribed, purchased a service, or made an inquiry. Of course, if you are starting in business, you won't have these, which is unfortunate, because this will be your best list. Magazines that decide to launch a newsletter always start with their house lists, as, of course, do multiple publishers. Just as soon as you get your first subscriber, start your house list. To it you will add the persons who inquire about your newsletter by phone or letter and, eventually, your expires—subscribers who do not renew at the end of the first year.

Mail Response Lists. These are the second best performing lists, made up of people in your subject area who have purchased something by mail, either a newsletter or a product. The important point is that they read mail and they respond. Suppose, for instance, you are trying to appeal to doctors. A doctor who has purchased something by mail, even if it is only a desk calendar, is a better prospect than one who has not, even though your newsletter may be directly in his field of interest. There are many people who just don't react to mail. By using a mail response list, you won't waste money mailing to such people. Mail response lists are really the house lists of other marketers.

Compiled Lists. If you can't find the kinds of names you want in mail response lists, you may turn to compiled lists. These are made up from various directories, including the telephone directory, of people in organizations and professional and occupational fields. There is a great volume. Your task is to test these lists to find if they are responsive to your offer.

It is safe to say that in most cases a mail response list will outperform a compiled list—and your house list will outperform both. I have said that some people do not respond to mail and, generally, these tend to be those under thirty-five years old, who are more likely to use the telephone than older generations. Those who have responded by mail within the past six months are called "hot-line" names, and they will be more productive. Likewise, new names added to a list usually outpull the rest of the list. And those who have purchased something from you two or more times will be livelier prospects than others who buy just once.

Where Do You Get Lists? You can either exchange or rent mailing lists. It is rare that you can purchase one, nor, usually, is there any reason why you should want to do so. You are interested in using only lists that produce enough orders and inquiries. These become names that you own for your house list.

List exchanges can sometimes be arranged with a publisher in a related field, even a direct competitor. You both benefit, and no money passes. You just trade an equal number of names.

More often you will rent through a list broker, a compiler, or a list manager.

A list broker does not own lists. He knows who has lists—he has experience in how they perform and what they cost. It costs you no more to do business with a list broker. He receives a 20 percent commission from the list owner but charges you only the price of the list as established by the owner.

A list compiler puts together lists from various sources and owns these lists. In certain special situations, a compiler can put together a list to your specifications.

A list manager handles the rental of lists for owners who do not want to be bothered by rental details: taking orders, shipping the lists, billing. The manager assumes these duties and deducts a charge for his services from the rental fees that he obtains for the list owner.

Currently, list rentals average between $45 and $60 per thousand and between $125 and $150 per thousand, depending on how specialized the list is. Even more highly specialized lists will cost more. You can consult the authoritative Standard Rate & Data's *Direct Mail List Rates & Data,* which contains descriptions of numerous lists. The compilers and list management companies also issue catalogs of lists, and many advertise in trade publications such as *Direct Marketing* magazine.

An advantage in dealing with a list broker is that once you become a customer, he acts as a consultant to you. He will help you develop a clear and concise description of the characteristics of your customer. A competent list broker wants to find lists for you that perform well, so that you will keep reordering. You should investigate a number of list brokers to find those of most help to you. In some cases, as with newsletter publishers, you will find that your needs for lists are not large enough to interest the broker. If you want ten thousand names and others are looking for a million names, you can see that you will not command as much attention from the broker. Look around for list brokers who understand the newsletter business. As the field grows, there will be more of them.

List brokers maintain data cards that give brief summaries of lists— list owners, descriptions, and sizes. This is a good way to learn the possibilities, but you will need a lot more information about the performance of the list before you rent it. Brokers will constantly look for new lists for you; they will verify information; they will clear with the owner the mailing piece you will want to send; and they will clear the mailing date you request.

You may not realize that there are 4,800 Yellow Pages telephone directories in the United States. They contain thousands of business categories, which may be useful in identifying companies in given industries that could become prospects for you. If you can put your hands on compilations of Yellow Pages advertisers in your field, you've found a more comprehensive listing than you'll find in normal business directories. For example, U.S. Business Directories (U.S.B.D.: 5707 S. 86th Circle, P.O. Box 27347, Omaha, NE 68127, 402-593-4593) provides over a thousand separate directory titles compiled annually from U.S. Yellow Pages.

Maintaining Your Lists   As I mentioned earlier, your first task is to build a house list. Once you have several thousand names, engage a service firm to put them on a computer. You'll have to do a lot of shopping to locate a firm that suits your needs. Before you have your list entered into the system, you must make some decisions as to the program you require. Each name will be given an identifying match code—a unique combination of numbers and letters to prevent duplications. You can also code in other information about your list. Generally, you will want to identify the names as subscribers, expires, and prospects, so that you can generate lists of any one of the three. This way, when you send a solicitation mailing, you won't annoy your current subscribers because you can eliminate them from the mailing. It is also useful to code in the source of the name, that is, the list from which you obtained it. Thus you can find out which lists produced the largest number of subscribers. Beyond that, coding depends on your specific needs. In any event, you will probably not need all of the demographic information that is so important in the vast mail order field that aims at the entire consumer market. However, if you also sell books, you might consider coding in information about purchases of books made by your subscribers, because this will tell you the dollar volume of a particular subscriber and will be of interest to persons wanting to rent your list.

Alternatively, you can obtain appropriate data base software and keep the list in-house. This gives you greater control, but you will have to determine whether it saves on costs.

Decoys.   Decoys are names scattered throughout the list that are known only to you. They may be invented names at addresses accessible to you—or friends or relatives. The process is sometimes called "seed-ing" or "salting." Be sure to scatter enough names throughout the list so that if only a portion is used it will still contain some decoy names. There are several reasons for decoys. They can tell you when the mailing is received in various parts of the country. By adding your own name and address as a decoy, you can know quickly if your letter has been mailed. The main purpose of decoys, however, is to detect illegal use of your list. They will give you sufficient evidence if you need to take legal action. It is also a good practice to insert some decoys when you rent another's list so that you know when the mailing has been received.

Merge/Purge. With the high cost of lists, it is obvious that duplicate names are wasteful and costly. Through match codes, rented lists can be run against your own list and duplicate names removed. This is called merge/purge and for large mailers it has been a godsend. The realities are, though, that it is only cost-effective in quantities of a million or more names. It is not economical for the average newsletter.

Keeping Lists Clean. This is a country on the move. At least 25 percent of the names and addresses on your list will change in one year. If you are able to keep up with the replacements, you will have a constant source of new names that will keep your list fresh. Someone in your organization will have to be responsible for making the changes on a regular basis. This is a frustrating job because many people are careless in notifying others when they move; many don't even bother to institute forwarding instructions. Companies will not inform you of deaths or retirements either. If there is a trade publication in your field, read it carefully for personnel changes. This is a time-consuming task, but worthwhile because names are money to you. When you start your own list, you will be part of the direct mail fraternity. Make sure *you* notify people who mail to you of changes within your own organization.

The best way to keep a list clean is to mail to it frequently and make the appropriate changes. Having a clean list is also an important factor if you rent your list to someone else.

Address Correction Requested. First-class mail is supposed to be for-warded, but you can't count on it. And third-class bulk, which is now generally used in large mailings, is not forwardable. You will get back from the post office those letters that can't be delivered—"nixies"—but you won't know where the addressee has moved. The best thing to do is to use the address correction service of the post office. On your en-velopes, you print three words—Address Correction Requested—and pay a deposit to your local post office. The post office will return to you either the entire envelope or a photocopy of the mailing portion of the envelope and charge your account 25¢ each. It is well worth the money. It would be worth even more, but unfortunately the post office gets only about half of all changes. But these are changes you wouldn't normally get on your own.

One word of caution: Do not use this service when you are mailing to rented lists. There's no point in paying for someone else's mistakes. If you forget, or your printer uses these envelopes by mistake, try to make a deal with the list renter so he will pay something for these nixies. If there are more than 10 percent nixies, notify your list broker and see if he can help you. At least the broker may be more careful in renting this list in the future.

Another list-cleaning device is to enclose a note in a mailing asking the recipient if he or she wants to remain on the list or if any changes should be made.

However, a list full of nixies is not necessarily bad. In the practical world of direct mail, what counts is results. Jack Oldstein of Dependable Lists says that some lists with lots of nixies will pull better for you—higher dollar return—than a clean list. So a list of good prospects, even if it has a lot of out-of-date addresses, is better than a completely up-to-date list of people who have no interest in your newsletter.

Lists as a Source of Income   Over time, your own house list will grow. One day you will have enough names to be attractive to other advertisers. You should then place these lists for rental. This can produce a welcome additional source of income. You can either handle the rentals yourself and notify list brokers or engage a list management firm to do it for you. Even though the outside firm will charge approximately 10 percent for its efforts, on top of the 20 percent brokerage fee, it is usually to your benefit to have it handle all of the details. The outside firm will bear the expenses of advertising the list, order processing, accounting, and payment collection. You are better off letting an expert represent you rather than getting immersed in something that is not your primary business.

Testing of Lists   Testing is a device essential in direct mail and it starts with lists. If you are considering renting a large list—20,000, 50,000, 100,000 names—you need some concrete evidence that it will perform. At this writing, the postage alone on a bulk third-class mailing of 100,000 would be $12,900. Even though a list has performed fantastically for other mailers, the only thing that counts is the results *you* will get. So you test a portion of the list.

How large should that portion be? The experts say, test enough names to produce thirty to forty subscriptions. Suppose, just to keep it simple, that you have been getting 1 percent returns from your mailings. This means 10 orders per thousand. To get forty orders, you would need 4,000 names. The minimum amount would probably be 5,000, and this should be safe.

Suppose that your test list returns just what you expected—0.80 percent. Does that mean that 100,000 will then return the same percentage? Not necessarily. According to probability tables it might pull more or less. You have to decide how much less you can accept and still have a successful mailing. Suppose you decide that you can afford a 0.25 percentage point limit of error. You consult a probability table based on 95 percent level of confidence. The table tells you that your large mailing would pull 0.55 to 1.05 percent ninety-five out of a hundred times.

These tables are purely statistical, but they help avoid costly mistakes in large mailings. You can find such tables in standard books such as Bob Stone's *Successful Direct Marketing Methods.*

To make a successful test, you first need to get a good sampling of the list. You don't test the first 5,000 names, or 5,000 names drawn from major cities. You test on an nth-name basis, which means that if you were using 5,000 names in a list of 25,000, the computer would select every fifth name (25,000 divided by 5,000). Of course, if the total size of the list is only 5,000, you don't bother to test a sampling. Just mail to the whole list.

Your list broker can help you set up the details of a test; you shouldn't have to work them out yourself. Just remember that you should never mail to a large list without testing.

Security of Your Lists   Your house list is a major asset in your business. Make sure that your computer house has adequate security against fire and theft. Make sure your mailing house provides security against theft of your list while it is in the mailing house's hands. Perhaps, to be certain, you should keep a magnetic tape of your list in your office safe.

Selling Subscriptions to Libraries   One list that is open to all newsletters is libraries. Some publishers refuse to sell to libraries, fearing that too many readers will use the library copy rather than subscribe on their own. Most publishers, however, are interested in selling to major public libraries, special libraries, and university libraries. These lists are easily available. One advantage to this market is that you have a chance of getting a much higher market penetration and can thus add perhaps as many as two thousand subscribers. Another advantage is that once a library likes your publication, it may place a standing order. This means that every year you simply send an invoice at the time of expiration and you will receive payment for renewal.

Keep in mind that libraries are inundated with periodicals and are always fighting budget limitations. So if there are several high-priced newsletters in a field, the library is unlikely to take them all. It will select the one that appears best for its readers.

Librarians agree on one thing—they expect your newsletter to have an index, at least annually. This is because libraries use newsletters to answer inquiries. Without an index, they believe the newsletter is useless to them. As I will discuss later, an index is a strong selling point in your promotion, and it will certainly become internally useful after you've been in business a year. You should have one.

Company libraries are a special case. Some publishers do not promote to them because, they observe, the sale is really made to an executive, who then asks the librarian to enter a subscription. This is not always so. Sometimes the executive asks the librarian for recommendations of newsletters in a special field. He or she cannot mention yours if it is not familiar.

A library will appreciate a discount, but whether it is necessary is a moot point.

How to Sell Subscriptions Through Direct Mail   Before discussing your actual mailing piece, let's first consider the strategy of your direct mail solicitation. I have defined direct mail as a medium that sells directly to one person. And in everything you write, you have one person in mind. Direct mail expert Denison Hatch, publisher of *Who's Mailing What!,* describes direct mail as intimate conversation—"the only truly participatory advertising art form." He says, "You find the envelope in your mailbox, and immediately have the option of participating or throwing it away. If you elect to go ahead and read it, *you* make it all happen—examining those elements you want to . . . in the order you choose. Free-lancer George Duncan uses a splendid term to describe direct mail: 'theater in print.' "

You take the first step when you decide the market for your newsletter and develop a profile of the kind of person who would have an interest in your subject matter and your approach to the subject matter. You take the next step when you find mailing lists—names and addresses of actual companies and people in your target audience.

Now your job is to tell that person that you have a newsletter available. And you must make an appealing offer that will cause him or her to respond favorably. On the surface, it would seem that all you have to do is mail a copy of your newsletter with a note saying, "Here it is. Send back the order card." Unhappily, it's not that simple. As Walter Prescott, a list broker, was fond of saying, "There's a vast difference between should and would." Many people who should respond never do—we're after those who would respond. Such is the perversity of people and the diversity of perception that you may find company A buys a hundred copies of a newsletter and company B in the same field won't buy even one.

Over the years, experts in the direct mail field have developed a variety of successful approaches. Particularly pertinent is *Success in Newsletter Publishing: A Practical Guide,* in which Frederick D. Goss has assembled a number of examples of effective promotions by newsletter publishers. Bob Stone has identified twenty-five basic offers, which he lists and describes in *Successful Direct Marketing Methods.* Keep in mind that many of these offers refer to products rather than to newsletter subscriptions. The offers listed below have some pertinence to newsletters. Rather than quoting Bob Stone's comments, I give my own as they apply to newsletters.

- *Free information.* This could be suitable in a space ad to get leads. A better way would be to assign a small charge, such as three issues for $1, in order to "qualify" the person as being more seriously interested. A mailing sending only free information would not be cost-effective.
- *Samples.* A sample swatch may be a great way to sell a pair of pants by mail. But a sample of the newsletter is not necessarily an effective method. Since this is one of the controversial points in newsletter promotion, I will discuss it in full in the section on the direct mail package starting on page 131.
- *Trial subscriptions.* There are two kinds of trials, paid and free. The purpose of a trial is to help your prospect meet you partway. Through a trial, the prospect can get acquainted with your newsletter over a period of weeks or months, and, you hope, get the habit. Trials usually have a limit of three months. They are best suited to dailies, weeklies, and twice monthlies.

A *free trial* will produce a larger response than a paid trial. However, the degree of interest will be less. You will attract more curiosity seekers, just as those who visit your for-sale house on the weekends are not usually as serious as someone who shows up on a Tuesday morning. For the lower-priced newsletters, the free trial is worth trying.

The *paid trial* is particularly suitable to the high-priced letter. You ask the prospect to put up a fraction of the cost of the subscription.

There is more likelihood that the prospect will read the trial issues carefully because he or she has made an investment of money.

With either type of trial, you will need another mailing package—a package designed to convert the reader from trial to full subscriber. This is usually done through a series of letters and order forms that accompany the trial issue. In each letter you call attention to a particular selling point and attempt to convert the reader to a full subscription. Keep records of the response to each of these conversion letters. Try to find out if a certain letter seems to have more appeal or if, for instance, more people always respond on the third letter. These statistics are invaluable in planning future promotions. Percentage conversions of trials are much higher than in your overall solicitation. You may draw a 1 percent response for the trial offer, but of those respondents 25 percent may convert to a full subscription.

Much care must go into selecting the right price and the right length of time for the trial subscription. For weeklies, thirteen weeks seems to be good. Again, don't take that as gospel. Test.

- *Conditional sale.* Stone describes this as prearranging the possibility of long-term acceptance based on a sample. He uses as an example: "Yes, please send me the current issue of *Psychology Today* and enter my name as a trial subscriber at the special introductory rate of $6 for 12 issues (half the regular price). However, if not delighted with the first issue, I will simply write 'cancel' on the bill and return it without paying or owing anything, keeping the first issue as a complimentary copy." This is a recognized offer in newsletters: I call them "paid trials."
- *Till forbid.* This means that the customer authorizes you to keep sending issues until he forbids it. This is, in effect, a "standing order," which is more common with libraries but certainly desirable for all subscribers. However, it is not suitable for initial orders. Your subscriber has to really believe in you before he or she would place such a standing order.
- *Yes-no.* Stone says that involvement—asking the prospect to respond through a token or stamp, whether or not he or she accepts or rejects—produces more favorable response than when no rejection option is provided. This is not used often in newsletters, but it should be tested.
- *Time limit.* This can be effective when tied to a special price or a special premium. It should generate a better response than a straight offer with no time constraint. It is better to be specific—July 31 rather than thirty days.

- *Friend-of-a-friend.* This asks the subscriber to recommend some friends to whom subscription information will be sent. This is an inexpensive way to get leads. It works for many newsletters, including Kiplinger. If you don't ask for too many names, you will get a good response. People like to be helpful. Some publishers offer a little gift or premium for the names. Others have found that a gift is not necessary. The gift smacks of bribery to some respondents. They would rather be approached as your friend and reply to your request as such. If you promise not to mention the subscriber's name, you will get more prospect names. If you ask the subscriber's permission to use his name, you will get fewer prospects, but subscription results are usually better.
- *Contests.* These are very successful with magazines, but not usually with newsletters. The reason for this is that magazines can afford to discount more heavily, since revenue comes from advertising. Contests and sweepstakes need huge mailings, again not suitable for newsletters. I do not deny the possibility that an inventive publisher can make them work, but it won't be for the small-universe publication.
- *Discounts.* These can be for cash, for an introductory offer, or for copies in bulk. But if you discount too often, prospects will conclude that this is your regular price and will resist paying the full price.
- *Lifetime membership.* These are used by clubs that sell merchandise at discounts. A few newsletters offer lifetime subscriptions in order to generate cash, but you don't want too much money tied up in this way.
- *Gifts.* These will almost always increase response. However, the selection of the gift, premium, or bonus offer is critical. The best premium is linked directly to the subject matter of your newsletter. A collection of back issues made up into a portfolio or binder, a book that you publish, or someone else's book in the field are all suitable premiums. Transistor radios, calculators, or pens are not suitable, because the recipient will usually be interested only in the gift, not your newsletter.
- *Deluxe alternative.* A classic example is a dictionary company offering either its regular edition or a thumb-indexed one for $2 more. By giving a choice, the advertiser often increases total response and total dollars. An appropriate offer for newsletters would be a set of back issues with a $6 binder for $2 more.
- *Charters.* These are widely used by newsletters when they begin. A charter subscriber receives a special rate over the regular rate. There is a time limit. Some charters guarantee a lower rate to charter sub-

scribers for the life of the subscription. Others are one-time offers.

- *Guaranteed buy-back.* This is not applicable, since a newsletter is not a product that you would take back and resell. However, you must guarantee satisfaction, either by refunding a portion or all of the subscription money upon the subscriber's request.
- *Multiproduct.* This may be a series of cards or sheets for several products, each with its own order form. It may apply to newsletters if you have several books or directories in addition to a newsletter. The idea is to increase the dollar value of your mailing.
- *Piggybacks.* These are "add-on" offers that ride along with major offers at no additional postage cost. They may even be for someone else's product if it is a logical fit for your prospects; you charge the other advertiser for including his offer in your mailing. However, Bob Stone advocates testing to find out whether piggybacks add to or steal from sales of the major offer.
- *Bounce-backs.* These are predicated on the premise that once a person buys a product he or she is in a better mood to buy more. You can include offers for other products you handle in your initial shipment or with the invoice.
- *Optional terms.* This gives the prospect the option of terms at varying rates. An example would be two- and three-year subscriptions that are a saving over the one-year rate.
- *Flexible terms.* This is used in the magazine business. A prospect is offered a bargain weekly rate for a minimum period of sixteen weeks. He or she is given the option of adding more weeks at the same low rate. Newsletter publishers must decide just how low they want to put their prices.
- *Exclusive rights.* This refers to syndicated newsletters, which were described in Chapter 1. The first subscriber in a trading area, perhaps a bank, has exclusive rights in the area.

Hard Offers versus Soft Offers   As you can see, many direct mail offers provide a variety of inducements to get the prospect to subscribe. In a hard offer you simply describe the publication, name the price, and enclose an order form—no charter, no premiums, no discounts. However, people are often so busy that they devote only a few seconds, if any, to looking at the mail that comes to them.

Aggressive mailers have learned that soft offers, such as discounts, premiums, and charters, improve response.

With the proliferation of soft offers, it becomes more and more difficult to get results from a hard offer. The customer has been spoiled. He or she expects more and more. But test a hard offer occasionally. Not only do you get a bigger profit, but those who accept the offer are more likely to renew, whereas those who act on soft offers may want another favor at renewal time.

Bill Me, Installments, and Credit Cards Anything you can do to ease the pain of paying will produce a higher response. Three magic words are "Send no money." Billing a subscriber increases your costs, but it may mean the difference between making the sale and not making it. Companies are used to being billed, for it often is a time-consuming procedure for an executive to get a check written by the accounts department. Government is the same way. Even if you demand cash with order, you will have difficulty in getting it.

As you gain experience, you will learn whether your universe consists of good credit risks or whether you are likely to lose more than 5 percent on no-pays. Usually, if you don't receive payment for a newsletter subscription within ninety days, you should cut the subscriber off your list.

If you expect to mail to the same lists several times during the year, keep a record of these no-pays. They are likely to show up again accepting your offer, counting on getting three months more of free service. There aren't many such people in the world, but they exist in every field.

Installment payments are rarely used. They would make sense primarily for a large ticket item of $300 or more. Paradoxically, companies that subscribe to such high-priced newsletters have the capacity to pay. It could be worthwhile to experiment with granting installment terms.

Credit card payments are certainly worth trying. They work best with members of consumer and professional groups in which an individual pays for the subscription. There are two types of credit cards: those that require the owner to pay in full each month and those that permit partial payments. Pick the partial payment cards because subscribers can pay off as they want, and hence are more likely to make the purchase on this kind of card. Of course, you share a few percentage points with the credit card company, but it can be worth it. While you have extended credit to your subscriber, you have the cash.

Toll-free 800 telephone numbers are also worth trying for the larger newsletter. The advantage is that you can give your prospect a chance to respond immediately while he is at the height of his interest. The disadvantage is that the minimum cost of the 800 service may be too steep to make it feasible.

What Percentage Return Should You Expect? This is the most frequently asked question in direct mail, and there has long been a myth that 2 percent is the average. This is completely false. There is no figure that is standard. Moreover, with the expansion of direct mail and the competition for the customer dollar, mailings do not pull as heavily as they once did.

There are several steps you can take in order to project the response rate you want for a mailing. First of all, your objective is to get your out-of-pocket expenses back. You do not consider your profit, your salary, your overhead. You simply aim to get back the money that it cost you to get into the mail. This cost is for the preparation of the mailing package: printing of envelopes, letters, enclosures, order forms, postage, and mailing-house charges for collating, stuffing, metering, and putting into the mail.

With postage and printing costs on the increase, plus general inflation, it costs more and more per thousand to get into the mail. Three hundred and fifty dollars is now a low figure. (This includes third-class bulk mail, not the prohibitively high first-class postage.) Let's say your cost is $350 per thousand and you are mailing 10,000 pieces. Your total expenditure will be $3,500. Divide that by the price of your newsletter. If your newsletter is $35 you will need 100 orders to get your money back. Now determine what percentage response produces 100 orders. One hundred divided by 10,000 equals 1.0 percent. It is certainly possible to get a 1.0 percent return, but if you get even a shade less, you are not going to recover costs. And you certainly have no room to make anything on the mailing.

Suppose instead that your newsletter's price is $100. Thirty-five orders will bring back your money and the percentage response needed is 0.035 percent. This would seem to be more prudent. And if you end up drawing 0.07 percent, you will double your money.

A common approach to establishing a price for your newsletter is to tally the estimated fixed costs and promotional costs and calculate how many subscribers are needed at various prices to cover these costs. Even though you have given yourself a salary, add in a profit factor of 10 to 30 percent. You are in business to make a profit, not just draw pay.

Most mailers, then, consider all of these factors. And you can see why newsletter subscription prices are higher than they were twenty years ago, when you could get into the mail for $100 per thousand.

Consider also the plight of the low-priced letters. A $10 newsletter in my example would need 350 orders, a response rate of 3.5 percent; a $15 newsletter would need 236 orders, a response rate of 2.36 percent.

It is always possible, of course, that your newsletter would produce a 5 percent response. However, if you make your assumptions on such a return, you have now left the field of direct mail marketing and entered the gambling arena.

Some Things You Should Know About Postal Regulations and Practices Almost every type of newsletter has to deal with the post office at various levels of complexity. Get to know the highest-level person possible in your local post office.

- *Second-Class Mail.* Your local postmaster can interpret the regulations on this special money-saving service.
- *Dual Addresses.* Many newsletters, as well as other businesses, have dual addresses (a street address and post office box). Mail will be delivered to the address appearing on the line immediately above the city and state of destination—and the ZIP code must correspond to the delivery address.
- *Where to Place Site and Apartment Numbers in Addresses.* The post office requests that these appear on the same line as the street address, or on the line above the street address.
- *How to Make Sure That Your Mailing Got Mailed.* If you use a lettershop, make sure that it returns to you the postal receipts it was given when it deposited the mail. Either of two receipts, Form 3602 or Form 3602 PC, will give the weight per piece mailed, total number of pieces, rate charged, and name of permit holder.
- *RMRS (remote meter setting).* If you use a postage meter, try to get RMRS service. This means that instead of taking your meter to the post office for payment and resetting, you can pay by mail and get the meter setting from a computer by telephone.
- *Solicitations in the Guise of Bills, Invoices, or Statements of Account.* You must put "Renewal Notice" rather than "Renewal Invoice" on your forms to conform to a postal regulation (Domestic Mail Manual 123.41). Sharpsters who have sent out phony invoices that unwitting people have paid made this regulation necessary. In the case of newsletter renewals, keep in mind that an invoice is for service ordered. If a subscriber is due for renewal you cannot send an invoice until he or she has expressly requested continuation of service.
- *Postal Permits.* If you use third-class bulk mail, you will need a permit from your local post office. The annual fee is $50. If you enclose in your mailing a business reply envelope (BRE) on which you pay the return postage, there are two methods of setting up the account with your post office. For an annual fee of $50, you pay 23¢ on top of the 22¢ first-class postage for each returned BRE; for $160 annually, you pay 7¢ plus the first-class postage. If you plan on receiving more than

a thousand BRE's a year, the higher annual fee is cost-effective. There is no fee for the address correction privilege. Charges will be made for each piece returned. Again, you may deposit money rather than paying each time. (Note: These were the fees at the time of writing. Always check with your post office.)

The Direct Mail Package The subscription solicitation that you send to your prospects is called a direct mail package because it has several elements.

The classic package consists of an envelope, a letter, a descriptive brochure or flier, an order form, and, possibly, a return envelope, either postage paid or without postage. Instead of a separate card and envelope, the order form may be part of a postcard, either business reply (postage paid) or requiring postage.

There are several variations to this package I will discuss later.

As I have said, direct mail has the advantage of being subject to testing. When you are puzzled as to which approach to take, test the alternatives and select the one that performs best for you.

There appears to be almost universal agreement on one alternative that has been tested over the years: a letter with a descriptive brochure will outperform either a letter or a brochure alone. The reason is that after a person reads your letter, he or she may want further details and reassurance that can best be provided in a brochure. A brochure alone lacks the personal effect of a letter.

The objectives of your mailing package are to tell a prospect about every benefit of your newsletter and to answer every possible question, just as if you were talking to the prospect in an office or in his or her home. That's why preparing the package takes so much time and skill. Leave nothing to the imagination. List every detail.

Before you begin to prepare the package or hire a consultant to do it for you, there is one thing you must do—one thing that only you, as the editor or publisher, can do. As I discussed in Chapter 3, you should write down a brief description of the unique characteristics and objectives of your newsletter. Then list every detail about your newsletter that produces a benefit for the reader. Examples are: "The only newsletter that reports the quarterly fisheries statistics." "Correspondents in major world capitals." "Digests the essence of 300 business publications." "Provides free telephone inquiry service." "Special reports of the industry annual trade show."

You should be able to come up with at least two dozen benefits. Be as specific as you can be. Avoid generalizations like "important," "newsworthy," or "timely," which can be said about hundreds of other publications. Only after you have gone through this exercise are you or your consultant ready to write persuasive copy.

Copywriter Don Hauptman, whose direct mail packages have won numerous awards, cites these five common *errors* in direct mail literature.

1. *Starting out with the product and not the prospect.* Remember, the prospect wants to make more money or get promoted. Show how your product does this for him or her.
2. *Absence of a big idea (sometimes called Unique Selling Proposition).* Say "This is the newsletter that . . ."
3. *Not digging deeply enough.* This creates a void of specifics and specifics help sell.
4. *Abstract, cloudy copy.* You need anecdotes and testimonials.
5. *Burying the strong selling point.* Keep stressing your strength, don't stray from it.

Keep in mind that what you are setting out to do is what thousands of direct mailers have accomplished selling tangible products. Next time you get a letter offering a shortwave radio, let's say, analyze it thoroughly. First is a letter that whets your appetite by telling you the uses for the radio. Next is a brochure—probably in color. It is designed to do everything except put the radio into your hands. It has a photo of the radio—actual size—and lists the dimensions. Every technical feature—inside and out—is described. In fact, a good product brochure will tell you more about the product than you could find out from a clerk in a store. When you get through reading it, there shouldn't be a single question left unanswered.

Your newsletter, however, is an intangible. A picture of it will look like many other newsletters. Therefore there is an even greater challenge to bring life into the description of your newsletter.

Now let's look at the various elements of your package and discuss the choices that you will have to make.

The Envelope The envelopes you choose will probably be number 10 with or without a window. You may include a corner card. Thus far it's simple. But the purpose of the envelope is not just to carry your material. It must get itself opened.

Many people in homes and offices open only what appears to be first-class mail—something that has a typed or handwritten address on the front—and discard advertising. So an important question to answer is, What addressing process will encourage people to open your mailing?

Remember that you may be mailing in the thousands, not the hundreds. Hand-typing envelopes is impractical and using a typing service is costly.

The answer lies in how your prospect names are kept. If the names are kept on stencils, they can be imprinted directly on the face of the envelope and will look just like what they are—stencil reproductions. However, if you rent lists that are kept on a computer, they will automatically be printed on Cheshire labels. The Cheshire label (see Glossary) can be placed on the face of the envelope or used with a window envelope. (I'll discuss the advantages of each envelope later.) Either method tells the person who opens the mail that this is not a personal letter. Will he or she open it or toss it?

No one knows, but many direct mailers take a bold step to "tease" the recipient into opening the envelope. They put an additional message on the envelope or make a promise about the contents.

This "teaser" can either be a simple descriptive line in typewriter type such as "Your Free Sweepstakes Entry Form Enclosed"—or a big brash typeface that screams "You Are Already a Winner. Find Out What Your Prize Is."

A look at your mail will tell you that there are hundreds of possibilities. Decide which mailings attract you and which repel you. Do not imitate the ones that claim "Important." Important to whom? Avoid the messages that are somewhat tricky, implying, for example, that they're government communications about your taxes when they're really about books on taxes.

However, something that appeals to you won't necessarily appeal to the recipient. Use your own tastes as a guide but be flexible and inventive. One of the great strengths of direct mail is being able to structure your appeal to your particular prospect's interest. You, as the publisher of your newsletter, know more than anyone else what interests the people who inhabit the narrow segment in which you operate. You know the technical language in the field. You know what turns them on; what makes them mad. Play on this knowledge.

By using your special knowledge of your newsletter field, you will probably develop a message that is really very much like the headline in an ad—the headline that compels you to read the copy underneath. Except that your copy is not underneath—it's inside the letter.

This is the rationale for envelope copy. You give up all pretense of a personal letter and identify it as advertising—but advertising that reaches out to the needs of your particular audience.

Look at the illustrations of envelope copy in Figures 33 A–C. Note

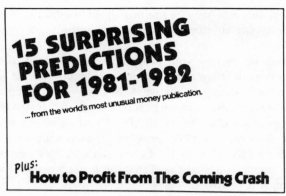

15 SURPRISING PREDICTIONS FOR 1981-1982

...from the world's most unusual money publication.

plus: **How to Profit From The Coming Crash**

Figure 33A

IS SOCIAL SECURITY DOOMED?

Open this envelope and learn the truth about America's most colossal fraud — and its effect on you!

Figure 33B

Figure 33C

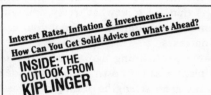

Interest Rates, Inflation & Investments...
How Can You Get Solid Advice on What's Ahead?
INSIDE: THE OUTLOOK FROM KIPLINGER

how they relate to the specific interests of the target audience. And note that there is a great promise of benefits. These envelopes were tested and are known to work.

The Letter If you use a headline on your envelope, it should be repeated at the top of the letter. This reminds people of the message. And repeating the headline makes the copy that follows more logical.

No book can teach you how to write a letter. You can learn through practice and through courses and seminars. Or you can hire a copywriter to do it for you. But you should at least understand the purpose of the letter.

Even the most experienced writer sometimes has difficulty in starting a letter. In *The Basics of Copy,* direct mail consultant Ed McLean identifies thirty-eight types of openers that have been successful in direct mail letters. You may find them useful in overcoming writer's block.

38 WAYS TO START A LETTER

1. *Reader benefit*
   Example: Now you can save up to one-third on your office supplies.
2. *On envelope—breakover*
   Example: To make a perfect party dinner in just 15 minutes, take 1 lb. crabmeat, 1 egg, 3 tbls. mayonnaise, 2 tbls. parsley, 1 . . . (con't. inside)
3. *Flattery*
   Example: If the list upon which I found your name . . .
4. *Quote—indirect*
   Example: According to a recent issue of the *Wall Street Journal,* a man in your income bracket can expect to have about $175,000 in his estate by the time he's 65.
5. *Quote—direct*
   Example: "Naturally curly hair and her own private income do wonders for a woman's disposition." Phyllis McGinley said it, and . . .
6. *Story*
   Example: It was a cold, blustery night, with the wind howling through the elms and the rain beating against the windowpanes. I was toasting my toes on the fender, feeling content, when Mabel said, "Harry, you've *got* to go out and get me some . . ."
7. *Case history*
   Example: The S_____ Company, a firm about the size of yours, recently cut their billing costs by 16%. They used a system so simple, it . . .
8. *Johnson box*
   Example:

> The Editors of Time-Life Books invite you
> to share their excitement in re-creating the
> **GREAT AGES OF MAN**
> by exploring the enthralling people . . .
> ideas . . . places . . . manners and morals of
> times as vital and creative as our own!
> Begin with an absorbing adventure in
> **CLASSICAL GREECE**

which you may read, use and discuss with
your family for 10 full days without
obligation or commitment to purchase it.

9. *How to*
   Example: How a new kind of cream makes the skin soft, clear,
   lovely—for reasons that every woman will understand!
10. *Request for assistance*
    Example: Will you give me the benefit of your judgment on a matter
    of considerable importance to us?
11. *Membership*
    Example: You have been elected to a full membership in our book
    club for one year. Here is your membership certificate. It is made out
    in your name and is nontransferable.
12. *Questionnaire*
    Example: An innocent-looking Questionnaire—just a little ink on a
    piece of paper—is enclosed with this letter. This Questionnaire,
    when answered and returned to us, will be able to tell you whether
    you rate as a drawing-room Sphinx, with whom conversation is a lost
    art unless the talk turns to business or . . .
13. *Gimme*
    Example: Give me two minutes of your time—and I'll give you the
    secret of profit without investment.
14. *Parable*
    Example: You've heard the story, I know, of the fisherman who was
    trying to impress a couple of guides with his piscatorial proficiency.
15. *Know it all*
    Example: Men who know it all don't need to read any further. This
    letter is not for them. Neither is it for those who are satisfied with
    the progress they've made in life.
16. *Shock*
    Example: You have thrown a million dollars into the gutter!
17. *Sure thing*
    Example: Some men are born gamblers, but . . .
18. *Gift*
    Example: Enclosed are a check for 50¢ and a ballpoint pen to en-
    dorse it with.
19. *Fantasy*
    Example: The other day, my horse turned around to me and said,
    "George, you need a new pair of riding boots."
20. *Sale*

Example: At the end of the season, space is more valuable than clothes. We must make room for the new spring collections so . . .

21. *Save money by spending it*
Example: That new fun fur you've longed for, but economically decided not to buy—That mink muff you resisted because it seemed extravagant—is now, you'll be happy to learn, a matter of plain commonsense economy.

22. *Request for information*
Example: Will you give me a little "inside information" about that boy of yours—just his height and weight and how old he is?

23. *Do you remember?*
Example: Do you remember when an East Side apartment rented for $75 a month?

24. *Hint of scandal*
Example: There's something I really feel you ought to know about your husband.

25. *Personality analysis*
Example: Have you ever been officially rated for personality and business traits—for your capacity to achieve, for your ability to direct your energies into the most productive channels?

26. *Question*
Example: Would you risk $1 for the most effective collection letter we have ever seen—a letter that brought in 85% of all past-due money when every other appeal had failed?

27. *Gadgets* (in this case, a mirror)
Example: Take a look at yourself! Typical New Yorkers look pretty much the same as everyone else. No horns. No strange identifying marks. But they do have one thing in common . . .

28. *Once-in-a-lifetime opportunity*
Example: Here's a bargain we'll never be able to offer you again . . .

29. *Offer of free demonstration*
Example: Will you let me put a fresh finish on the walls of any room in P.S. 106—*without cost to you?*

30. *Can you qualify?*
Example: Here is an amazingly easy way to end money worries for your family—if you can qualify as a "Preferred Risk."

31. *Snob appeal*
Example: Will you be one of the "first families" of Scarsdale—the dozen or more who, by their unusual generosity, are making the lives of the sick and unfortunate in our community happier and brighter?

32. *Announcement*

    Example: On Thursday, December 3, a remarkable new product will be introduced in the New York area.

33. *Sweepstakes*

    Example: You may have won Procter & Gamble's $100,000 Soap Stakes!

34. *Satisfied user*

    Example: I'd like to tell you how I lost 73 pounds *without ever going hungry* . . .

35. *Reservation*

    Example: Because I know you are seriously interested in the arts, I have reserved a copy of Morton Weinstein's new book, *Contemporary Sculpture,* for you . . .

36. *Emotional*

    Example: Many people live to regret the things they didn't do for their mothers.

37. *Reasons why*

    Example: Here are 43 reasons why you should have read *U.S. News & World Report* last week.

38. *Choice*

    Example: I would like to send you a gift next week, but don't know whether you'd prefer Shakespeare's *Comedies* or his *Tragedies.*

The essential in any letter is getting the attention of the reader. The letter must immediately identify a benefit, usually by posing a problem that you know is troublesome to the reader. For instance, you might strike a sympathetic chord in writing to a middle-aged business person about the high costs of college education. You then state the solution—a newsletter that has hundreds of money-saving ideas that will enable the person to accumulate the funds needed. Now you must prove your assertion—describing the newsletter, telling the expert sources you use, mentioning other people who have found the publication invaluable. And then you must ask for the order and explain how simple it is to send in the order form and get the first copy by return mail.

You will also want to make a guarantee of satisfaction. The usual guarantee is money back for the unexpired portion of the subscription. A better guarantee is money back at any time for the full amount. This is not as risky as it might sound. Few people, if any, ever wait until the eleventh month to ask for a full refund.

P.S. Don't forget it. The P.S. gets high readership. It's your chance to throw in another benefit, such as "If you send a check with your order, I'll give you two extra issues free."

The Publisher's Letter. Many authorities say that this device lifts response 10 percent or more. Hence some call it the "lift" letter. It's either a folded letter or a letter in a separate sealed envelope that carries the message "Open this letter *only* if you have decided not to respond to this offer." Everyone looks at it, of course, and it gives the reader the publisher's assurance that the newsletter is indeed a very special publication and that the prospect will only gain by responding. If you use the device, try to show some originality. Lately all of the publisher's letters I've seen seem to say exactly the same thing.

Other Devices. Bob Stone writes that form letters using indented paragraphs will usually outpull those in which paragraphs are not indented and that underlining important phrases and sentences usually increases results slightly. Using color ink for underlining or bracketing key paragraphs in simulated handwriting can create an even better effect.

As to the length of the letter, Stone says a two-page letter outpulls a one-page letter. More bluntly, a one-page letter just isn't long enough to do the job. Two, three, and four pages are common and can be effective. Some newsletters have been highly successful in using sixteen pagers. The key point is that prospects decide when they read your opener whether they're interested. If not interested, they toss the letter, so it makes no difference what length it is. But if they're interested, they want every bit of information you can give them.

The Descriptive Brochure or Enclosure The enclosure can be a two-page flier, a four-page folder in color—anything you desire. Its purpose is to reinforce the claims you have made in your letter. If your letter boasts of the high caliber of the expert editors, you can run photos and biographical sketches of these editors. If you have been recognized in the press, you can run reproductions of the press clippings. And for any newsletter you can give tantalizing one-line descriptions of the types of information that you will be offering in the months ahead. This is the place to list important testimonials, signed by people who are known in a particular field or industry. (Be sure that you have written permission from such people in your files in case the Federal Trade Commission comes calling.) If you are offering back issues in a binder, a photo of this would be appropriate. In fact, everything tangible about your newsletter should be described and illustrated in the brochure.

One of the most effective enclosures is an index of past issues. It tells the reader the range of subject matter—and it is proof of what you do.

At this stage, the question usually arises, why bother with an enclosure, why not just enclose a sample of the newsletter? The surprising answer is that nine out of ten publishers who have tested this method have found that it doesn't work as well. Let's examine some of the reasons.

On a practical note, if your newsletter is more than four pages, it could make your mailing package overweight. In addition, there is not only a disadvantage, but also a danger, in enclosing the newsletter. This danger requires some explanation.

People read a newsletter for various reasons—perhaps for a monthly feature that summarizes valuable information. Some people will find a subscription worthwhile for this reason alone. By looking at one issue of a newsletter, however, many people are unable to imagine the wealth of information it is going to give them over the years and the various tips that will help them. All they see is four pages. No single issue portrays all of the benefits of an individual newsletter. These benefits appear over time.

There's also a matter of sales psychology. You cannot sell anyone anything against his will. People help sell themselves if they are given the right clues from your sales letter. They will visualize the benefits you mention in all kinds of ways, and establish preconceived notions of your newsletter. Then when they have been brought to the point where they're ready to order and they glance at this four-page typewritten letter, they might feel a letdown. Later, of course, when they receive their first copy in the mail, they will have forgotten all of your breathless prose and will settle down to judge the newsletter on its merits.

I said nine out of ten publishers do not enclose a sample. What kind of newsletter publisher is the tenth who does? In most cases, he or she publishes a newsletter that stands on its own. Let's take as an example a financial information newsletter that offers a series of charts each issue. The same charts are there all the time, only the figures change. A sample issue will tell the prospect everything he or she wants to know. Other publishers develop a composite—a sample issue that combines the strongest features of the newsletter.

All I can do is tell you what other publishers have learned. This doesn't mean that you should follow their practice with your newsletter. I recommend that you prepare a simple flier or brochure, as I have described. Select a portion of your prospects. Send the flier or brochure to 50 percent of the portion and send a sample letter to the other 50 percent. Code your order forms accordingly and keep a careful record of the returns. The results will guide you to the best approach for your newsletter. That's another benefit of testing.

The Order Form   You not only have to ask for the order, you also have to provide a convenient way for the prospect to place it. Here are the essentials that must be placed on the order form.

Your name, address, phone number
A brief statement of the offer such as:

_____Yes, I want to receive XYZ newsletter twice each month at the limited charter rate of $3 a month on an annual basis. I understand that I will receive your Portfolio of 500 Selling Ideas. And if I am not completely satisfied, I may write "cancel" across your invoice without any further obligation, but I may keep the Portfolio.

_____Check for $36 enclosed.

_____Please bill me.

Name (of prospect)_____

Address_____

City, State, ZIP_____

It is important to repeat the offer on the order form for two reasons. The first is to make sure that the prospect understands the terms of the offer. The second is that if the prospect throws away the rest of the letter and forgets what it said, the order form will serve as a reminder.

It is important that you make it as easy as possible for the prospect to reply. Anything that slows him or her down may cause a change of mind—"too much trouble." This brings up a reason for using window envelopes. With a regular envelope, the prospect has to fill in all of the blanks of the order form. With a window envelope, you can place the Cheshire mailing label on the order form and insert it into the envelope. There is nothing for the prospect to do except check the appropriate blanks and return.

The question now arises, should you enclose a return envelope? This is another matter that you should test with your particular universe. Generally speaking, if you are mailing to a business audience, an executive will forward the order to the accounting department or give it to a secretary to mail. Business firms generally don't use other people's envelopes.

If you are mailing to someone at a home address, then the return envelope—with postage paid—is important. Make it easy for the prospect at home. Don't make him or her go hunting for an envelope and a stamp.

Many publishers believe in creating an order form that reflects a special offer. It might be called a "savings certificate" if the offer provides a discount. Or "charter registration." In fact, anything that avoids the words "order form."

Don't Fall Into This Trap   For purposes of design, publishers sometimes use the same color stock for all elements of the mailing package. This is a mistake. Use different colors instead so that each element will be more readily identifiable.

Also, make sure that your newsletter name, address, and phone number are on the letter, the enclosure, the order form, and the return envelope. People have a habit of separating the elements, so each element should tell them where you are and what you are offering.

Renewals   It is truly said that the newsletter business is not a subscription business—it's a renewal business. Whether you make money or not on a first-year subscription is not as important—pleasant though it may be—as the income from that subscriber, year after year, through renewals.

In fact, the publisher of a new newsletter cannot say with any degree of certainty that the venture is successful until the first renewal period is past. You may be getting an unusually high response to your promotion mailings and receiving enthusiastic letters from readers. But the moment of truth is when you invite the subscriber to renew. Only then will you be able to open the reader's mind and learn his or her real view of your newsletter. Even though very few may have accepted your guarantee to cancel and receive a refund, you cannot assume that you are home free. The business audience is particularly uncertain in this respect. Very few business subscribers will ask for a refund because it causes internal problems. The company has already written the subscription off as a business expense. When a refund appears, the company's accounting department may not know where to put it. So the executive finds it's easiest to let it ride. But when you send your renewal notice you may find he or she has decided against you.

If your first-year renewal rate turns out to be 75 percent, you will have to replace 25 percent just to stay where you were. If it's 50 percent, you will need to replace half of your subscribers. If renewals are under 50 percent, many publishers believe that the newsletter won't make it. Others say they can still get by with less. I would think that there's something very wrong if you get less than 50 percent of your subscribers to stay with you.

First-year renewals behave differently from second-year renewals. The first year brings the major shakeout of those people who took a chance with you but weren't really committed. However, of those who

The Newsletter Direct Mail Package: A Checklist
by George Duncan

The following is a checklist of the components of a direct mail package, together with certain other creative, special offer, or marketing elements that you will want to include, or at least consider, in planning a direct mail promotion.

Outer Envelope
1. Format.
   a. Number 10 business envelope
   b. 9″ × 12″ business envelope
   c. 6″ × 9″ "promotion" envelope
   d. Monarch "personal" envelope
   e. Self-mailer
2. Postage.
   a. Stamp (first class or precancelled third class)
   b. Metered postage
   c. Printed third-class indicia
3. Mail class.
   a. First class
   b. Third class
4. Corner card. (Name and address or none)
5. Label. (Label on envelope or a show-through window)
6. Copy blurb.
   a. "Teaser" or "Pitch"
   b. Benefit, Premium, or Price
7. Overall look.
   a. Color
   b. Illustration
   c. Stock and texture

Letter
8. Headline.
   a. Typeset, typewritten, or penscript
   b. Benefit, Premium, or Price
9. Overall look.
   a. Typescript
   b. Computer Letter
   c. Illustrations (Letter or brochure)
10. Subheads, second color, bullets, etc.
11. Price and guarantee.
12. Number of pages. (Separate sheets or 11″ × 17″ folded)

13. P.S. (Typewritten or penscript)
14. Letterhead or address.

Brochure
15. Include or omit.
16. Size. 8½ " × 11", 11" × 17", or 11" × 22"
17. Color.
18. Illustrations.
19. Testimonials.
20. Second order form.
21. Name and address.

Order Card or Offer
22. Certificate.
23. Boilerplate copy.
24. Stub.
25. Action device.
26. Guarantee.
27. Signature.
28. Deadline date.
29. Billing.
    a. Bill me or Payment with order
    b. Credit card (toll-free number)
    c. Bill company (P.O. Box number)
30. Two-year term.
31. Offer.
    a. Short-term trial, payment with order, or bill P.O. Box number)
    b. Full year, first issue(s) free
32. Premium.

Other
33. Sample issue.
    a. Actual
    b. Generic
34. "Lift" letter.
35. Premium insert.
36. Business reply envelope.

renew the first time, the odds are that they will remain with you three or four or more years. Thus, each year you are in business, your overall renewal rate, as opposed to the first-year renewals, will rise.

Certain types of newsletters have different renewal histories. Business newsletters usually have steady renewals. Certain consumer newsletters—travel, for instance—have subscribers who come and go. Subscribers may take an extended trip, arrive home broke, and cancel the letter. A couple of years later their pocketbooks and interest may have revived, and they will come back to the newsletter.

Regardless of how subscribers come and go, the expires (ex-subscribers) will produce a list that will prove to be better than any other list you will obtain. Newcomers to newsletter publishing find this hard to grasp. This is because they persist in believing that people are always rational and always make logical decisions. A subscriber may have been going through an emotional crisis, such as a divorce. This crisis has to be resolved before you can get that person's attention. This is a reason to keep on mailing to your expires, usually as part of your house list, or, sometimes, in a mailing designed only for them. Consultant René Gnam is one who advocates developing a series of mailings targeted to expires.

Alfred M. Goodloe, Jr., international marketing consultant and publisher of the newsletter *Publishers Multinational Direct,* is a specialist in renewals. He believes that not enough publishers think through the psychological effects of their renewal efforts. In particular, he is opposed to sending a final notice stamped in big letters, "Your subscription has expired." He says that this changes the game completely. You have cut off your reader so abruptly that he is inclined to say to himself, "OK, I can live without your newsletter. I got along without it before; I can get along without it forever." Instead, Goodloe continues to write to his expires without ever bluntly telling them that they are no longer in good standing; just reminding them that it's time to renew.

Other publishers who follow a variation of this technique will wait a few months after the final notice, then start the series all over again. Since so much of your income depends on renewals, every bit of time and ingenuity spent on them is well worthwhile.

Goodloe has found six major factors that affect renewals. Here they are, with some explanatory comments of my own.

1. *Your product and its quality.* Take a good look at your newsletter. Is the content really as good as it should be? Is it well written? Are the graphics appropriate? Does your editorial content match what you claim it covers in your promotion letters? Even though good techniques sell newsletter subscriptions, the product itself has to be first-rate. All the expertise in the world won't sell a poor letter—nor will a poor letter entice renewals.

2. *Quality of your service.* If your mailing labels for subscribers have

misspellings, if you fail to note a change of address, or if you fail to send the extra copy that you promised, you are irritating your subscriber. You are conveying the message that perhaps the rest of your service is not too good, either. At renewal time, these slippages of quality can produce a negative effect on the reader.

3. *Quality of renewal effort.* This simply means that you should pay just as much attention—perhaps more—to retaining subscribers through a carefully scheduled series of mailings as you do to your original promotion effort. Most publishers agree that they could do better with their renewal efforts. A survey some years ago revealed that life insurance salesmen rarely returned to their original policyholders to offer additional coverage. They preferred to make new calls rather than take advantage of the goodwill they had worked so hard to establish. Don't make the same mistake.

4. *Seasonal timing of expiration.* This will not apply to all newsletters. However, if your subject area has seasonal characteristics, such as a period when all plants are closed for vacation, take those into account when you send renewals. If you deal with accountants, for instance, don't approach them for subscriptions or renewals in April, the heavy tax month.

5. *Quality of subscriber source.* Earlier I mentioned that it is useful to code your subscribers by the source of the mailing lists upon which you found their names, then rank them in importance. It is reasonable to expect that if some lists don't perform as well as others in the initial promotion, they may not renew as well either. If so, you should avoid some of these marginal lists in the future.

6. *Quality of initial offer.* If you gave a clear picture of your service in your new subscriber promotion package, this will be reflected in your subsequent renewal rate. Introduce the good elements of that initial package in your renewal series.

In short, renewal time is when the voters go alone into the polling booths and make their private decisions. You will never know what influenced their decisions, but paying attention to these six factors can help put you in the winning column.

Copywriter and newsletter consultant Richard Silverman gives these six tips for boosting renewal response:

• *Send "love letters."* A few weeks before your renewal series starts, let the subscribers know you love them with an inexpensive gift, article, booklet, and so forth, they will find of interest. But *no sell!* Just a note or memo to the effect that "we came across this article and think you'll enjoy it. Please accept it with our compliments." You may be pleasantly surprised at how much this can increase your renewal response.

- *Never number your renewal series.* Writing "First Renewal" anywhere on your renewal package is like putting up a red flag warning the subscriber more letters are coming, no need to answer now.
- *Step up frequency of renewals.* There's nothing sacred about spacing them a month apart. Especially with charge-card subscribers, who are your best customers, and those most likely to pay before the subscription runs out.
- *Try for automatic renewals.* The subscription continues from year to year, billable annually against the credit card indicated, unless cancelled by either party. People pay for everything else that way: insurance, rent, phone bills, electricity. Why not subscriptions?
- *Don't refer to previous notices* reminding the subscriber he or she hasn't answered. Make each communication sound fresh, important, and urgent.
- *Always write as if the subscriber is current*—even in postexpire mailings. Use—or hire—the best creative people to plan and write your renewal series. If you want first-class response, give subscribers first-class treatment.

You should start your renewal effort about three months in advance of expiration. Keep *careful records* of your results. Through a code or date, record how many respond to each renewal notice. When you are through, you may find that you have gotten 50 percent of your total number of renewals from the first renewal notice.

Stop your renewal series when it becomes more expensive than getting a new order. Keep good records so you will know when the renewal effort has reached this point.

Some publishers, particularly those who offer a premium at the start, offer another premium for renewal. And some of these offer the premium at the end of the series after all else has failed. This can be a fatal mistake. The word gets out fast. In subsequent years, people will wait until the end to see what gift you will have for them. More important, it is not fair to those cooperative subscribers who pay on the first notice. The rule is, if you offer a premium, offer it only with the first renewal notice and state firmly that there is a time limit for the gift.

Many publishers have learned that a simple renewal notice, with no letter or premium, works very well as the first item in the series. Try it. It saves a lot of time and effort. However, please be aware that it is against the law to send this notice in the form of an invoice. In 1985 Time Inc. was penalized approximately $100,000 for sending *Time* magazine renewal notices in the guise of invoices. U.S. Postal Service regulations—in Section 123.41 of the Domestic Mail Manual—prohibit sending solicitations in the guise of bills, invoices, or statements of account.

Renewing by Telephone   When you have satisfied yourself that it no longer pays to send further renewal letters, it is time to consider the telephone. If you have only a few names left on your outstanding renewal list for the month, you may want to undertake the telephoning yourself. You will be recognized as the editor, so you won't have to explain who you are. If you listen carefully, you will find out why the reader has hesitated thus far—and may even find a very legitimate complaint that you can straighten out. At the very least, you will understand better how your readers react to your newsletter.

If you are dealing with numerous subscribers, you may want to investigate some of the telephone services available and pay close attention to the costs. The best short piece on the subject was written by Al Goodloe, detailing his experience with his own telephone renewal program. Here is a summary.

The rule for renewal by direct mail is: Mail your renewal efforts up to a point where cost equals income. In other words, continue to mail individual renewal efforts up to a point where the last renewal effort is a break-even. It is usually cheaper to buy a renewal at break-even than to go out into the market and buy a new order. The rule for renewal by telephone is: Telephone up to a point where total telephone operations cost equals 60 to 65 percent of the gross dollar value of the orders. Here are the reasons:

- Since telephone renewals were not obtained by direct mail, they will not renew as well when they are followed up by mail the next year.
- Cancellation and bad debts on telephone operations can run 20 to 30 percent higher. Since there is no signed contract between you and your customer, he can change his mind or "forget" that he agreed to renew his subscription.
- Telephone operations require more managerial time, and you should be compensated for that time. You will have to hire

telephone salespeople, supervise them, pay them, and control the overall economics of the operation.

Goodloe says that to get one hundred orders, he has to make four hundred calls. About one hundred are what are called "contacts," such as when the spouse answers or the subscriber answers but does not want to talk about the matter at that time. There are other time-consuming delays in using the telephone. In addition to the four hundred calls, there are six hundred additional calls that do not go through—"no answers"; "busy signals"; "operational difficulties on the line." You don't pay the telephone company for them, but you are paying the salesman.

By all means try the telephone for renewals, but ground yourself thoroughly in the techniques and economics.

Scheduling of Mailings Promotional and renewal mailings require careful scheduling. Start first with your list selections. When you learn when the lists can be delivered, you know that this date is the earliest you can schedule the mailing. You also know how many copies you'll need of the package and the envelopes, and you can get an estimate from the printer as to the time he'll need. With this done, set a mailing date and put in motion the steps required to get the mailing out on time.

Once you have gotten some experience with results on lists and have tested copy variations, you are reaching the point where you can begin to schedule your mailings for an entire year (Fig. 34).

Selling Subscriptions Through Subscription Agencies Subscription agencies got their start in the magazine field and can be a great advantage

Figure 34

to a magazine. They work closely with libraries and with businesses that require a variety of periodicals.

These agencies operate on a commission basis, usually about 20 percent, sometimes higher. Also, I am told, they sometimes receive a fee for handling the subscriptions for a large organization.

One advantage to the publisher is that an agency can find subscribers that the publisher might not. Another is that the subscription payment accompanies the order. The advantage to the large user of periodicals is that all orders can be placed with one agency and paid for with one check, rather than having to deal with hundreds of individual publishers. Subscription agencies keep complete records on periodicals, update them regularly, and make sure they have all the facts about overseas postage and the like. They recommend publications to their clients, and at renewal time they do their best to collect for another year.

Yet in the years I've been in the newsletter field, I haven't found publishers wildly enthusiastic about the agencies. Some publishers aren't willing to pay them any commission and others won't deal with them at all.

The reasons reflect the specialized nature of newsletters. Newsletter publishers work hard to develop their prospect lists and they spend a lot of money on promotion. Some resent sharing money with an agency that picks up a subscription at the same time that a company library is ordering *Time, Newsweek,* and the like. Newsletter publishers set up a carefully targeted program of renewals. They may resent it when they send a renewal notice, the company turns it over to a subscription agency, and 20 percent is knocked off the price. They may notify the agency that they will not pay the commission. They do this with the knowledge that if the agency has a good client, it will still place the order without the commission in order to keep the client happy. And subscription agencies are understandably irritated at being put on this spot. So there is resentment on both sides.

Many publishers take a middle ground. They will pay the 20 percent on a new subscription, figuring that this might not have come to them otherwise. But arguing that it is the performance of the newsletter during the year that earns the renewal, they limit the renewal commission to 5 percent. Incidentally, 5 percent of a $100 newsletter subscription earns the agency more, in fact, than does 20 percent of a $20 magazine subscription, with no more work involved for the agency.

There is one specialized subscription service for newsletters alone that should be mentioned. It is Select Information Exchange (SIE), specializing in investment and business letters. George Wein, its principal, maintains extensive mailing lists of purchasers of business services and prospects to whom he mails catalogs. The catalogs list a large number of newsletters, with a full description of each, but no addresses. He has an arrangement with each publisher that he may offer his catalog readers trial subscriptions to newsletters that interest them. These trials are offered in variously priced packages—three for $11, for example—so that prospects can sample several newsletters at a small price. This fee is kept by SIE. The names and addresses of inquiries are sent to the appropriate publishers, who furnish one or more months of service at no charge. The publishers now own the prospect names and they are free to promote to the inquiries. If a subscription results, a 20 percent commission is paid. SIE also advertises in magazines and has taken a number of full-page ads in the *New York Times*. This has been mutually beneficial to a number of publishers.

Names and addresses of subscription agencies are in the Bibliography.

Selling Subscriptions Through Publicity   Newsletters can generate a lot of publicity for themselves. Because newsletters are so specialized and have so much in-depth information, the press finds them valuable resources for stories. The press likes to quote authorities and many newsletter editors are authorities in their fields. When the energy crisis hit, Louis Lundberg restarted his newsletter on oil, which he had folded to concentrate on consulting, and he has since been the subject of many major stories. When you have specialized information on events of national consequence, get it to the press.

Better still, start a regular publicity program, putting key newspeople on your list and sending them information regularly. You may give the press a hot item that you have just published and then find it featured all over the country on the wire services. But make sure your readers read it first, before they see it in the paper. Seeing it in the paper will reinforce your relationship with your subscriber because it confirms that you are the expert you claim to be. This is called third-party endorsement and it's hard to beat.

Just to make sure that your subscribers get the news story, reproduce it as an enclosure in your next letter. And be sure to use it in your subscription promotional material. This is called merchandising your publicity and it works.

What if a paper uses your material but attributes it to "a newsletter" rather than naming you? There's no point in suing, but you can drop the paper from your press list. One publisher took a more refined approach. He kept the paper on the press list but made sure that releases got there one day late.

Publicity may bring invitations to appear on radio and TV talk shows or to make a speech. Make sure that additional publicity stories result.

It is difficult to predict how many direct subscriptions will result from publicity, particularly for the business letter. Newspapers rarely give the addresses of publications that they mention and most readers won't bother to call or write the paper about it. William Donoghue took an inventive approach. He incorporated his city and ZIP code as part of the name of the newsletter—*Money Market Report of Holliston, MA 01746.*

Don't neglect sending your material, when suitable, to other newsletters. A newsletter that was mentioned some years ago in the *Kiplinger Washington Letter* received sackfuls of mail.

Certain consumer newsletters get a substantial number of subscriptions through feature stories in newspapers and magazines. If your subject matter is something that has broad appeal, such as winning contests or saving through store coupons, a story in a major publication may bring thousands of orders. Lifestyle, Weekend, Travel, and other feature sections of newspapers and magazines regularly highlight one or more newsletters of interest to their readers. If you publish a letter on food, nutrition, cooking, travel, retirement, fitness, or other common subjects of the mass media's editorial fare, you should pursue these media outlets for your own public relations and promotional advantage.

Other publications, including house organs of corporations, run features on interesting things to write for. Try to get yourself listed in as many of these publications as possible. You may get responses that will bolster your prospect list.

One word of caution when dealing with the press: If a reporter calls and wants to interview you on the phone, drop everything you're doing. If you think you're going to get such calls, keep at hand a reference of brief key phrases describing your newsletter, so that you can react fast. You may find, for instance, that what you say is being recorded for a radio broadcast, so you won't have much time to make your points. It follows, if you respond to reporters' calls immediately, that you may be fortunate enough to find some reporters who like to quote you regularly. Otherwise it might be the last call you get.

The Big Three: Creativity, Testing, and Records

Creativity   The successful selling of your newsletter calls for every ounce of creativity you can muster. Read constantly about the direct marketing field. Attend seminars. How you handle the mundane will make the difference, many times, between profit and loss.

For example, how do you handle a price increase? (With inflation, you must constantly review your subscription prices.) One way is to announce it to your readers and give them a chance to extend their subscriptions for one, two, or three years at the old rate. The result may be a sudden influx of cash. This sounds good, but it may complicate your tax situation. Another way is not to mention it at all—just raise the price one month and change all your forms accordingly. Experience shows that both will work.

How you say the same thing can make a big difference. For instance, Kiplinger has stated the same offer four different ways: 26 issues for $15; six months for $15; 26 weeks, 60¢ a week; six months, 60¢ a week. More and more newsletters state their subscription prices by the month, for example, $3 a month on an annual basis (for a $36 newsletter). And a few also add "plus postage."

Does this mean that you should do likewise? There's a common two-word phrase in direct mail that answers it: it depends.

How do you decide how to deal with issues such as price increases? Test.

Testing This doesn't mean that you should test everything. Start with your lists. Make sure you have a good representation of names. For instance, if you find that 20 percent of the names are in New York, order the same percentage in your test.

You can test price in a new newsletter. Select two prices and find out which pulls best. To avoid having people in adjoining offices get different prices—or having the same person receive two solicitation letters in one week with two different prices—send one price to those whose ZIP code ends in an even number and the other price to those whose ZIP ends in an odd number.

As time goes on, you may want to try another direct mail package. If it's professionally prepared, there's no need to test it. Simply send it to the same lists as you did for your first package, now known as the *control,* and find out whether it beats the first package.

Don't be test happy. You don't need to test first-class versus third-class mail, stamps versus metering, or color. And don't pay any attention to the test results of another mailer. The only thing that counts is what your tests reveal about your mailings.

Records Keep records of your tests and of your full promotions. If you keep a daily return of responses and money amounts, you will have an experience record of your mailings. And you will need an accurate measure of your out-of-pocket costs so that you can apply it to your total cash received. The checklist below (Fig. 35) is from the November 1979 issue of the *Januz Direct Marketing Letter.* (Note in particular line 23, Refunds, and line 24, Uncollectables. Do not get too euphoric about your response until you make deductions for these items.)

Unless you keep accurate records, the only person who will be fooled is you.

Fulfillment To most people entering the newsletter field, "fulfillment" is a brand-new word. Understanding the word and setting up a proper fulfillment procedure is critical to your success. When someone sends you a subscription order, you have an obligation to fulfill that order—to send the subscriber the promised issues on designated dates for the life of the subscription.

A mailing list is only the start. The fulfillment process involves your record keeping, your bank account, your subscription statistics, and a host of other items.

At start-up, says Walter G. Caroll, there are a number of policy decisions that you will have to make which are directly or indirectly related to fulfillment.

CHECKLI$T:

HOW TO ESTIMATE YOUR DIRECT MAIL CAMPAIGN COSTS

TO ASSIST YOU IN BUDGETING YOUR DIRECT MAIL PROMOTION THE FOLLOWING BUDGET OUTLINE IS PROVIDED.

OPERATION	COST PER 1,000	TOTAL COST
1 ARTWORK AND CREATION		
2 MAILING LISTS		
3 PRINTING BROCHURE		
4 PRINTING LETTER		
5 PRINTING BUSINESS REPLY CARD		
6 PRINTING BUSINESS REPLY ENVELOPE		
7 PRINTING OUTER ENVELOPE		
8 FOLDING BROCHURE		
9 FOLDING LETTER		
10 LABELING		
11 INSERTING		
12 TIE, BAG, MAIL		
13 METERING POSTAGE		
14 POSTAGE FIRST CLASS		
15 POSTAGE THIRD CLASS		
16 TOTAL COST	$	$

		TOTAL COST
17	COST OF PRODUCT	
18	FULFILLMENT, SHIPPING, POSTAGE COSTS	
19	TOTAL FULFILLMENT, PRODUCT COST PER ORDER—LINE 17 PLUS LINE 18	$
20	NUMBER OF ORDERS RECEIVED	
21	TOTAL COST FOR ORDERS RECEIVED LINE 19 MULTIPLY LINE 20	
22	TOTAL MAILING PROMOTION COSTS LINE 16	
22A	OVERHEAD—SALARIES, PHONE, RENT, ETC	
23	TOTAL COST FOR REFUNDS	
24	TOTAL UNCOLLECTABLES / SELLING PRICE	
25	GRAND TOTAL MAILING PROGRAMS COSTS ADD LINES 21, 22, 22A, 23, 24	
26	NUMBER OF INQUIRIES	
27	PER ORDER OR INQUIRY COSTS LINE 25 DIVIDED BY LINE 20 OR 26	$
28	CASH RECEIVED PER ORDER	
29	TOTAL CASH RECEIVED LINE 20 TIMES LINE 28	
30	TOTAL MAILING PROGRAM COSTS LINE 25	
31	NET PROFIT FOR MAILING PROGRAM SUBTRACT LINE 30 FROM LINE 29	$

Figure 35

- *Length of subscription periods.* Annual, multiyear, semiannual, and short-term trial subscriptions can be offered. One-year terms are standard; multiyear periods are used to get a longer commitment from the subscriber and get more money up front for the publisher. Trials are used by stock market–oriented letters, for example, to allow the reader to get a flavor of the publication and test the expertise of the writers. Six-month terms are shunned by most publishers, since they probably cut into the number of annual subscriptions, but they may be viewed by readers as a more desirable long-term trial. The nature of the product and the frequency of publication come into play here.
- *Pricing.* Many factors must be considered: size of the potential audience, consumer/business orientation of the publication, production and mailing costs, frequency of publication, value to the reader. Much testing of various offers will be required to determine the price that yields maximum revenue. "Charter" rates may be considered to quickly build up a subscriber base. Group rates may yield additional revenues for business-oriented publications by reducing the amount of copying. Special foreign rates compensate for higher postage costs. Discounts to subscription agencies may yield additional subscribers.
- *Billing.* Decisions to be made concerning billing procedures include the following:

  Will we accept credit-card orders?

  Will we accept "bill me" orders?

  How long before we terminate no-pays?

  Format, frequency, and timing of invoices.

  Will we offer an incentive (discount; bonus issues) for cash-with-order?
- *Cancellations.* Do we offer a full refund or pro rata refund? The former may result in additional subscribers.
- *Renewals.* Considerations include:

  Format, frequency, and timing of notices.

  Use personalized messages?

  Upper-/lowercase printing?

  Automatic renewal option?

  Number (if any) of grace issues after end of subscription while still trying to elicit renewal.
- *Promotion file.* You will want to create a promotion file of likely subscribers to use in your marketing efforts. You will want to add the names of people who have inquired and your own expires. You may want to consider renting the list out for additional revenues and, if so, may want to add the active subscribers as well. If your

policy is *not* to rent the active subscribers, you will periodically need to purge the actives by matching the subscriber list against the promotion file.

The answers to many of the questions here will be determined by the nature of your publication and your intended market. Others must be answered by thorough testing of the alternatives.

If you are going to be using a computer system (a given if you're at all successful), make sure it's flexible enough to handle all of the requirements you've so carefully thought out. And maintain close communications with your computer people (in or out of house). You must decide whether you are going to maintain these files manually or through a computer. Herbert Messing developed a comprehensive list of the elements involved. I have incorporated his ideas in the following discussion of fulfillment procedures.

New Orders and Renewals   When your first check arrives with a subscription order, yes, you deposit the check. But before you rush to the bank there are some procedures you must establish and carry out. What follows is a review of essential steps and ways many publishers handle them in a manual (noncomputer) system.

- *Record order on a master card.* This gives full name and address, term of subscription, date paid or billed.
- *If check accompanies order.* Enter the name of the suscriber, check number, and date in cash ledger.
- *If "bill me."* Assign an identifying number to the order (chronologically) and place the same number on the bill. When the bill is paid, it is easier to find the bill in the file by the number rather than the name.
- *Acknowledge order.* A welcoming form letter is an easy way to help cement the new relationship. It gives you a chance to reinforce your offer. Remind the subscriber of the benefits he or she will receive. Some believe that the cordiality expressed in such a letter is the first step toward a renewal next year.
- *Bonus; back issues.* If you promised a bonus and/or back issues, set up a procedure to send this promptly, perhaps with the welcoming letter.
- *Special handling.* If the first three issues are to be sent to the subscriber's summer home, for instance, make sure this is done.
- *Expiration date, subscription term.* Note on the master card the expiration date and whether the subscription is for one, two, or three years.

- *Pricing.* If you are testing several prices, note the price for a specific order. Or perhaps an order comes in at an earlier price no longer current. You must have a policy either to accept or to send a form letter asking for the additional amount. If someone sends you an additional payment even though he is paid up for most of the year, you must also have a policy to deal with this. Most publishers keep the check and credit the subscriber with the additional paid-up issues.
- *Number of copies.* This must be noted on the master card and in instructions for the mailing house.
- *Commission.* If a commission is owed, arrange to pay it promptly.
- *Gift.* If the order was a gift, note this in your records. You may want to send renewal notices to both donor and donee.
- *Standing order.* This must be isolated from all others who will receive renewal series. A standing order gives you the right to send an invoice for payment at expiration time.
- *Trial repeaters.* Some people who order trial subscriptions do not pay. Maintain a list of such no-pays. When you get future trial orders, check these against the list of no-pays for people attempting to get another trial at your expense. Develop a form letter that you will send explaining why you can't accept the second trial.
- *Check credit.* If a "bill me," you may have a list of no-pays to whom you will not extend credit.
- *Calculate sales tax and postage.* Sales tax varies by state. Many newsletters do not have to pay it. Check carefully with your state to find whether you are required to pay. Don't just take the word of your accountant, who, while professionally qualified, may not understand the difference between newsletters and other kinds of publications subject to tax. If postage is to be added to the bill, it must be calculated.
- *Special billing address.* If the billing address is different from the ship-to address, note that fact. All bills should be sent to the billing address with the name of the subscriber also shown on the bill.
- *Complete purchase order.* Large companies and the government are likely to require you to fill out voluminous purchase order forms before you get paid. I know one state that upon receipt of your invoice will return it to you with a form for you to have notarized, swearing that your invoice is indeed a correct invoice. It's best to do what is required if you want to get paid.
- *Prepare invoice.* A two-part form, providing a record for the payer and a copy sent back to you for identification of payment, is common. Another type of form is a single card, with a portion that can be torn

off by the payer and kept as a receipt. A possible difficulty with this is that the payer may return to you his receipt portion instead of the invoice portion. Either way, set up your form so that you can use a window envelope, which eliminates typing or stenciling the address twice.

- *Post receivable to subscriber balance.* When a renewal check is received, record it promptly to avoid sending a second notice, which may lead to lengthy correspondence on the fact that the bill has been paid.
- *Prepare bank deposit.* Develop some shorthand of your own to identify deposits as newsletter subscriptions, books, or other products you sell.
- *New subscribers.* Add these to your records, delete them from your promotion file, and prepare the necessary number of labels for the bonus, welcome letter, and first issue.
- *Renewals.* Adjust the expiration date on the master card.
- *When you receive payments.* Make a clear identification of the subscriber through your accounts receivable file. Then record the check as paid—or *reduce the subscriber's balance owed*—and deposit. Be prepared for unidentified checks.
- *Address changes.* Be sure to note any that require special handling. Also note the *effective date.* Some companies send out changes three months in advance, for instance, but they expect to receive their copies at the old address until they move. *Calculate the postage charge or refund, issue credit or invoice,* and *adjust the balance.* A subscriber may be moving overseas, so you'll charge more for postage, or he may be returning to the United States. Adjustments either way are in order. Make sure you *correct the address.*
- *Cancellations.* Whatever the policy you have determined—full money back or balance of unexpired subscription—calculate the difference, and issue a check or invoice for the amount owed if still unpaid. *Delete the name* from active subscribers. You may also want to send a letter responding to the reason for the cancellation.
- *Issue date.* When you send out your issue, labels must be ready, sorting provided, the mode of transportation determined, and provisions made for multiple copies.
- *Periodical fulfillment procedures.* A calendar should be prepared showing the periods when you:

Issue statements.
Cancel delinquents.

Prepare sales tax report.
Delete cancels.
Move expires to promotion lists.
Prepare renewal notices.
Prepare alphabetical listings.
Select labels for promotion mailings and list sales.

Not all of these procedures are necessary for everyone. This is merely a checklist reminder.

Management Statistics Depending on the system you use and your own business needs, here are some statistics that can be generated.

- Orders received by advertising source. (This helps in future promotion lists selection.)
- Cash received. (This is a cash-flow business.)
- Sales by customer type.
- Renewals by expiration date.
- Renewals by subscriber type.
- Renewals by letter number. (This refers to your renewal series. You want to know if the subscriber renewed on the first or subsequent notices.)
- Accounts receivable balance.
- Subscriber count.
- Cancellation report. (If there is a surge in cancellations, you want to find out why.)
- Mailing counts.
- Geographic analysis.
- Term analysis. (How many expirations in each month?)
- Orders received by offer terms. (This helps to determine which offers are most profitable.)
- Unearned income. (See Chapter 8 on newsletter management.)
- Profit and loss statement.

Caution: You must reduce to the minimum errors that will be perpetuated in your system. One way is to use three- or four-part labels—sheets of gummed labels with carbons in between. If you record correctly the name and address of the subscriber, then all of the carbons will also be correct. You can use these for your master card, for labels for welcoming letters, for bonus or back issues, and for stencil conversions. And, of course, you must carefully proofread the stencil.

Fulfillment Methods What fulfillment method is best for you? Here are your choices.

1. *In-house, manual.* You will need some equipment. Scriptomatic, Elliott, and Xerox-Cheshire are recognized systems suitable for the small publisher. You will have to type accurately on the stencil, whatever the system, and purchase a machine that will generate labels from the stencil or address directly on envelopes. When you send out issues, you also have to stuff your newsletter into the mailing envelope and affix postage. Some publishers are able to accomplish this with part-time help when the subscription list is in the hundreds. When you move into the thousands, you may want to consider another system.

2. *In-house, computer.* Until recently, it was unrealistic for the small publisher to consider a computer system. However, prices have dropped drastically and this trend promises to continue. Some publishers have installed such systems for as little as $3,000 or $5,000. The essential is the software programming. Toronto-based Rolf Brauch, longtime computer services consultant and publisher of *Brauch & Neville File Newsletter,* has developed a desktop subscription fulfillment and circulation management system for files from 1,000 to 100,000. Designed for the Macintosh Plus, it's called *Mac-SUB.* Many other programs for relatively small circulation management are also available.

Management consultant Tom Stevenson, of New York City, offers seven rules for installing an in-house computer circulation system.

- *The Second Engine Rule.* A plane with two engines is safer than a plane with one. Buy two computers so that your publishing enterprise does not have to close down for three days because a $4 chip goes bad.
- *The "What If It Breaks" Rule.* Go ahead and buy discount from a California mail-order firm, but before you write out the check, ask these two questions: If it breaks down, who will repair it? What will happen to my business if it takes more than two or three days for repairs?
- *The Pioneer Rule.* Don't be one. Let others be the trailblazers and purchase the new hardware and software. Once the trail is well worn and clear, then you may safely follow it.
- *The "Bad Bet" Rule.* When you buy insurance you hope you will never get your money back. You should have the same attitude about your circulation system: Back up your circulation data every week hoping that every minute you spend on this boring task is eventually proved unnecessary.
- *The First-String Quarterback Rule.* No football team can be successful unless it has a good quarterback. No computer installation will be

successful unless you have one person on your staff who has the aptitude and the interest to master computers.

- *The Second-String Quarterback Rule.* No matter how good the person is running your computer installation, some day that person may no longer be available. Make sure there is a second person who has at least some familiarity with the system.
- *The "I'm the Boss" Rule.* You don't have to know how your system operates—but each week (or month) you should receive printouts reconciling the number of new subscribers, expires, past dues, and all other accounts on your system. Plus a copy of your backup tape.

3. *Outside, manual.* For the small publisher there are some mailing houses that have manual systems based on the types I have mentioned. If a mailing house does a good job at a reasonable price, consider its recommendations in setting up your fulfillment operation. Compare the system recommended with the elements of fulfillment I have noted and find out what it can and cannot do. Generally, however, such systems are inflexible and obsolete.

4. *Outside, computer.* When you have several thousand subscribers and it looks as if you will continue to grow, or if you plan additional newsletters, an outside fulfillment house may be for you. Discuss the list of functions that you will require with the firm and compare costs with alternative systems. Expect to pay about 60¢ per subscriber per year.

Naturally you want a foolproof system at the lowest possible price. Publishers who neglect the fulfillment process because it's boring to them pay a price. One publisher I know turned to an outside fulfillment service when he found that he honestly didn't know how many subscribers he had. He was still sending issues to hundreds of subscribers who were no longer current. Another publisher who set up an in-house computer system with the wrong programming lost six thousand subscribers at the push of a button.

In weighing the differences between outside and inside fulfillment, either manual or computer, remember that you have to hire and pay people if you keep it in-house. If you do some of the work yourself, you are getting away from your essential job of writing and promoting your newsletter. Your time is worth money even if it isn't shown in dollars in your records.

8

Newsletter Management

The Number One Management Problem—Time This sounds obvious and it is. But the obvious is often overlooked. At the simplest level of being involved with a newsletter, you will quickly learn that time is what everyone else is thinking about, too. If you agree to do a newsletter for the local PTA, you will be asked, "When will it be done?" And this is the question you'll be asking the printer. Many informal newsletters for a group never get beyond the first issue, because someone didn't realize how much time it would take.

The editor must determine quickly how long it will take to write the letter, how long it will take to get into production, how long it will take to print, and how long it will take to deliver. If your company requests that you take over a newsletter, ask yourself how much time it will take. If you are a free-lancer and offer to do newsletters for hire, base your charge on time. When I was first hired as a moonlighter to do a newsletter, there was a fixed fee. The faster I completed the letter, the higher my hourly rate became. This was not only a boost to the ego, but it also prepared me to handle more newsletters and constantly increase my fees.

If you start a one-person newsletter, as so many have, you will need to report, research, and write. You produce the letter, take it to the printer, pick it up, run off stencils, collate, stuff, and mail. The faster you can dispose of the purely mechanical functions, the more time you will have for writing and editing.

When you work for a large newsletter firm, time will be imperative. Subscription newsletters work as close to the printing deadline as possible. With word-processing equipment, it is possible for the editor of an eight-page letter to lay out the finished stories in camera-ready form in twenty-five minutes.

Newsletters, as a branch of journalism, must manage time above all.

Management Operations What follows in this chapter is a discussion of some of the management functions that you are likely to encounter, depending on the type of newsletter. You should be aware of them to make the most efficient use of your time and to maximize your profit.

Legal Form of Newsletter Business If you start a newsletter on your own, there's no need to incorporate at the beginning. You may operate as a *sole owner and proprietor,* and this is how you identify yourself on any legal or tax forms. At tax time, declare your income and state your expenses in the deductions section. You don't declare a salary, just income.

If you are starting a newsletter you may also be talking to a partner. But with the divorce rate of partnerships probably surpassing the fifty-fifty odds of marriage, you'd better take a close look at your prospective partner. Tom Stevenson, management correspondent for *The Newsletter on Newsletters,* has devised an eight-point scale for weighing the chances of your partnerships surviving the rocky years of a business start-up. Answer each question yes or no.

1. Will each of you contribute a set of skills that the other lacks?
2. If each of you were to list who should be placed in charge of each of the ten major functions of your newsletter, would the two lists be basically similar?
3. Have you disagreed sharply on some issues?
4. Does one of you think "Look before you leap" and the other "He who hesitates is lost" when confronted with a decision?
5. Are you reasonably certain that the other person's ethical standards are at least equal to your own?
6. Are you getting a partner for partly psychological reasons?
7. Are you willing to give your partner an equal number of shares—fifty-fifty—if you are the only stockholders?
8. Will you draft a buy-out procedure that either partner can invoke for any reason?

If you have answered no to any one of these questions, think again about matrimony. Here's why:

- Duplicate skills usually equal fat in a small company—and increase the odds of bickering (number 1).
- Each partner should recognize the other's strengths—and his or her own weaknesses. Once you start working, it may be too late—or too costly—to discover them through trial and error (number 2).

- Disagreements? You'll have dozens. So better see now whether they deepen respect or foster animosity (number 3).
- One inevitable conflict will be over the "let's do it" versus "let's research it" decision. But that's a conflict that can produce serendipitous results (number 4).
- In contrast, ethical disagreements spell disaster (number 5).
- While each of your contributions of equity and skills are important, don't kid yourself: you could probably obtain them more cheaply elsewhere. Recognize that the main reason for pairing together is psychological and there is far less chance of a miscalculation (number 6).
- If you choose a fifty-fifty stock arrangement, then the chances of one partner's outweighing the other in a disagreement are eliminated (number 7).
- To avoid a deadlock that destroys your company, simply draw up an agreement that either partner may buy the other out at any time (number 8). But avoid a book-value or earnings formula in your agreement. Instead, agree in advance to hold a two-person auction for all outstanding shares.

If your business grows, you should then investigate the advantage of becoming a Sub Chapter S corporation. As such, you would be able, as corporations are, to limit your liability by putting your business assets into the corporation. But on your corporate form you merely declare income and expenses and whatever is left—plus or minus—and carry this forward on your personal income form. You are getting the advantages corporations have in limiting liability, in setting up an attractive pension plan (also a form of tax shelter), and getting an assist on medical expenses. You have the advantage of the sole proprietorship in that you still operate pretty much as before, with firm control of your money.

It is only if you grow still larger and add employees that your business life becomes more complicated, and a regular corporation may be the answer.

There are two professional people you should get acquainted with as early as possible in your career—an accountant and a lawyer. All things being equal, it would help if both of these people had some knowledge of the publishing industry. If this is not possible, you will have to educate them about the special nature of the business.

Tax Accounting for Newsletters There are two Internal Revenue Code sections that are key to all publishers: number 455 allows publishers to spread income over the life of the subscription; and number 173 permits spreading costs of acquiring subscriptions over the life of the subscriptions. In reality, publishers use only number 455, spreading out income, and deduct all promotion costs in full as they are paid. This gives publications the effect of a tax shelter, especially in the early years.

Here's the way it works. Let's say that in November you spend $10,000 on a promotion mailing. You list it as an expense for the tax (in this case, calendar) year. Let's say also that you received $20,040 in new subscription revenue, derived from 167 subscriptions at $120 each. By spreading these subscriptions over the one-year life, you can push the bulk of the revenue into the following year. For tax purposes, you declare as income in the first year, one-twelfth each month. So, for November you would list as income $10 per subscription—$1,670—and the same for December, a total of $3,340 for the year. The following year you would be liable for the balance, $16,700, but you would have the use of that money until tax return time the year after that. The key point is that as of the first year, your gain ($20,040 income minus $10,000 expenses) of $10,040 has been translated into a loss ($3,340 taxable income minus $10,000 expenses) of $6,660. For several years, then, as you promote heavily, you would run at a tax loss. Eventually, of course, like all tax shelters, this will even out. But it is a tremendous benefit in starting a newsletter.

Your accountant and your lawyer should understand this point. They should work together in helping you reap legitimate tax savings.

Deducting Expenses for an Office in Your Home Recent tax law changes offer some deductions, both for moonlighters and full-time newsletter writers, for office space in your home. There are important restrictions on taking such deductions that you should know about.

As a self-employed newsletterer, you must be able to prove that you use your designated office space on an *exclusive* and *regular* basis, either as your principal place of business or as an established place where you meet with clients or customers in the normal course of your business. (Exclusive use requires that you use your designated office space *strictly for business purposes;* regular use requires that you use such space on more than an incidental or occasional basis.)

Pro rata deductions for home businesses may include rent or mortgage, heat, light, electricity, telephone service, depreciation, and miscellaneous operating expenses. Detailed record keeping and physical proof that you use the area regularly and exclusively for business are essential. Consult your accountant or the IRS to be sure you are aware of all relevant regulations.

Profit-and-Loss Statements, and Your Banker There is a third professional you will encounter in your newsletter business—your banker. When you visit him for a loan for expansion of your business, he will want to see your profit-and-loss statement. When he sees the large loss you have accumulated because of the tax structure, he will not be impressed. All your banker will see is what appears to be a big liability.

Under the publishing industry's accounting procedures (as described above), all cash received in advance (deferred subscription revenue) is shown on the liability side of the balance sheet. In the words of accountant Jerry Huss, publisher of a number of newsletters for accountants, "Bankers tend to view all liabilities as negatives, even though some liabilities are different from others."

Huss goes on to say, "So, it's *crucial* that you're prepared to explain your business to the banker. In many cases, you actually must educate your banker about accounting for publishers." Because few bankers understand publishing and fewer still understand newsletter publishing, it's important to make a strong impression about your operation to your banker. Huss offers these suggestions.

- Stress cash flow. That's what will repay your bank, so prepare projections of your cash flow.
- Have a CPA firm prepare your financial statements and projections. Be sure that these are on your CPA firm's letterhead.
- Ask your CPA to explain the peculiarities of publishing statements to your banker.
- Be sure your balance sheet shows the caption "deferred subscription revenue," not "unearned subscription liability." Stress the facts that (1) this account merely represents funds collected in advance, not amounts that must be repaid, and (2) your costs to produce future issues will be much less than the amounts you've already collected. At worst, you can probably get another publisher to take over your unfulfilled subscriptions—so this amount will never be a real liability.
- Give your banker an estimate of the value of your subscriber base.
- Tell your banker exactly how much you want and when you plan to pay it back. This shows the banker that you've thought through your financial needs.
- Impress your banker with your publishing knowledge. Pepper your conversation with actual examples from your experience and what your plans are. More than anything else, your banker wants to be assured that you're capable of running a successful business.

Photocopying   The newsletter publisher is concerned about photocopying because it is easy for a company with one subscription to make multiple copies for its executives. This not only causes a loss of potential revenue, but it's also against the law. Copying has become so much a part of our everyday life that many people do not understand that they are violating the law when they photocopy something that is copyrighted. Technically, a photocopying shop should refuse to copy such a document, but such photocopying is done all the time and cannot be policed.

There has been a lot of tilting at windmills in trying to find a paper that doesn't photocopy or an ink that foils the copier. Certain color combinations will be uncopyable on some machines but not on all. The technology of the copying industry is such that it will always overcome such devices.

London-based publisher Mike Hyde, impatient with both illegal photocopiers and the dark-colored papers designed to thwart them, has proposed a watermark "which on introduction to a photocopier comes out loud and clear with the following statement, 'This photocopy is illegal, you cheapskate!' "

Perhaps one day a newsletter publisher will collect enough evidence to take a company to court and be prepared to go to the Supreme Court if necessary. Meanwhile, there are only two things that you, as a publisher, can do.

• Remind your subscribers from time to time about the copyright law— point out to them that it is a criminal offense to photocopy your newsletter willfully. Display your copyright notice prominently.
• Work out a reasonable rate for additional subscriptions to the same company. If yours is a popular newsletter within the company, the chances are good that you will get some additional subscriptions without ever raising the copyright point.

There's no single formula for bulk orders. Here's the discount schedule of the experienced *Bureau of National Affairs, Inc.,* in Washington, D.C.: two to five copies, 10 percent; six to fourteen, 15 percent; fifteen to twenty-four, 20 percent; twenty-five or more, 25 percent. If the order is really big, such as 10,000, the rate is five-sixths of unit price.

Copyrights The Copyright Act of 1978 recognized the vulnerability of newsletters to photocopying and the potential loss in revenues. This was due in part to efforts by the Newsletter Clearinghouse and, later, the Newsletter Association of America in acquainting Congress with the needs of the newsletter industry.

The basics of the law are the same as they have always been. If you want to copyright your newsletter, you claim copyright. This is done by printing on your newsletter the copyright symbol, ©, or Copyright, (date) (name of claimant); e.g., "© 1988 The Newsletter Clearing-house." The symbol © is preferred, because this simultaneously entitles you to international copyright protection. If you want to register your copyright claim, you need a form from the U.S. copyright office and you must include two copies of your newsletter. (This is in part how the Library of Congress obtains its huge collection of books and periodicals.) If you publish only through print, and your work is primarily textual in nature and is published periodically, there is only one form you need—SE. This form is the one to use for serial works—a work issued in successive numbered or chronological parts—which are intended to be issued indefinitely. However, if you are registering a copyright claim for an individual contribution to a periodical, then you should use form TX instead.

According to James Reisman, Esq., of the law firm of Gottlieb, Rack-man, and Reisman, New York, specialists in copyrights for publications, there are two main points in the copyright act of pertinence to newsletters.

- *Filing.* You don't have to file for copyright. However, there is now a greater incentive for you to file. If you file within three months of your publication date and if you later want to sue for infringement of copyright, there are statutory damage provisions up to $10,000 available plus compensation for attorneys' fees. If you do not file in this period, you can still obtain an injunction and the infringer's illicit profits, but not attorneys' fees or statutory damages. The filing fee is $10. There is also a provision for multiple registration (using Form GR/CP) to cover the same author for works published during a twelve-month period. But if additional people write your newsletter as independent contributors, you cannot take advantage of this provision.

- *Fair use.* It is now considered "fair use" if someone uses your material or makes a photocopy for the purpose of criticism, reporting, or research. However, there are exceptions if the purpose is actually commercial, especially if the copying would affect the market for the original work. The amount of copying (1 percent or 100 percent, for instance) is also a factor. This new doctrine of fair use gives better protection to newsletters, Reisman says. Further, he points to Section 107 of the copyright act, in which the legislative history discussing newsletters shows congressional intent to give us greater protection because of the nature of our business. These statements in Section 107 would be valuable ammunition for your lawyer if you had to sue.

There is one exception to be noted. A library may make one copy if there is no financial advantage and it shows your notice of copyright on the newsletter. For full instructions on filling in forms, write Register of Copyrights, Library of Congress, Washington, DC 20559.

You should also investigate the services of the not-for-profit Copyright Clearance Center, Inc. (CCC), 21 Congress St., Salem, MA 01970. It operates a centralized photocopy permissions and payments system for authors and publishers.

Trademarks You should do a trademark search to find out whether the name of your newsletter is registered by someone else, which would make it rather risky for you to adopt that mark. A trademark search takes time and many people find that hiring an attorney will help speed the process, especially to interpret the results.

It is not absolutely necessary to register your newsletter name; once you begin to use it, you establish a common-law right to the name. The advantage of formal trademark registration is that it puts third parties on notice of your trademark rights and gives you certain procedural advantages in any possible court battle over the name. In the event of a court case, if you have not registered, you may have difficulty in proving that the name should be yours. In such an event, you might be forced to stop using it.

You may obtain trademark application forms by either writing to the Patent and Trademark Office, U.S. Department of Commerce, Washington, DC 20231, or by visiting Crystal Plaza, Arlington, Virginia. Again, hiring an attorney may produce results faster.

If it is found that no one is already using the name you have chosen, or one similar to it, you will usually get approval unless:

your name is immoral or deceptive;
you have used the U.S. flag or any other governmental logos;
you have used the names or pictures or signatures of any living
    persons without their consent.

You cannot register a company name—only the name of your product or service, e.g., the newsletter name. Moreover, "descriptive" terms (which literally "describe" the product or service) are also hard to register.

To fulfill application requirements for a registration, you will have to include:

a drawing of the mark;
your completed application;

five specimens of the mark as it is now being used, e.g., letterhead,
newsletter logo;
the $200 application fee.

The process is not speedy. It may take a year or more. You can,
however, alert your competition to the fact that you are claiming rights
in your trademark. This is done by placing "TM" after your product
name. This indicates a common-law "ownership" of the mark.

The "TM" can be upgraded to an "R" within a circle, once the patent
office approves and the mark becomes registered. After registration, your
trademark is valid for as long as you continue to use it, provided you file
a maintenance affidavit by the sixth anniversary of the registration and
then renew it every twenty years.

The ISSN and What You Should Know About It   The ISSN (International Standard Serial Number) is the tiny number that appears on the
front page of many newsletters or sometimes in mastheads. An ISSN will
help you in many ways; for example, in sales to libraries and overseas—
and it is free. A single ISSN identifies the title of your newsletter regardless of language or the country in which it is published. It results in an
accurate citing of serials by scholars, researchers, abstracters, and librarians. It helps publishers and suppliers to communicate. If you deal with
the Copyright Clearance Center, the number will help to monitor payments. The ISSN is used by libraries to identify titles. It is also suitable
for computer use in fulfilling updates, retrieval, and transmittal of data.
The U.S. Postal Service uses the ISSN to regulate certain publications
mailed at second-class rates.

The various and constant changes to which serials are subject, com-
bined with the large growth in the world's publishing output, have made
necessary the development of a standard for the identification of serials.

The coordination of the code is international, with registration initi-
ated at the national level where serials are published. To coordinate this
two-level network, the International Serials Data System (ISDS), with
an International Center in Paris, was established within the framework
of UNESCO's World Science Information Program. The National Serials Data Program (NSDP), within the Library of Congress, is the U.S.
center of the ISDS. NSDP is responsible for registering and numbering
serials published in the United States and for promoting the use of and
fulfilling requests for ISSNs.

Assignment of ISSN. For the purpose of assigning ISSNs, a serial is
defined as a publication in print or in nonprint form, issued in successive

parts, usually having numerical or chronological designations, and intended to be continued indefinitely. Newsletters fit this definition.

An ISSN is composed of eight digits—seven digits that act as a unique title number, plus an eighth "check" digit, which guards against incorrect transcription of the number. The system used for calculating the check digit sometimes requires a check number of ten, in which case, to prevent a nine-digit ISSN, the roman numeral X is substituted.

For each serial with an ISSN there is a corresponding "key title"—a commonly acceptable form of the title established at the time of ISSN assignment. The title provides a benchmark that serves to regulate the assignment of ISSN.

The ISSN does not incorporate any significance other than the unique identification of a serial.

How to Obtain an ISSN   There is no charge for an ISSN assignment. An ISSN application form can be requested from the National Serials Data Program. Instructions for supplying the desired bibliographic information for registering the serial in the International Serials Data System data base appear on the form. Whether or not a form is submitted with the ISSN request, a suitable representation of the publication must be included. Telephone requests for an ISSN are honored when publication deadlines are imminent.

When requesting an ISSN for an already published serial, send NSDP a sample issue or copy of the cover, title page, and masthead as appropriate. For prepublication requests, a mock-up or artist's conception of the same identifying parts of the publication should be sent. A follow-up sample issue or surrogate of the actual publication must be sent directly to NSDP.

How to Use the ISSN   To fulfill the purpose of its assignment, the ISSN should be displayed prominently on every issue, preferably in the top right corner of the cover. It is acceptable, however, for the number to appear elsewhere on the publication (usually in the masthead area).

The typeface and size can be set at the publisher's discretion. The recommended style of printing the ISSN is to divide it into two groups of four digits separated by a hyphen and preceded by the letters ISSN; e.g., ISSN 1234-5679.

The ISSN should appear on publisher's advertisements (both direct mail and space ads) and catalogs, on the serials themselves, and in all other places where details of books and serials normally appear. Multijournal publishers also should have an "Index to Journals" in the back of their catalogs, in which the journals are listed alphabetically followed by their ISSN. This makes it very easy for a library to be certain it subscribes to all the journals it wants.

Changes Affecting ISSN   Serials often undergo changes, many of which result in a change of key title. When this occurs a new ISSN must be assigned. The earlier ISSN is not discarded, however, because it is a permanent attribute of the serial when it was issued under the earlier key title. To avoid unnecessary confusion NSDP must be notified in advance of a pending title change—especially one affecting the cover title (which is often the source for the key title). The notification will be treated as a request for a new ISSN, and the procedure is the same as that for the original ISSN request. Other changes to a serial, such as those affecting publisher, imprint, and frequency, do not affect the ISSN assignment.

You can get an application form from the National Serials Data Program (NSDP), Library of Congress, Washington, DC 20540.

How to Put a Value on a Newsletter   At some point, publishers want to know what their newsletters are worth. They may want to know for estate planning, for drawing up a will, out of curiosity, or because they want to buy or sell a newsletter. An authoritative booklet is *How to Buy, Sell, and Price Newsletter Properties* by Thomas J. Gilgut, Jr. A brief summary of Gilgut's key points follows.

First, although the financial figures for two different newsletters may seem to be the same, there are seven factors that have a bearing on the true worth.

1. *Age of the newsletters*—old or young?
2. *Profit performance*—steady or erratic?
3. *Size of universe*—large or small?
4. *Competition*—how does the newsletter stand in relation to others in the field?
5. *Growing or dying industry*—growth possibilities or decline due to new technology?
6. *Market penetration*—5 percent or 20 percent, for instance?
7. *How editorial content is generated*—can any competent journalist do the newsletter or does it depend on the unique expertise of the founding editor?

One-Time Sales   This simple formula holds that a multiple of sales, usually one-time, gives a good approximation of worth. For example, a newsletter grossing $50,000 would be worth $50,000. In newsletters grossing less than $100,000 this sometimes turns out to be true. The reason, Gilgut says, is that "a newsletter *grossing* $50,000 is apt to be earning a level of *profit* that a buyer would be willing to pay $50,000 for."

Regardless, there is one reason to study the annual gross, to find out if the bulk of the subscribers are one-year. If a newsletter has a high proportion of two- and three-year subscriptions, the annual value is lower.

The Sum of the Next Two Years' Renewals   This formula recognizes that usually a newsletter with a high renewal rate is worth more than one with low renewals. This formula would value a $50,000-sales newsletter with a 60 percent renewal rate at $48,000; with an 80 percent renewal rate at $72,000. There is quite a difference. The formula, while useful in pinpointing such differences, still does not take into account profitability and growth.

Multiple of Earnings   A multiple of earnings tells you how much you have to pay to own something producing annual earnings of a certain amount. A 5 percent savings account has a twenty-times-earnings multiple. (Multiple of earnings is the reciprocal of return on investment: a multiple of twenty is the reciprocal of 5 percent, or one-twentieth.) You might pay twenty times earnings to put money into a bank because of safety. In something more speculative, such as publishing, you might pay five times earnings to achieve 20 percent on your investment.

How Do You Find Earnings?   You look at the profit-and-loss statement. Figure 36 (page 174) is a typical example.

There is much more to the valuation of newsletters than this brief summary provides. However, these are the main points to consider.

Some Common Newsletter Management Problems

Libel   Libel is not generally a problem for newsletters. However, in this increasingly litigious society, more and more publishers are becoming concerned. Consult the booklet *Libel: An ABP Practical Guide,* by Faustin F. Jehle, former counsel, McGraw-Hill. As for libel insurance, and the perhaps more important errors and misprints coverage, contact the Newsletter Association (NA) and the Newsletter Clearinghouse (NLCH).

How to Survey Your Subscribers for Sensitive Information   The editor of a business newsletter needs to know all he can about the particular industry he is serving. Subscriber companies may be reluctant to give out information. One way to get information is to prepare an anonymous questionnaire and have it returned in an envelope addressed to an accounting firm that will tabulate the results. A second envelope or card can be enclosed that the subscriber returns to you so you know the questionnaire has been sent. This way you know who responded, but the replies are not linked to the respondents.

```
                        XYZ CORP

                PROFIT AND LOSS STATEMENT

GROSS SUBSCRIPTION INCOME                        $100,000

EXPENSES

Officer salaries              ......             20,000

Salary, editor                ......             17,000

Salary, business manager      ......              7,000

Taxes (Payroll)               ......              3,000

Publishing (printing, postage)......              8,000

Rent                          ......              2,000

Office Supplies               ......              2,000

Marketing Costs               ......             20,000

Telephone                     ......              2,000

Legal and Accounting Fees     ......              2,000

Other Editorial Costs         ......              1,000

Insurance                     ......                500

Depreciation                  ......                500

                              TOTAL            $ 85,000

PRETAX PROFIT                                  $ 15,000
```

Figure 36

List Maintenance for the Free Newsletter If your newsletter is free—
controlled circulation—to customers, sales prospects, opinion leaders,
and donors, you will get requests from people wanting to get on the list.
At first you may be flattered and agree. One day, you may find you are
no longer in control, that you have more names than you intended, and
you don't know how to cut back. One way is to publish a subscription
price in your masthead for people outside the field, and add names only
if you receive a payment.

Professional Services Disclaimer If you deal with elements of the legal, accounting, or other professional areas, you may be accused of practicing without a license—in extreme instances, you may be forced out of business. You should add something like the following to your masthead:

> This publication is designed to provide information in regard to the subject matter covered. It is sold with the understanding that neither the editor nor the publisher is engaged in rendering legal or accounting service. If legal advice or other expert assistance is required, the services of a competent professional person should be sought.

How Am I Doing?   This is the question every publisher must keep answering. A properly programmed computer can provide answers fast. Or you can use the simple form in Figure 37 (page 176).

Providing for Your Successor   The one-person newsletter publisher who doesn't aspire to adding staff has a successor problem. If he dies with no plan to keep the newsletter going, or if his heirs can't keep issues coming out on time, the newsletter may have to be sold at a distress price. If the publisher sells out when he retires, the new owner may require that the publisher stay on longer than he chooses so that a successor can be found. What happens if you are run over by a car and spend six months in the hospital? How will the newsletter get written and printed on schedule? There are some preliminary steps that can be taken to avoid such big problems.

One way is to seek out a competent free-lancer. Train the free-lancer to write your stories and to learn your procedures. This will force you to do something else that you've doubtless neglected to do: writing down your procedures so that someone else can follow them in your absence. Train this person for the day when you feel like taking a vacation. (In the first couple of years, newsletter publishers usually don't think about vacations.) Then take off for a couple of weeks and brace yourself for what you find upon your return: it is likely everything will be just fine. You may not be indispensable after all.

A variation is to arrange with another newsletter publisher in a similar situation to spend a little time learning each other's business. Or you might find someone at a larger newsletter who may one day aspire to join you and who would be willing to make a small investment in your business toward the day he or she could succeed you as publisher.

No one of these suggestions is an easy solution to your problem, but they are all better than just hoping that the worst won't happen. Oh yes,

A SIMPLE SCORECARD FOR MEASURING YOUR NEWSLETTER'S PROGRESS

NEWSLETTER _____   YEAR _____

	MONTH:			YEAR TO DATE (months)			
	Average, Last Year	Budget This Year	Actual This Year	Actual Last Year	Budget This Year	Actual This Year	% Change vs. Last Year
1. RECEIPTS New subs. Renewals Back copies Other							
2. EDITORIAL Salaries/fees Telephone Misc.							
3. PUBLISHING Print, mail Postage							
4. PROMOTION Direct mail Space ads Other							
5. GEN. & ADMIN. Salaries Rent Legal, Acctg Office, Postage Payroll tax, insur. Business machines Misc.							
6. TOTAL EXPENSES							
7. PROFIT							

8. VERIFICATION: ADD:
Cash balance, end of prev. month: ☐
= Cash balance, end of this month: ☐

Figure 37

make sure your spouse is aware of your contingency plans. It will make for peace of mind.

Professional Development   The failure rate in newsletters is high. The reason, in many cases, is bad management—marketing, editorial, promotional, and financial. You need information about the management of your own business. Shoptalk with other newsletter editors and publishers can be productive. Newsletters are still in an exciting stage in which they have not realized their full potential. So you may find others in the field eager to share their knowledge with you.

There are some more formal opportunities that you should investigate. Seek out newsletters and magazines that offer information you need—in editorial, promotional, financial, and technological areas. (Naturally, I think that *The Newsletter on Newsletters* should be first on your list.) Attend seminars. Attend the annual conference sponsored by the Newsletter Association. If you are eligible to join NA, by all means do so. Look on it as a privilege, not an obligation.

If you are in association work, the American Society of Association Executives can help. If you are in a company, the International Association of Business Communicators has practical programs. And there are helpful publications sections in the various nonprofit groups. See the Bibliography for these groups and publications.

Making Extra Income From Supplemental Services

Once your newsletter is established, your subscribers should be viewed as satisfied customers who trust you and who will give consideration to other products you have for sale. This chapter describes some of the supplemental services and products that you can offer.

A Classified Ad Section　If your readers need equipment, reports, or services in their field, they may have a difficult time meeting their special needs through the normal classified ad sections. You can develop an ad section in your newsletter in which outside suppliers and your customers can communicate with each other. When you set up such a section, do not eliminate any editorial pages. Make it an additional section. You will be giving your readers what they contracted for—plus an extra feature. You may find that readers like such ad sections and find them an extra benefit of your newsletter.

Special Reports and Back Issues　From your intimate knowledge of your field you can develop special reports that you can sell. Back issues on a certain subject—or just back issues—may make good offers to your readers. None of these items need to be elaborately printed or bound. Put on a cover or assemble them in a folder.

Selling Other People's Books　It is more and more difficult for people with special interests to get books they want from bookstores. Even large bookstores cannot stock the many thousands of new books printed each year, let alone older books. You can assemble a number of titles to appeal to your readers' interests and promote them through fliers in your newsletter.

Make an arrangement with a publisher in which you get a commission for each book sold. Try to get a 50 percent commission; don't go below 20 percent; and don't offer books under $10. After you receive an order, type a mailing label, send it to the publisher with your check, less commission, and the publisher will do the shipping. (This is called drop shipping.) Some newsletter publishers have not found bookselling worth the effort. Keep a careful record of your costs, returns, and time spent. Then evaluate the effort after a year.

Following is a case history of one publisher, Warren Blanding, Marketing Publications, Inc., Washington, D.C., who has made a success of selling books.

Introduction. By way of explanation I should start by saying that our firm specializes in the field of physical distribution management, which comprises freight transportation, warehousing, order processing, inventory management, materials handling, industrial location, and customer service. Our newsletters are primarily "state of the art" newsletters dealing with technology and management rather than news as such. We publish four newsletters of our own, plus a number of external corporate newsletters for others. We have developed a dozen or so books of our own, in some cases from material we have already published, in others from scratch to use as premiums in connection with circulation promotion. We find a continuing market for back issues bound into sets. We have also developed specialized computer programs in our field which we service on a timesharing basis. We also hold frequent seminars both for income purposes and to maintain our image of leadership in our field.

Until a few years ago we handled a few books, mostly our own, through our "book department," which like most departments in a small firm, existed only on paper. We had some problems with our firm name—Marketing Publications—because this did not convey the type of books we actually carried, and in any event most of our subscribers knew us by the names of our individual newsletters. Thus we decided to change the name of our book department to "The Physical Distribution Bookstore" and to conduct all future books sales under that name. I would like to say that we gave a lot of thought to the name, but in fact it was quite casual—I was working at the light table and picked up a sheet of Prestype and said something to the effect of "Hey! Let's call ourselves the Physical Distribution Bookstore," made up a letterhead on the spot, embellished it by sketching a shelf of books—and we were in business. Incredibly, this resulted in almost immediate identification, and with our first mailing under this heading we knew we were in the book business for real. The following observations reflect what we have learned since then.

Assuming that your newsletter reaches an audience with reasonably homogeneous interests, you may have the potential for grossing nearly as much in book sales as you do from the newsletter itself.

The first step is to find the books your readers are most likely to buy in connection with the subject matter of your newsletter. This is not as easy as it sounds, because many publishers do not catalog their books by subject matter, and the Xerox (Bowker) directories do not cover all subjects. Of course you will learn about some books through releases, the press, etc., but to build a good offering it is almost essential to go through a large number of publishers' catalogs. Once you have set up your basic list, you can keep track of new titles in your field simply by subscribing to the *American Book Publishing Record* (also Xerox/Bowker), which comes out every month and lists all new titles.

We found it very helpful to join the American Booksellers Association at a nominal fee (about $50 for the first year) because as part of our membership we got a directory of all major publishers whom we could contact for catalogues; the directory also shows the discount rates each publisher offers for different categories of books.

Another source of new-book information is people in the field who have written books and are anxious to support their sales. We are currently handling titles from a number of people in our field, and they have been quite cooperative—in some cases they have gotten us special consideration for improved cooperative discounts because of the support we give their books.

One other point: in our field, we find that the spectrum of interests is relatively narrow. That is, books dealing with specialized subjects within the discipline tend to sell better than general management books or books we think our readers "ought to" be interested in. We do handle a few titles that are highly theoretical, or dealing with management "philosophy," but they are primarily window-dressing; they do not sell very well.

Negotiating With Publishers. Setting up arrangements with publishers can run the gamut from very easy to extremely frustrating. If you have the author's support, it is usually easier, but not always. Some publishers are extremely cooperative and will give you a good discount in return for the promotional support you will be giving their titles. Others will give you the standard discount and will want to research your credit back to your great-grandparents.

Our own box-score: very good relationships with McGraw-Hill, Wm. C. Brown, Wiley, Irwin, Dow Jones-Irwin, Prentice-Hall, and others. The smaller publishers in our field are generally quite good. Bear in mind that many of the specialized publishers deal primarily with college book stores or have direct mail programs of their own. The relatively few books you buy from them are small potatoes, although some of them are smart enough to see that it's all gravy because you are reaching special markets they probably don't reach. Bear in mind, too, that once a technical book goes out of print the publisher isn't likely to reprint it . . . and usually won't even warn you that a book *is* about to go out of print. This can be embarrassing and costly if you have just invested heavily in promoting a particular title!

Although many publishers will drop-ship for you, we have chosen to buy books in quantity and have them shipped to us. That way, we control the shipment and we also keep our lists intact.

Promotion Folders. If you are mailing a four-page newsletter, you can also mail a four-page book promotion folder and stay within the first class postage limit. This has been our practice with several of our newsletters. Although we thought at first that our subscribers might resent this "commercialism," we found that it produced excellent sales and over a number of years has brought only four or five complaints. We initially inserted folders only occasionally; now we send them with every issue of every newsletter. They are very productive.

Our general format is to feature a single book (or set) on the first three pages of the folder, with the first page devoted to a large illustration of the book and a recital of its benefits, etc. The inside we will usually devote to a rather detailed listing of the table of contents; if the table of contents is too general, we go through the book and make a detailed subject outline. We consider this very important.

The fourth page of the folder is used to list and briefly describe four or five related titles. The coupon is on this page also. Although we find that these secondary listings do not pull nearly as well as the main book, they do produce enough incremental income to be worthwhile. Sometimes we will sell all the titles listed on a folder as a "special" with a 10 percent discount. Again, the results are not very spectacular but if the books are closely enough related without overlapping, it may be worthwhile.

We also prepare a short-form catalog, which is essentially a folder (in our case 8½" × 14" folded down) listing all our titles and a one-line description. In our case, we find it useful to classify these titles by general subject matter. We also have a coupon on this folder, of the circle-the-number type. This is used primarily for an enclosure with correspondence, invoices, and book shipment. It does reasonably well.

Promotion Catalog. If you carry any substantial number of titles, sooner or later you will want to publish a catalog, complete with illustrations. We published our first real catalog of this type in early 1974, and wish we had done it sooner. Ours was relatively inexpensive; we used a good amateur photographer to take the pictures (which are quite difficult to take, incidentally) and were able to get some photos from publishers as well. We set the type ourselves and did the pasteup. It took us a long time to complete a 16-page catalog, but the actual printing (10,000 copies) was relatively inexpensive. We have since gone to a second color, but we aren't entirely sure this is cost-effective.

We also publicize our catalogs to the trade press in our field. Several editors placed our catalogs on their bingo cards, and we got reasonably good response in terms of requests for catalogs as well as subsequent traceable sales.

The main virtue of the catalog, and what justifies a difficult undertaking, is that it usually more than doubles average order size. When you mail a four-page folder describing one book, you usually sell one book, with occasionally some of the secondary titles thrown in. This doesn't bring you a whole lot of profit. When we started mailing our catalog (to people who had previously bought books from us, as well as subscribers—who are very often the same people), the average order just about doubled, and we got some orders (from business libraries) for almost every book in our catalog.

General Guidelines. It is almost axiomatic that you give all potential buyers a ten-day or two-week free examination of any book you offer. This is a built-in damper against overselling or misrepresenting the book in your promotion. We have found that the best way to sell is to make the promotion as factual as possible, and also give a great deal of detail about the contents. This screens out most of the people who think the book is something other than what it is, who are often your main source of returns. There are a few people who will order every book on your list on this trial basis, we suppose, but we haven't seen them. We have experienced remarkably few returns, and very few deadbeats. If an order seems suspicious, i.e., not on our coupon or a purchase order or company letterhead, we may do a little checking before we send books out. If we can't be sure of the bona fides, we will hold the order for a while; if there is no follow up, we will discard the order on the assumption that it was phony to begin with. There are probably more sophisticated ways to do this, but since we deal 99 percent with companies—i.e., executives at a business address, with purchases paid for by the company—we have very few losses. If we had to credit check all orders, we would lose our shirts because of the added expense.

Phone Orders. We say in our catalog, "Phone orders accepted from rated firms in U.S. and Canada." In practice, anybody at a business address who calls in an order will get it on the same basis as if he or she had ordered from the catalog. We get a fair amount of business over the phone in this way, with virtually no returns, since the person phoning is usually in a hurry to get the book. We also give a name to call—Sharon—to make it less impersonal. This appears to be a plus.

Shipping Charges. We absorb shipping charges when payment accompanies an order, but we protect the buyer's return right and issue him a refund check if he decides not to keep the book. We thus get a lot of payments with orders but in practice have to issue very few refunds. When books are shipped on open account, we use a formula for shipping charges which relates to the number of books rather than the actual postage. With current high costs of postage and UPS we are considering assessing shipping charges in *all* sales.

Canadian Market. We have found this quite good in our field, as there are almost no books published in Canada on our subjects. Book purchases are duty-free below a certain dollar limit, so only the larger orders require customs documentation.

Overseas Markets. We have done quite well in Australia and Japan. Surface rates for shipping books go by the Postal Union and are quite cheap, but transit time is terrible—a month or six weeks is not unusual. We usually require payment with orders from overseas, although here again we may make exceptions if the circumstances seem to warrant it. Our reason is not mistrust; it just takes a long time to get payment otherwise! Some of our overseas customers are willing to pay airmail shipping charges for books, although these can be quite steep.

Mailing Lists. Your best prospects for buying books are people who have already bought books. Thus, even though your mailings may be confined to subscribers, it will pay to generate a separate bookbuyers list to capture these names. We use a Scriptomatic system and our procedure is very simple: when we type a Scripto card for a bookbuyer and file it, if there is already a card there, we throw out the old one. The date on the new card thus controls when we get around to cleaning the list and sorting our inactives from actives. We do not generally identify bookbuyers by the titles of the books they buy, although we would like to. We have done this for one cost workbook which we ourselves publish, and it has provided us with an excellent mailing list for some seminars we will be giving on the same subject. At this writing, we are converting our lists to computers, which will give us much more flexibility.

General Comments. Selling books to supplement newsletter income can be a major undertaking (as we have made it), or it can be merely a hitchhike type operation where you use envelope stuffers and anything you sell is gravy. In our case, we had to recognize that there were practical limits to how many newsletter subscriptions we could profitably sell, and thus it seemed desirable to do the job large-scale. We find that by concentrating on people who as subscribers already know us, we can increase per-subscriber revenue by close to 100 percent, and in our opinion this is more economic than trying to double our circulation to achieve the same result.

Pricing. We sell at the publisher's recommended list price, although there is no compulsion to do so and we are considering changing this practice. We occasionally discount for special combinations of three or more books, but have found that this doesn't work particularly well. We suspect that the people who buy the combination probably would have bought all the books anyway at the regular price.

Of course it doesn't really pay to handle many books under $10, unless you are going to sell in multiple orders. We try to arrange our "mix" of books offered so that those with the lowest discounts (20 percent) are in the higher-price range, while any in the lower-price range are high-discount titles. Of course, a high-discount title in the high-price range is ideal, particularly if it sells well. Even so, there are some short-discount books in the low-price range that you almost have to handle because they are standards, or the only available title on the subject.

Don't be afraid of high prices. We have some books that move very well at $37.50, and also some at $17.50 that move well. We handle some audio-visual training programs that sell for $150 and do exceptionally well. And we enjoy steady sales of our own books at prices ranging from $9.95 to over $100.

Seminars Seminars are a big business, although they are sharply sensitive to the economy. When the economic outlook is good, attendance will be good. If the outlook is uncertain, attendance will drop. However, you should investigate seminars for their income potential.

James Marsh, *The Washington Monitor,* Washington, D.C., has some excellent advice on seminars.

Before you sit down to consider the arithmetic of putting on seminars or conferences, you owe it to yourself to weigh certain qualitative questions first.

Do I have the time to do this the way it ought to be done? How can I organize things in order to do it properly? What are the opportunities and what are the risks?

The opportunities, if you can do a good job of designing and bringing off the seminar, are substantial.

- You will increase the size and the quality of your reputation. As a newsletter publisher you are automatically an expert in your field—but perhaps neither you nor enough other people recognize that fact. If you put on a useful, timely, informative, or thought-provoking seminar or symposium, you will do wonders for your reputation—*and* your self-esteem.
- Paradoxically, you will learn much about your subject matter. The necessity of presenting yourself as an expert will make you act more like one. You will sharpen concepts and ideas, and you will fill in the gaps in your knowledge—whether or not you are carrying the full speaking load yourself.
- Finally, you will get more practice at taking the well-calculated risk. This is a crucial factor in the long-term development of your business.

The risks:

- If you do a poor job—if you produce a seminar or conference that disappoints, that does not fulfill expectations—you will damage rather than enhance your reputation. And you will hurt your newsletter business.
- Another risk is that you will make the mistake of creating an event that you can't repeat. Don't put on a conference that you can do only once; in fact, once every two years isn't often enough. You need to be repaid for the time and attention you diverted from other tasks and opportunities.
- Let's say you spend $15,000 designing, planning, promoting, and holding a conference on which you gross $30,000. The resulting $15,000 seems like a tidy profit. But ask yourself this: would you spend all that time and effort to create a new newsletter that had only a $15,000 potential? Of course not. So try to conceive and develop an event that you can hold *at least* once a year—and preferably two, four, or even a dozen times a year.

This is why we at *The Washington Monitor* prefer seminars over conferences or symposia. The purer the instructional value of the program, the more likely you will be able to repeat it frequently enough to make it interesting financially. We do one of our seminars twenty times a year, and each of two others ten times a year. As a consequence we gross about $300,000 a year on seminars.

Now what about the arithmetic of seminars and conferences?

Development Costs   Depending on the nature of your program, you can spend anywhere from nothing up to $50,000. By development costs I mean the salaries and fees involved in conceiving, planning, and coordinating all aspects of the program. Normally these costs should range between $5,000 and $15,000, but if you are creating original written materials for the program, they can quickly go higher.

Promotion Costs   The number of pieces of direct mail advertising you will need to mail out to be successful can range from 15,000 to 75,000, but aim for 20,000 to 30,000. The cost for such a number will be reasonable and the mailing should be large enough to guarantee a response. Of course, the higher your registration fee the more promotion you can afford. The unit cost for the promotion piece should range between 15¢ and 25¢—including the conception, design, printing, labeling, and delivery (by bulk rate). You can spend a little less, and you can spend much, much more. But don't fool yourself that an expensive, elegant-looking mailing piece will persuade people to register for your program. With thought and care, you can produce an economical, attractive, informative, and, above all, convincing self-mailer that will encourage people to attend. It's what you tell them that counts, not how pretty the package looks.

What kind of response rate should you expect? Hope for a minimum of 0.3 percent overall. That way, if you mail out 25,000 you'll probably get enough responses to cover most of your costs. If you get a very large response you may have to schedule an overflow session, which is a nice problem to have.

Pricing Your Program   This is the most difficult thing to be scientific about, but, happily, it's probably the least important to be scientific about. Most one-day programs cost between $125 and $200. Most two-day programs range between $175 and $500. Some of these prices are bargains and some are not; it all depends on the program. The important thing to remember is that if your seminar is valuable, you're entitled to charge a reasonable price.

If you insist on a rule of thumb, however, price it so that you'll *net* $15,000 if response meets your most wildly optimistic expectation, and $5,000 if it meets your most pessimistic. Does this mean you should abandon the idea if with your most pessimistic projection you will break even and you are prevented by some outside constraint from charging more? Yes!

Hotels and Meeting Halls   Bear in mind that the principal difference between the Chateau Fleabag and the Ritz may not be the price but the degree of training and commitment of the hotel employees. The Ritz may cost more, but its quality of service may help your program go smoothly, which makes the cost worthwhile.

Actually you don't have to choose the most expensive site. Although I hold my seminars at Washington's most elegant hotel, I would be just as well served at any one of a half-dozen others. I hold them where I do because the other hotels in town insist on charging for meals or sleeping accommodations. I hold half-day seminars for people who come largely from the Washington metropolitan area and don't need the meals or rooms.

Choose a half-dozen hotels that are conveniently located and have a variety of meeting rooms. Visit them and talk with the sales staff. Narrow the list down to two or three, ask for the names of a few organizations that have held daytime functions at each recently, and check with these references. Here are some typical charges as of June 1987.

Coffee, $1.75 per cup
Danish, $2 each and up
Lunch, $4 to $20 each
Cocktail party (open bar), $5 to $15 per person
Meeting rooms: generally no charge if you serve meals or have registrants staying at hotel; otherwise $250 to $500

As a bonus, you may be able to get one complimentary hotel room for every fifty rooms rented by your registrants.

Speakers, Faculty, Honoraria Try to avoid paying honoraria and pay only expenses. Use your own staff whenever possible. And never, ever use big-name speakers.

You may be surprised at how little a well-qualified speaker is willing to accept. Why are good but not so well known speakers usually the cheapest? They have reputations to build, and speaking to your group is a way of doing that. You get their best effort because they'll be working as much for themselves as for you. People with established reputations generally made their reputations some years ago. You want someone who's going to establish a reputation in the near future—in the next couple of years. And since you're familiar with most of the people in your field, you ought to know who these people are.

If you're thinking of a symposium, or some other kind of program with markedly less instructional value, then you may not be able to afford the luxury of this kind of speaker. You may be forced to pay for a well-known speaker in order to get people to attend. In such cases, your costs are apt to be quite high.

Fees generally range between $100 and $500 for presentations lasting from thirty minutes to a couple of hours. Of course the fees may be higher if you go after the big-name speakers I've urged you to avoid.

Materials   The cost of furnishing printed materials can be expensive. Try to limit this cost to between $5 and $10 per person. It's not the volume of the materials that counts, it's the quality. One reason for the explosive growth of the seminar business in recent years is that people have developed an aversion to reading. So reams and reams of printed material just aren't necessary.

All the foregoing are predictable and measurable costs. They'll all show up on your year-end statement. But don't forget about the intangible but very significant costs of your own involvement in launching a seminar or conference. You'll spend time and take attention away from the rest of your business, and you'll be concentrating on this project instead of others that might be profitable.

Ask yourself these questions before you plunge ahead:

- Are we inspired and prepared organizationally to do a really first-rate job with this project, or will other pressures force us to cut corners? Are we being realistic about how much time it will take to do it right?
- Can we repeat this program often enough to make this substantial diversion of our time and attention worthwhile?

If the answers to these simple but essential questions are yes, then go to it—and have fun!

(Note: Be sure to tell prospects that your seminar is a tax-deductible expense under the Internal Revenue Code.)

Directories   Newsletters that cover a particular industry are in a good position to develop a directory of companies in the field and other industry information. A directory can command a good price, sometimes $100 or more per copy. It may also generate advertising revenue. On the negative side, a large directory is very time consuming, may require extra staff, and may have substantial printing costs.

10 The Future for Newsletters

Keeping Up With Technology Newsletters are facing a technological revolution that will continue through this century. As I discussed earlier, the big trend is the blending of word processors and computers—what is called desktop publishing. Incredibly rapid printing processes that use lasers and ink jets continue to evolve; these are particularly suitable for mass mailings. These developments will upgrade the entire industry. Costs for equipment will continue to decrease (do you remember when a calculator sold for more than $100?). So-called obsolete equipment, far better than many of us have ever seen, will be available. Even the volunteer-staffed newsletters for schools or community organizations may be able to obtain equipment they never dreamed of—and may, finally, get rid of those beat-up manual typewriters with those dirty keys.

The technological revolution started with electronic transmission. Once companies were able to receive text on their PCs via a modem, newsletters were able to tap a new market.

McGraw-Hill, for instance, continues to sell some of its statistical-type newsletters via electronic transmission. The subscriber company can either call up the text on its screen or request that the text be sent in a printout, as the old-fashioned teletypewriter used to do. Subscribers receive portions of the material each day, rather than waiting a week to get an entire newsletter. Subscribers who receive multiple copies are charged a fee for each person who has access to a receiving terminal.

It's easy to see how there would be a big demand for the electronic reception of news involving a time factor—financial information, for example, has much more value if it is transmitted instantly. It's also easy to see what a boon this is to all of us as collectors of information to be able to have access to the vast data bases that already are in operation.

The interest in receiving information electronically has not extended much beyond the workplace. In fact, the day I am writing this, September 15, 1987, finds Andrew Pollack writing in the *New York Times* that "the vision of an electronic society in which consumers read the news, pay bills, and make airplane reservations on their home computers has proved an illusory one."

What, then, is going to happen to the vast majority of newsletters that don't have sharp news, that are twice weekly or monthly in frequency, and that interpret in depth? Will readers want these in video format? I don't think so—nor is a simple printout an attractive alternative. Reading words on a video screen is not nearly as efficient as reading words in print, and it can produce eyestrain. Also, a newsletter would appear in small bits. A column from the *New York Times,* for instance, would probably fill fourteen screens' worth of information. The printed newsletter has a long life expectancy, in my opinion.

Ultimately, technology has another answer, the intelligent copier. It is possible to send your subscriber your newsletter via electronics, laid out as you want it and with color, and have it printed out the same way. Thus the electronic devices would become the printer—you would get your newsletter to your subscriber in the form you want and on time. In that sense the electronic revolution will bring us back to where we were when the post office was able to deliver efficiently!

Meanwhile, most newsletterers who aspire to electronic transmission have an easy choice. In January 1982, John H. Buhsmer founded a company named NewsNet to specialize in electronic editions for newsletters. One hundred newsletters signed up and, as of this writing, there are more than five hundred in the system. Publishers service manager Andrew S. Elston says that most of these newsletters transmit to subscribers at their business addresses.

The first step that publishers should take to learn how to capitalize on the information they own is to get it in *machine-readable* form. This means some form of computer storage, tape, or disk, for instance, or conversion from print by optical scanning. This is the first step for eventual storage in a data base.

If you are interested in an electronic edition of your newsletter and want to know about royalties and profits, contact NewsNet at 945 Haverford Rd., Bryn Mawr, PA 19010.

For many publishers it'll be a waiting game, just as in the early days of TV, until there are enough receivers in homes and offices to indicate the time to switch. Certainly the day that Kiplinger goes electronic will be a significant signal.

To summarize, the electronic age for newsletters is in full swing.

Electric typewriters are being replaced by electronic versions and PCs and word processors. Keyboarded material can be transmitted by modem to a typesetting machine next door or across the country. Your manuscript can be delivered electronically to any PC for reception. Or it can be transmitted by satellite to a printing plant thousands of miles away. And, as we have noted, there are many electronic editions of newsletters.

But despite this, paper is not yet obsolete. One way or another, all of these electronic procedures and devices are primarily steps toward the printed page. And those who have been waiting for the paperless office are advised to hold on to their wastebaskets for probably another decade.

In Conclusion   Since the entire newsletter field as we know it started with one man, Willard M. Kiplinger, it seems fitting to conclude with some observations by his son, Austin Kiplinger, at the 1980 International Newsletter Conference in Washington. He stressed that newsletters are utilitarian, reader-minded, forward-looking, and based on the need of the reader to make decisions. Newsletters are in business to help people adjust to the realities of life. And he concluded with one word that is his key to newsletter success—"Survivability."

In 1988, this is still the key word.

Glossary

action devices Items and techniques used in a mailing to initiate the desired response.

active subscriber One who has committed himself for regular delivery of magazines, books, or other goods or services for a period of time still in effect.

address correction requested An endorsement that, when printed below the return address in the upper left-hand corner of the address portion of the mailing piece, authorizes the U.S. Postal Service, for a fee, to provide the new address, if known, of a person no longer at the address of the mailing piece.

advance renewal A subscription that has been renewed prior to its expiration.

AIDA The most popular formula for the preparation of direct mail copy. The letters stand for Get *Attention,* Arouse *Interest,* Stimulate *Desire,* Ask for *Action.*

assigned mailing date(s) The date(s) on which the list user has the obligation to mail a specific list based on prior agreement between the list owner and the user. No other date is acceptable without specific approval of the list owner.

bingo card A reply card inserted in a publication and used by readers to request literature and samples from companies whose products and services are either advertised or mentioned in editorial columns.

bleed A printing method in which the ink color appears to run off the edges of the paper. This is achieved by trimming the edges. Most magazines have covers that bleed.

blue line A proof the printer provides on which errors are corrected (sometimes called a brown line).

blue nonreproducing pencil A pencil that does not photograph; it "washes out" and disappears.

193

BRE   Business reply envelope.

buyer   One who orders merchandise, books, records, information, or services. Unless a modifying word is used, it is assumed that a buyer has paid for all merchandise to date.

camera-ready copy   Text or art ready to be shot by the printer's camera; should be free of smudges, unclear type, or faint type.

caps   Short for capitals or uppercase.

caption   A legend or explanation that identifies an illustration or photograph.

cash-with-order   A requirement for full or part payment at the time the order is placed.

character (printing)   The term applied to a single printed or typewritten letter, number, or symbol.

Cheshire labels   Specially prepared paper (rolls, fanfold, or accordion fold) used to reproduce names and addresses to be mechanically affixed, one at a time, to a mailing piece.

cleaning   The process of correcting or removing a name or address from a mailing list because it is no longer correct or because the listing is to be shifted from one category to another.

cluster selection   A selection routine based upon taking a group of names in a series, skipping a group, taking another group, and so on. For example, a cluster selection on an nth-name basis might be the first 10 out of every 100 or the first 125 out of 175, and so on. A cluster selection using ZIP codes might be the first 200 names in each of the specified ZIP codes, and so on. Cluster selection is useful for testing.

coding   (1) Identification devices used on reply materials to identify the mailing list or other source from which the address was obtained. (2) A structure of letters and numbers used to classify characteristics of an address on a list.

cold type   Typesetting accomplished without the use of molten lead or "hot metal." Cold type includes photographic, rub-on, direct-impression, and so on. It is the most popular method used today.

collate   To assemble individual elements of a mailing in sequence for inserting in a mailing envelope.

compiled list   Names and addresses derived from directories, newspapers, public records, retail sales slips, trade show registration, and so on, to identify groups of people with something in common.

computer service bureau   An internal or external facility providing general or specific data-processing services.

controlled circulation   Distribution at no charge of a publication to individuals or companies on the basis of their title or occupation.

Typically, recipients are asked from time to time to verify the information that qualifies them to receive the publication.

co-op mailing A mailing in which two or more offers are included in the same envelope or other carrier with each participating mailer sharing mailing costs according to a predetermined formula.

corner card Your name and address imprinted in the top left corner of an envelope or on the back flap.

cost per inquiry (CPI) A simple arithmetic formula—total cost of mailing or advertisement divided by the number of inquiries received.

cost per order (CPO) Similar to cost per inquiry but based on actual orders rather than inquiries.

cost per thousand (CPM) Refers to total cost per thousand pieces of direct mail "in the mail."

coupon clipper One who has given evidence of responding to free or nominal-cost offers out of curiosity, with little or no serious interest or buying intent.

cropping Placing black or red pencil (or crayon) marks at the margins and corners of a photo or illustration to indicate what portion is to be reproduced.

daisy-wheel printer A type of strike-on printer that uses an interchangeable typing element and produces letter-quality printing.

DBA Doing business as.

deadbeat One who has ordered a product or service and, without just cause, hasn't paid for it.

decoy A name specially inserted in a mailing list for verification of list usage.

delinquent One who has fallen behind or has stopped scheduled payment for a product or service.

demographics Socioeconomic characteristics pertaining to a geographic unit (county, city, sectional center, ZIP code, group of households, and so on).

desktop publishing The process by which microcomputers are used to typeset and lay out camera-ready copy.

direct mail advertising A promotional effort using the postal service or other direct delivery service for distribution of an advertising message.

Direct Mail/Marketing Association (DMMA) mail preference service (MPS) A service provided by DMMA, MPS enables individuals to have their names and addresses removed from or added to mailing lists. These names are made available to both members and nonmembers of the association.

direct response advertising Advertising, through any medium, designed to generate a response by any means (such as mail, telephone, or telegraph) that is measurable.

dot-matrix printer A type of strike-on computer printer that uses dots in series to produce characters.

dummy (1) A preliminary mock-up of a printed piece showing placement and nature of the material to be printed. (2) A fictitious name with an actual address inserted into a mailing list to check on use of that list.

envelope corner card Return address printed in the upper left-hand corner of an envelope.

expire A subscriber (see *active subscriber*) who has let a subscription run out without renewing.

font Complete assortment of the different characters of a particular style and size of type.

friend-of-a-friend (friend recommendation) The result of one party's sending in the name of someone considered to be interested in a specific advertiser's product or service (a third-party inquiry).

galley proof A proof pulled after type has been composed or set and before the publication has been compiled or made up into pages.

halftones Photos and illustrations reproduced in one color, as compared with two-color duotones and full-color photos.

hardware A term used to describe the mechanical, electrical, and electronic elements of a data-processing system.

hot-line list The most recent names available on a specific list—no older than three months. *Hot-line* should be modified by such terms as *weekly* or *monthly*.

house list Any list of names owned by a company as a result of compilation, inquiry, buyer action, or acquisition that is used to promote that company's products or services.

ink jet Method of printing by spraying droplets of ink through computer-controlled nozzles.

inquiry A request for literature or other information about a product or service. Unless stated otherwise, it is assumed no payment has been made for the literature or other information. A catalog request is generally considered a specific type of inquiry.

ISSN International Standard Serial Number (for full discussion, see pages 170–72).

key code (key) A group of letters and/or numbers, colors, or other marking used to measure specific effectiveness of media, lists, advertisements, offers, and so on (or any parts thereof).

keyline Essentially the same as a pasteup. The original composite art of offset printing.

laser printer Method of photocopying or printing, using a laser beam to charge the drum.

layout An artist's sketch showing the relative positioning of illustrations, headlines, and copy on a press sheet for most efficient production.

lc (lowercase) Uncapitalized letters of the alphabet.

lettershop A business that handles the mechanical details of mailings, such as addressing, imprinting, and collating. Most lettershops offer printing facilities and many offer direct-mail services.

light table A table with a glass top and a diffused light underneath to facilitate pasteup.

list broker A specialist who makes all necessary arrangements for one company to make use of a list of another company. A broker's services may include some or all of the following: research, selection, recommendation, and subsequent evaluation.

list cleaning The process of correcting or removing a name and address from a mailing list. Information for the change may come from the postal service (see *address correction requested*) or the individual.

list compiler One who develops lists of names and addresses from directories, newspapers, public records, sales slips, trade show registrations, and other sources of groups of people or companies with something in common.

list maintenance Any manual, mechanical, or electronic system for keeping name and address records (with or without other data) so that they are up-to-date at a specific time.

list manager One who, as an employee of a list owner or as an outside agent, is responsible for the use by others of a specific mailing list. The list manager generally serves the list owner in some or all of the following: list maintenance (or advice thereon), list promotion and marketing, list clearance and record keeping, and collection for use of the list by others.

list rental An arrangement in which a list owner furnishes names on his or her list to a mailer, who has the privilege of using the list on a one-time basis only (unless otherwise specified in advance). For this privilege, the mailer pays a royalty to the list owner. (*List rental* is the term most often used, although *list reproduction* and *list usage* more accurately describe the transaction, since *rental* is not used in the sense of leasing property.)

list sequence   The order in which names and addresses appear in a list. While most lists today are in ZIP-code sequence, some are alphabetical by name within the ZIP code, others are in carrier sequence (postal delivery), and still others have another (or no) order within a ZIP code. Some lists are still arranged alphabetically by state (and city within the state), alphabetically by name, or chronologically (with many variations or combinations).

logotype   The characteristic signature of a firm or product.

nameplate   Name of a periodical as it appears on the first page and at the top of the other pages.

nixie   A mailing piece returned to a mailer (under proper authorization) by the U.S. Postal Service because of an incorrect or undeliverable name and address.

no-pay   A person who has not paid (wholly or in part) for goods or services ordered. *Uncollectible, deadbeat,* and *delinquent* are often used to describe this person.

nth-name selection   A fractional unit that is repeated in sampling a mailing list. For example, in an *every tenth* sample, you would select the first, eleventh, twenty-first, thirty-first, and so on, records.

pasteup   A mechanical of illustrations, headlines, and copy prepared for printing.

photo offset   Method of lithographic printing that transfers ink from a plate to a blanket, then from the blanket to paper.

piggyback   An offer that hitches a free ride with another offer.

pyramiding   A method of testing mailing lists, in which one starts with a small quantity and, based on positive indications, follows with larger and larger quantities of the balance of the list until, finally, one mails the entire list.

RMRS   Remote meter setting.

salting   Deliberate placing of decoy or dummy names in a list to trace list usage and delivery (see also *decoy* and *dummy*).

SASE   Self-addressed stamped envelope.

sectional center (SCF or SEC Center)   A postal service distribution unit comprising post offices whose ZIP codes have the same first three digits.

self-mailer   Newsletter mailed without an envelope.

SIC (Standard Industrial Classification)   Classification of businesses, as defined by the U.S. Department of Commerce.

software   A set of programs, procedures, and associated documentation concerned with the operation of a data-processing system.

source code   Unique alphabetical or numerical identification for distinguishing one list or media source from another (see also *key code*).

split list   A technique in which two or more samples from the same list—each considered to be representative of the entire list—are used for package tests or as a test of the homogeneity of the list.

stet   A proofreader's term meaning "let it stand." Used when a word or sentence is changed or deleted and later changed back to the original.

teaser   An advertisement or promotion planned to excite curiosity about a later advertisement or promotion.

till forbid   An order for ongoing service that is to continue until specifically cancelled by the buyer.

trial subscriber   One who orders a publication or service on a conditional basis. The condition may relate to delayed payment, the right to cancel, a shorter than normal term, or special introductory price.

universe   Total number of individuals who might be included in a mailing list.

uppercase   Capital letters, as distinct from lowercase and small caps.

white mail   Incoming mail that is not on a form sent out by the advertiser.

Bibliography, Sources, and Resources

Books and Pamphlets

Associated University Bureau of Business and Economic Research Bulletin. University of Oregon, Eugene, OR 97403.

Bacon's Publicity Checker: Vol. 1 Magazines. Annual. 332 S. Michigan Ave., Chicago, IL 60604.
Lists a number of newsletters.

The Basics of Copy. Ed McLean. 1975. Thistle Hill, P.O. Box 218, Ghent, NY 12075. Also available from The Newsletter Clearinghouse.

The Basics of Testing. Ed McLean. 1978. Thistle Hill, P.O. Box 218, Ghent, NY 12075. Also available from The Newsletter Clearinghouse.

The Best of Impact, *"A Newsletter on Trends, Techniques, and Tools for Communicators."* Robert L. Baker. 1981. P.O. Box 1896, Chicago, IL 60604.

The Chicago Manual of Style. 13th ed. 1982. The University of Chicago Press, 5801 S. Ellis Ave., Chicago, IL 60637.

Copyright Handbook. 3rd ed. 1987. R. R. Bowker Co., 245 W. 17th St., New York, NY 10011.

Desktop Publishing With PageMaker. Tony Bove and Cheryl Rhodes. 1987. John Wiley & Sons, 605 Third Ave., New York, NY 10158.

Direct Mail and Mail Order Handbook. Richard S. Hodgson. 3rd ed. 1981. The Dartnell Corporation, 4660 Ravenswood Ave., Chicago, IL 60640.
A basic book for all in the direct mail field. Particularly valuable for its encyclopedic qualities and details you won't find anywhere else.

Direct Mail Copy That Sells. Herschell Gordon Lewis. 1984. Prentice-Hall, Inc., Englewood Cliffs, NJ 07632.

Directory of Editorial Resources. 1981. Editorial Experts, Inc., 85 S. Bragg St., Alexandria, VA 22312.

The Do-It-Yourself Direct Mail Handbook. Murray Raphel and Ken Erdman. 1986. The Marketers Bookshelf, 402 Bethlehem Pike, Philadelphia, PA 19118.

Editing Your Newsletter: A Guide to Writing, Design, and Production. Mark Beach. 3rd ed. 1987. Coast to Coast Books, 2934 NE 16th Ave., Portland, OR 97212. Also available from The Newsletter Clearinghouse.

Encyclopedia of Associations. Annual. Gale Research Co., Book Tower, Detroit, MI 48226.

Encyclopedia of Mailing List Terminology and Techniques: A Practical Guide for Marketers. Nat G. Bodian. 1986. Bret Scott Press, Winchester, MA 01890.

59 Response/Profit Tips, Tricks, & Techniques to Help You Achieve Major Mail Order Success. Galen Stilson. 1984. Premier Publishers, Box 16254, Fort Worth, TX 76133.

Form Book for IBM Selectric and Remington SR-101 Typewriters. Richard L. Clement. 1979. The Aurelian Press, Wilmette, IL 60091.
　　Useful to anyone who uses typewriter composition.

Getting It Printed: How to Work With Printers and Graphic Art Services to Assure Quality, Stay on Schedule, and Control Costs. Mark Beach, Steve Shepro, and Ken Russon. Coast to Coast Books, 2934 NE 16th Ave., Portland, OR 97212. Also available from The Newsletter Clearinghouse.

Harnessing Desktop Publishing. 1987. Scott Tilden. Scott Tilden, Inc., 4 W. Franklin Ave., Pennington, NJ 08534.

How to Buy, Sell and Price Newsletter Properties. Thomas J. Gilgut, Jr. 1980. Foreword by Howard Penn Hudson. The Newsletter Clearinghouse, P.O. Box 311, Rhinebeck, NY 12572.

How to Put Out a Newsletter. Peter S. Nagan. 1987. Newsletter Services, Inc., 1545 New York Ave., NE, Washington, DC 20002.
　　Free sixteen-page pamphlet prepared by the publisher and printer of a number of Washington newsletters.

How to Start Publishing Newsletters. 1976. TOWERS Club Bookstore, P.O. Box 2038, Vancouver, WA 98668.

Packs a lot of reliable, basic information into a few pages. TOWERS Club also publishes *TOWERS Club USA Newsletter* for self-publishers and writers.

How to Work With Mailing Lists. Richard S. Hodgson. 1976. Direct Mail Marketing Association, 6 E. 43rd St., New York, NY 10017.

How to Write Company Newsletters. Gerene Reid. 1985. Reid Publications, 8429 Sale Ave., Canoga Park, CA 91304.

Hudson's Newsletter Directory. Annual. The Newsletter Clearinghouse. P.O. Box 311, Rhinebeck, NY 12572.

Hudson's Washington News Media Contacts Directory. Annual. P.O. Box 311, Rhinebeck, NY 12572.

Lists the Washington, D.C., newsletters.

The Illustrated Handbook of Desktop Publishing and Typesetting. Michael L. Kleper. 1987. Tab Professional and Reference Books, P.O. Box 40, Blue Ridge Summit, PA 17214.

Inside Xerox Ventura. James Cavuoto and Jesse Berst. 1987. New Riders Publishing, P.O. Box 4846, Thousand Oaks, CA 91360. Also available from The Newsletter Clearinghouse.

Investment Newsletters. Annual. Larimi Communications, Inc., 246 W. 38th St., New York, NY 10018. Also available from The Newsletter Clearinghouse.

Directory of more than 770 publications for financial executives and investors. Updated weekly.

LaserPrint It! A Desktop Publishing Guide to Reports, Resumes, Newsletters, Directories, Business Forms and More. James Cavuoto. 1986. Addison-Wesley Publishing Co., Reading, MA 01867. Also available from The Newsletter Clearinghouse.

Legal Aspects for Newsletter Publishers. 1986. The Newsletter Association, 1401 Wilson Blvd., Arlington, VA 22209.

Special report on plagiarism, publishing law, copyright, trademarks, Freedom of Information Act, fair use, libel, ISSN, incorporation, taxes, and international currency.

Libel: An ABP Practical Guide. Faustin F. Jehle. 1981. American Business Press, New York, NY 10017.

Mailer's Guide. 1980. U.S. Postal Service, Washington, DC 20260.

Marketing With Seminars and Newsletters. Herman Holtz. 1986. Quorum Books, Greenwood Press, 88 Post Road West, Westport, CT 06881.

Mastering Graphics: Design and Production Made Easy. Jan V. White. 1983. R. R. Bowker Co., 245 W. 17th St., New York, NY 10011.

The Monthly Catalog of United States Government Publications and **The Monthly Checklist of State Publications.** Superintendent of Documents, U.S. Government Printing Office, Washington, DC 20402.

The National Directory of Investment Newsletters. 1987–88. Idea Publishing Corporation, 55 E. Afton Ave., Yardley, PA 19067.

The Newsletter Editor's Desk Book. Marvin Arth and Helen Ashmore. 3rd ed. 1984. Parkway Press, Box 8158, Shawnee Mission, KS 66208.

Newsletter Publishing: A Guide to Techniques and Tactics. Howard Penn Hudson and contributors. 1987. Knowledge Industry Publications, Inc., 701 Westchester Ave., White Plains, NY 10604.

Contributors include Thomas Gilgut, Jr., Don Hauptman, Jerry Huss, Stephen Sahlein, Richard Silverman, Beverley Walker, and Richard Wambach.

Newsletters Directory. 3rd ed. 1987. Gale Research Co., Book Tower, Detroit, MI 48226.

NewsNet Directory of Electronic Publishers. Annual. NewsNet, 945 Haverford Rd., Bryn Mawr, PA 19010.

Lists hundreds of publications, mostly newsletters, transmitted electronically to subscribers.

Oxbridge Directory of Newsletters. 1987. Oxbridge Communications, Inc., 150 Fifth Ave., New York, NY 10011.

Pocket Pal. International Paper Co., 220 E. 42nd St., New York, NY 10017.

Since 1934, this handy graphics art digest has been serving people in printing.

Proofreading Manual and Reference Guide. 1981. Editorial Experts, Inc., 85 S. Bragg St., Alexandria, VA 22312.

The Publisher's Direct Mail Handbook. Nat G. Bodian. 1987. ISI Press, 3501 Market St., Philadelphia, PA 19104.

Quick & Easy Newsletter Guide. Phyllis L. Stover. 1986. P.O. Box 822, Solana Beach, CA 92075. Also available from The Newsletter Clearinghouse.

A kit of clip art, nameplates, quotations, story heads, and paste-up boards for the low-budget organization newsletter operation.

Renewals. Eliot Schein. 1984. Folio Publishing Corp., P.O. Box 4006, New Canaan, CT 06840.

Secrets of Successful Direct Mail. Richard V. Benson. 1987. The Benson Organization, 4 Baywood Ln., Skidaway Island, Savannah, GA 31411. Also available from The Newsletter Clearinghouse.

Stet! Tricks of the Trade for Writers and Editors. Edited by Bruce O. Boston. 1986. Editorial Experts, Inc., 85 S. Bragg St., Alexandria, VA 22312.

Stylebook for Writers and Editors. 1987. *U.S. News & World Report,* 2400 N St., NW, Washington, DC 20037.

Success in Newsletter Publishing: A Practical Guide. Frederick D. Goss. 2nd ed. 1986. The Newsletter Association, 1401 Wilson Blvd., Arlington, VA 22209.

Successful Direct Marketing Methods. Bob Stone. 3rd ed. 1984. Crain Books, an imprint of NTC Business Books, 4255 Touhy Ave., Lincolnwood, IL 60646.

A basic book that explains the why as well as the how of direct mail. Considered by many as a classic in the field.

The TypEncyclopedia: A User's Guide to Better Typography. Frank J. Romano. 1984. R. R. Bowker Co., 245 W. 17th St., New York, NY 10011.

The UK Newsletter Directory. 1987. UK Newsletter Association, IBC Ltd., Bath House, 56 Holborn Viaduct, London EC1A 2EX, England.

Ulrich's International Periodicals Directory. Annual. R. R. Bowker Co., 245 W. 17th St., New York, NY 10011.

Using Direct Mail to Increase Sales & Profits. Ed McLean. 1978. Bill Communications, Inc., New York, NY 10017. Also available from The Newsletter Clearinghouse.

The Wall Street Gurus: How You Can Profit From Investment Newsletters. Peter Brimelow. 1986. Random House, Inc., New York, NY 10022.

Washington Newsletters and Federal Information Sources. Brian Sheehan. 1967. Unpublished master's thesis. American University, Washington, DC 20016.

Who's Who in Direct Response Creative Services. Denison Hatch. 1988. P.O. Box 8180, Stamford, CT 06905.

Directory of writers, designers, and consultants published by the editor of *Who's Mailing What!* newsletter.

Wilson Library Bulletin, untitled article. Gail Pool. Vol. 58, No. 8, April 1984. 950 University Ave., Bronx, NY 10452.

Discussion of "the quirky and untidy" newsletter field from a librarian's point of view.

Newsletters and Other Periodicals

In addition to *The Newsletter on Newsletters* and *Newsletter Design* (The Newsletter Clearinghouse, pages 209–10), the following are useful sources of information.

EDITORIAL AND GRAPHICS

Communications Briefings
806 Westminster Blvd.
Blackwood, NJ   08012

Communications Concepts
1377 K Street, NW, #840
Washington, DC   20005

Contacts
Larimi Communications, Inc.
246 W. 38th St.
New York, NY   10018

The Desktop
In House Graphics, Inc.
342 E. Third St.
Loveland, CO   80537

Desktop Graphics
Dynamic Graphics, Inc.
6000 N. Forest Park Dr.
Peoria, IL   61614

The Editorial Eye
85 S. Bragg St.
Alexandria, VA   22312

Editor's Digest
Douglas & Laabs Publications
4510 Regent St.
Madison, WI   53705

Editor's Forum
P.O. Box 1806
Kansas City, MO   64141

Editor's Health Article Service
Berry Publishing
300 N. State
Chicago, IL   60610

Editors Only
P.O. Box 2597
Waterbury, CT   06723

Editor's Revenge
Box 805
Morristown, NJ   07960

Editor's Workbook
Ink Art Publications
P.O. Box 36070
Indianapolis, IN   46236

Fillers for Publications
1220 Maple Ave.
Los Angeles, CA   90015

Impact
P.O. Box 1896
Evanston, IL   60204

**The Kiplinger Washington
   Letter**
1729 H St., NW
Washington, DC   20006

Media News Keys
Television Index, Inc.
40-29 27th St.
Long Island City, NY   11101

MicroPublishing Report
2004 Curtis Ave.
Redondo Beach, CA   90278

Personal Publishing
P.O. Box 390
Itasca, IL   60143

Publish!
*The How-To Magazine of Desktop
   Publishing*
501 Second St., #600
San Francisco, CA   94107

The Ragan Report and
   The Reporter's Report
Lawrence Ragan
   Communications, Inc.
407 S. Dearborn St.
Chicago, IL   60605

TOWERS Club USA Newsletter
Jerry Buchanan Advertising
   Agency
P.O. Box 2038
Vancouver, WA   98668

ADVERTISING AND
PROMOTION

Advertising Age
740 N. Rush St.
Chicago, IL   60611

Business Mailers Review
1813 Shepherd St., NW
Washington, DC   20011

The Copley Mail Order Advisor
Copley Communications
Box 405 Prudential Center
Boston, MA   02199

Creative Forum
Direct Marketing Creative
   Guild
516 Fifth Ave.
New York, NY   10036

**Dependable's List Marketing
   Newsletter**
Dependable Lists, Inc.
33 Irving Pl.
New York, NY   10003

Direct Marketing Magazine
224 Seventh St.
Garden City, NY   11530

Direct Marketing News Digest
Infomat
708 Silver Spur Rd.
Rolling Hills Estates,
   CA   90274

The Direct Response Specialist
P.O. Box 1075
Tarpon Springs, FL   34286

Editor & Publisher
575 Lexington Ave.
New York, NY   10022

Folio
125 Elm St.
P.O. Box 697
New Canaan, CT   06840

Friday Report (direct mail)
Hoke Communications, Inc.
224 Seventh St.
Garden City, NY   11530

Per Inquiry Advertising
A & T Promotions
167 Main
Gurley, AL   35748

Postal World
United Communications Group
4550 Montgomery Ave., #700N
Bethesda, MD   20814

Prescott's List Insights
Prescott Lists, Inc.
17 E. 26th St.
New York, NY   10010

Promotion Power
Reuben H. Donnelley
825 Third Ave.
New York, NY   10022

Publishers Multinational Direct
150 E. 74th St.
New York, NY   10021

Who's Mailing What!
P.O. Box 8180
Stamford, CT   06905

Organizations

American Society of Association Executives
1575 Eye St., NW
Washington, DC   20005
R. William Taylor, president
    Conducts seminars and workshops on association newsletters.

California State University
Northridge, CA   91330
    First course on newsletters was given in 1977 by James Joseph; it is still offered on an occasional basis.

Direct Mail/Marketing Association, Inc.
6 E. 43rd St.
New York, NY   10017
212-689-4977
Jonah Gitlitz, president
    Has an excellent information center and is a good source for books and seminars on direct mail.

Ebsco
P.O. Box 1943
Birmingham, AL   35201
  Subscription agency.

Faxon
15 Southwest Park
Westwood, MA   02090
  Subscription agency.

International Association of Business Communicators
870 Market St.
San Francisco, CA   94102
Norman G. Leaper, president
  Conducts seminars on editorial practices and graphics of sponsored newsletters—industrial, trade, association, or fraternal.

National Serials Data Program (NSDP)
Library of Congress
Washington, DC   20540

The Newsletter Association
1401 Wilson Blvd.
Arlington, VA   22209
703-527-2333
Frederick D. Goss, executive director
  Nonprofit association of professional newsletter publishers founded in 1977. It conducts the annual International Newsletter Conference and numerous seminars on publishing and editorial and promotion and management topics. Members receive "The Guidebook to Newsletter Publishing" (which is an ongoing loose-leaf service of articles and reports on various aspects of newslettering) and the twice-monthly newsletter *Hotline*. NA also sponsors an annual Newsletter Journalism Awards program.

The Newsletter Clearinghouse
44 W. Market St., P.O. Box 311
Rhinebeck, NY   12572
914-876-2081
Howard Penn Hudson, president
  Private service organization for the newsletter industry worldwide, founded in Chicago in 1964. The present ownership took over in 1968. NLCH established the annual Newsletter Conference and the annual

Newsletter Awards and Promotion Awards competitions and acted as a prototype association. In 1975, Howard Hudson invited several other publishers to join him in founding the Newsletter Association of America and transferred to the new group the rights to the International Conference. Publications include *An Inside Look at the Newsletter Field, How to Buy, Sell, and Price Newsletter Properties,* and *Hudson's Newsletter Directory.* Publishes *The Newsletter on Newsletter* twice monthly and *Newsletter Design* monthly. Subscribers receive the *Executive Portfolio of Newsletter Ideas That Work.* Since 1969, NLCH has conducted seminars under the name "How to Start a Newsletter."

Patent and Trademark Office
U.S. Department of Commerce
Washington, DC   20231

Register of Copyrights
Library of Congress
Washington, DC   20559

Select Information Exchange
2095 Broadway
New York, NY   10023
George Wein, president
  Subscription agency specializing in business newsletters.

Standard Rate & Data Service
5201 Old Orchard Rd.
Skokie, IL   60076
  Publications include *Direct Mail List Rates & Data, Business Publication Rates & Data,* and *Consumer Magazine Rates & Data.*

University of Wisconsin–Extension
Madison, WI   53706
  Conducts an annual conference on newsletters.

Gallery of Newsletters

1. **Energy Design Update,** Cutter Information Corp., 1100 Massachusetts Ave., Arlington, MA 02174. Founded 1983.
2. **BrushUp,** Oral-B Laboratories, One Lagoon Dr., Redwood City, CA 94065. Founded 1986.
3. **TOWERS Club USA Newsletter,** Jerry Buchanan, P.O. Box 2038, Vancouver, WA 98668. Founded 1974.
4. **Hotline,** Newsletter Association, 1401 Wilson Blvd., #403, Arlington, VA 22209. Founded 1977.
5. **Corpus Chemical Report,** Corpus Information Services, 1450 Don Mills Rd., Don Mills, Ontario, Canada M3B 2X7. Founded 1969.
6. **Money Reporter,** Marpep Publishing Ltd., 133 Richmond St. W., Toronto, Canada M5H 3M8. Founded 1978.
7. **The TeleManagement Report,** Angus TeleManagement Group Inc., 1400 Bayly St., Office Mall Two, #3, Pickering, Ontario, Canada L1W 3R2. Founded 1983.
8. **Television Digest,** Television Digest Inc., 1836 Jefferson Pl., NW, Washington, DC 20036. Founded 1945.
9. **Beer Marketer's Insights,** Beer Marketer's Insights Inc., 51 Virginia Ave., West Nyack, NY 10994. Founded 1970.
10. **Harvard Medical School Health Letter,** Harvard Medical School, 79 Garden St., Cambridge, MA 02138. Founded 1975.
11. **Media Mergers & Acquisitions,** Paul Kagan Associates Inc., 126 Clock Tower Pl., Carmel, CA 93923. Founded 1987.
12. **The AIDS Law Reporter,** National Legal Research Group Inc., 2421 Ivy Rd., P.O. Box 7187, Charlottesville, VA 22906. Founded 1987.
13. **PetroChemical News,** William F. Bland Co., 1435 Bedford St., #1F, P.O. Box 1421, Stamford, CT 06904. Founded 1963.
14. **Men's Health,** Rodale Press, 33 E. Minor St., Emmaus, PA 18098. Founded 1985.

15. **Human Resource Management News,** Enterprise Publications, 20 N. Wacker Dr., Chicago, IL 60606. Founded 1951.

16. **Contest News-Letter,** Park Avenue Publishing, 500 Fifth Ave., New York, NY 10036. Founded 1975.

17. **Kovels on Antiques and Collectibles,** Ralph and Terry Kovel, P.O. Box 22200, Beachwood, OH 44122. Founded 1974.

18. **Real Estate Investing Letter,** Management Resources Inc., 96 Morton St., New York, NY 10014. Founded 1976.

19. **PR Reporter,** PR Publishing Co. Inc., Dudley House, P.O. Box 600, Exeter, NH 03833. Founded 1958.

20. **Chemical Insight,** Hyde Chemical Publications Ltd., 6 W. Grove, Greenwich, London SE10 8QT, England. Founded 1972.

21. **Crime Control Digest,** Washington Crime News Services, 7043 Wimsatt Rd., Springfield, VA 22151. Founded 1967.

22. **Random Lengths,** Random Length Publications Inc., P.O. Box 867, Eugene, OR 97440. Founded 1951.

23. **The Community Relations Report,** Joe Williams Communications, P.O. Box 924, Bartlesville, OK 74005. Founded 1981.

24. **Hideaway Report,** Harper Associates Inc., Box 50, Sun Valley, ID 83353. Founded 1979.

25. **Hospital Peer Review,** American Health Consultants Inc., 67 Peachtree Park Dr., Atlanta, GA 30309. Founded 1976.

26. **The Direct Response Specialist,** Stilson & Stilson, P.O. Box 1075, Tarpon Springs, FL 34688. Founded 1982.

27. **Home Video Publisher,** Knowledge Industry Publications Inc., 701 Westchester Ave., White Plains, NY 10604. Founded 1984.

28. **Business Mailers Review,** Business Mailers Review Inc., 1813 Shepherd St., NW, Washington, DC 20011. Founded 1980.

29. **Inside R&D,** Technical Insights Inc., 32 North Dean St., Englewood, NJ 07631. Founded 1972.

30. **Micrographics Newsletter,** Microfilm Publishing Inc., P.O. Box 950, Larchmont, NY 10538. Founded 1969.

31. **The John & Mable Ringling Museum of Art,** The John & Mable Ringling Museum of Art, 5401 Bayshore Rd., Sarasota, FL 34243. Founded 1964.

32. **Pratt's Letter,** A. S. Pratt & Sons Inc., P.O. Box 9655, Arlington, VA 22209. Founded 1934.

33. **Washington Drug Letter,** Washington Business Information Inc., 1117 N. 19th St., Arlington, VA 22209. Founded 1969.

34. **Doane's Agricultural Report,** Doane Information Services, 11701 Borman Dr., St. Louis, MO 63146. Founded 1938.

35. **Ragan Report,** Lawrence Ragan Communications Inc., 407 S. Dearborn St., Chicago, IL 60605. Founded 1970.

36. **The Bank President's Letter,** United Communications Group, 4550 Montgomery Ave., #700N, Bethesda, MD 20814. Founded 1982.

37. **News-Letter of the American Antiquarian Society,** American Antiquarian Society, 185 Salisbury St., Worcester, MA 01609. Founded 1968.

38. **Advanced Composites Bulletin,** Elsevier International Bulletins, Mayfair House, 256 Banbury Rd., Oxford OX2 7DH, England. Founded 1987.

39. **Bulletin on Training,** The Bureau of National Affairs Inc., 1231 25th St., NW, Washington, DC 20037. Founded 1976.

40. **Coal Outlook,** Pasha Publications, 1401 Wilson Blvd., #900, Arlington, VA 22209. Founded 1975.

41. **Care World Report,** Care Headquarters, 660 First Ave., New York, NY 10016. Founded 1972.

42. **Air/Water Pollution Report,** Business Publishers Inc., 951 Pershing Dr., Silver Spring, MD 20910. Founded 1963.

43. **Recruitment and Retention,** Magna Publications Inc., 2718 Dryden Dr., Madison, WI 53704. Founded 1987.

44. **Research Recommendations,** National Institute of Business Management Inc., 1328 Broadway, New York, NY 10001. Founded 1947.

45. **Shipyard Weekly,** Shipbuilders Council of America, 1110 Vermont Ave., NW, Washington, DC 20005. Founded 1962.

46. **Telecommunications Reports,** Business Research Publications Inc., 1036 National Press Building, Washington, DC 20045. Founded 1934.

47. **Mutual Fund Forecaster,** Institute for Econometric Research, 3471 N. Federal Highway, Ft. Lauderdale, FL 33306. Founded 1984.

48. **Telephone News,** Phillips Publishing Inc., 7811 Montrose Rd., Potomac, MD 20854. Founded 1980.

49. **Impact,** Impact Publications, P.O. Box 1896, Evanston, IL 60204. Founded 1959.

50. **Western Tanager,** Los Angeles Audubon Society, 10336 Cheviot Dr., Los Angeles, CA 90064. Founded 1934.

51. **AI Nikkei Artificial Intelligence,** Nikkei–McGraw-Hill, 1-1, Ogawamachi, Kanda, Chiyoda-ku, Tokyo, Japan 101. Founded 1986.

52. **Electric Utility Week,** McGraw-Hill Inc., 1221 Avenue of the Americas, New York, NY 10020. Founded 1970.

53. **The Hulbert Financial Digest,** Hulbert Financial Digest Inc., 643 S. Carolina Ave., SE, Washington, DC 20003. Founded 1987.
54. **The Gallagher Report,** The Gallagher Report Inc., 230 Park Ave., New York, NY 10017. Founded 1953.
55. **Competition,** Council for a Competitive Economy, 122 C St., NW, Washington, DC 20001. Founded 1979.
56. **Hazardous Waste and Toxic Torts Law and Strategy,** Leader Publications, 111 Eighth Ave., New York, NY 10011. Founded 1984.
57. **Washington Memo,** The Alan Guttmacher Institute, 2010 Massachusetts Ave., NW, Washington, DC 20036. Founded 1971.
58. **The Lawyer's PC,** Shepard's/McGraw-Hill Inc., P.O. Box 1235, Colorado Springs, CO 80901. Founded 1983.
59. **Privatization,** Alexander Research & Communications Inc., 1133 Broadway, #1407, New York, NY 10010. Founded 1986.
60. **NASNewsletter,** National Association of School Nurses Inc., P.O. Box 1300, Scarborough, ME 04074. Founded 1986.
61. **Health Care Competition Week,** Capitol Publications Inc., 1101 King St., P.O. Box 1454, Alexandria, VA 22313. Founded 1983.
62. **New England Farm Bulletin,** Jacob's Meadow Inc., Box 147, Cohasset, MA 02025. Founded 1976.
63. **Latvian News Digest,** American Latvian Association, P.O. Box 4578, 400 Hurley Ave., Rockville, MD 20850. Founded 1976.
64. **Pulp & Paper International News This Week,** Miller Freeman Publications, 500 Howard St., San Francisco, CA 94105. Founded 1986.
65. **Cardiogram,** Franklin Communications, 288 Old Briarcliff Rd., Briarcliff Manor, NY 10510. Founded 1982.
66. **The Executive Letter,** Insurance Information Institute, 110 William St., New York, NY 10038. Founded 1967.
67. **Chamber of Commerce Executive,** American Chamber of Commerce Executives, 1454 Duke St., Alexandria, VA 22314. Founded 1974.
68. **Waterfront World,** Waterfront Center, 1536 44th St., NW, Washington, DC 20007. Founded 1981.

2. *BrushUp*

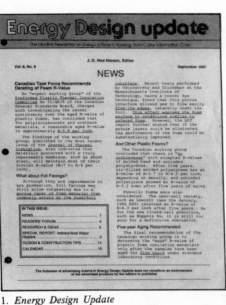

1. *Energy Design Update*

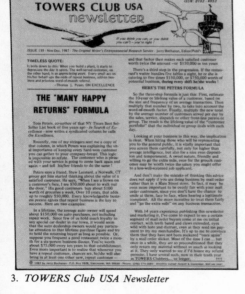

3. *TOWERS Club USA Newsletter*

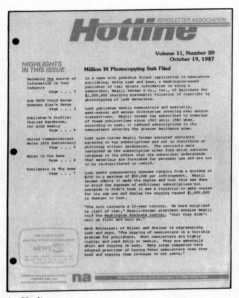

4. *Hotline*

Corpus Chemical Report

A WEEKLY MARKET LETTER ON CANADA'S CHEMICAL PROCESS INDUSTRIES

September 21, 1987

5. *Corpus Chemical Report*

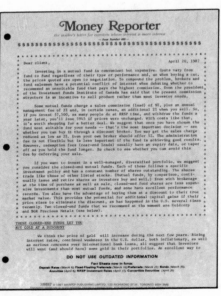

6. *Money Reporter*

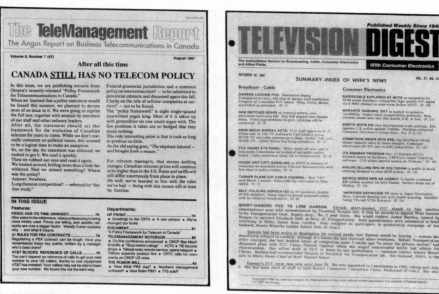

7. *The TeleManagement Report*

8. *Television Digest*

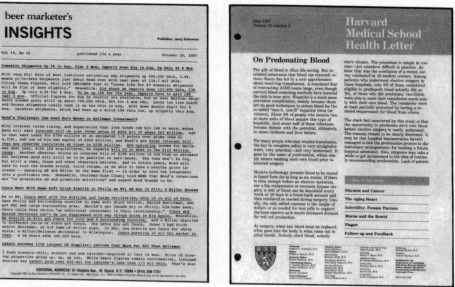

9. *Beer Marketer's Insights*

10. *Harvard Medical School Health Letter*

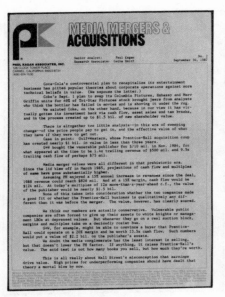

11. *Media Mergers & Acquisitions*

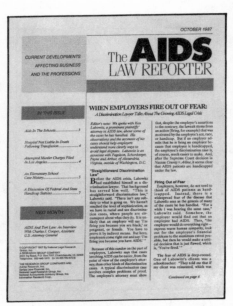

12. *The AIDS Law Reporter*

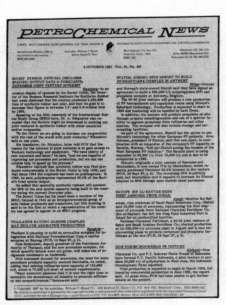

13. *PetroChemical News*

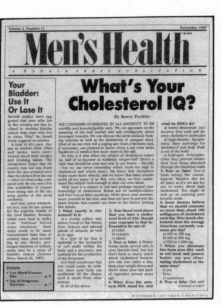

14. *Men's Health*

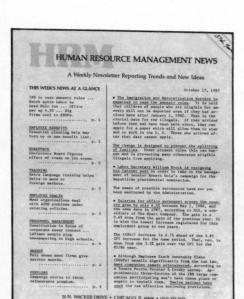

15. *Human Resource Management News*

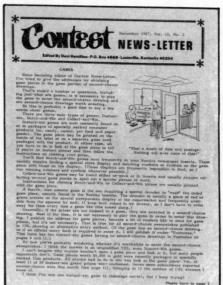

16. *Contest News-Letter*

17. *Kovels on Antiques and Collectibles*

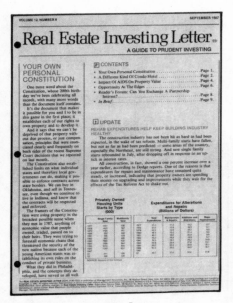

18. *Real Estate Investing Letter*

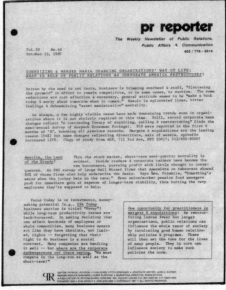

19. *PR Reporter*

20. *Chemical Insight*

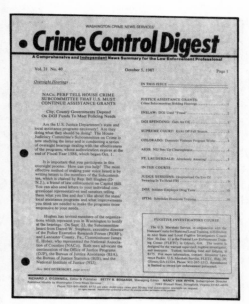

21. *Crime Control Digest*

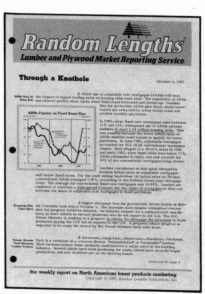

22. *Random Lengths*

23. *The Community Relations Report*

24. *Hideaway Report*

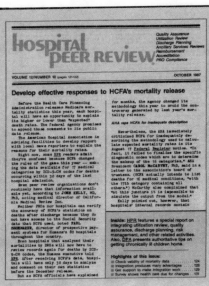

25. *Hospital Peer Review*

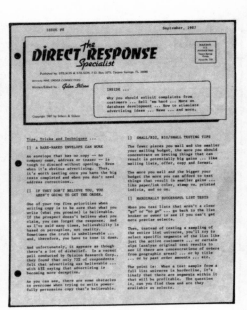

26. *The Direct Response Specialist*

27. *Home Video Publisher*

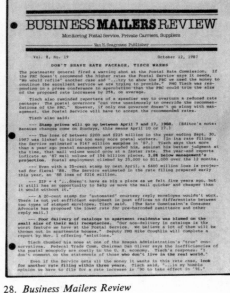

28. *Business Mailers Review*

INSIDE R&D
THE WEEKLY REPORT ON TECHNICAL INNOVATION

Volume 16, Number 39 · September 30, 1987

Ion Implantation Method Treats Large Areas Simultaneously: Like traditional ion implantation, new method enhances materials such as plastics, metal, and semiconductors by adding ions to surface layer. But unlike usual methods, in which implantation is line-of-sight, Applied Science and Technology approach is to bombard all surfaces. It eliminates use of masks, manipulation of beam or target, and size restrictions on targets. Limitations: Only ion species that are gaseous at room temperature can be used, and system lacks mass analysis. First limitation may be alleviated by mixing gas with non-gaseous ion species you want to use.
Here's how it works: Target is placed inside a plasma source and pulse-biased to a high (-10 kV to -100 kV) negative potential relative to chamber walls. Iron sheath is placed around target. Ions in plasma then bombard all surfaces of the target simultaneously. Typically, production run takes 30 min at 0.0002 Torr and reaches peak temperature of 150°C. Method is suited to in-house treatment since equipment is smaller, less expensive, and easier to maintain and operate than conventional implantation units. Details: John Tarrh, Senior Vice President, Applied Science and Technology, Inc., 37 Cedar St., Newton, MA 02159. Phone: 617-527-6345.

Explore Versatility of Reversed Micelles for Enzymatic Reactions: While you can usually perform enzymatic reactions in organic solvents, there are limitations, compared to aqueous solutions. New approach promises to lift these limitations. It uses reverse micelles -- enzymes embedded in tiny droplets of water encased in a surfactant layer -- to conduct chemical reactions in solvent solutions. Reversed micelles are 100 Å in diameter and remain stable after solution is mixed or shaken to free them.
Major promise of reversed micelles -- as yet unproved -- is that they can be used in sequential reactions. Theoretically, during collisions of reversed micelles caused by Brownian motion, reaction products of one reversed micelle could be transferred to a reversed micelle containing a different enzyme to conduct a secondary reaction. Researchers are now attempting to perform such a sequential reaction, the oxidation of aromatic aldehydes to benzoic acid and hydrogen peroxide.
High solubility of micelles in organic solvents lends technique to use in any hydrophobic substrate, including steroids, fatty acids, aromatic compounds, and organic esters. Details: Andreas S. Bommarius, Graduate Student, Dept. of Chemical Engineering, Massachusetts Institute of Technology, Cambridge, MA 02139. Phone: 617-253-8509.

Simplified Enzyme Immobilization Aids Bioreactor, Biosensors: Frustrated by complex processes required to immobilize enzymes? Look into licensing DuPont's Perflex™ immobilization technology. It frees you from need to chemically modify fluorocarbon membranes or to use secondary support membrane before immobilization. Instead, you perfluoroalkylate the enzyme to enhance adsorption. Then, simply wet membrane in solution of surfactants and immerse it in enzyme solution for several seconds.
Besides enzymes, technique can be used to immobilize other proteins, particles, films, and fibers. Most important industrial use will likely be stabilizing proteins and enzymes in bioreactors and biosensors. In addition, DuPont has recently introduced an application in affinity column purification of antibodies. Company has applied for patents and is interested in licensing the technology. Details: Dr. Robert K. Kobos, Senior Research Chemist, E. I. du Pont de Nemours, Glasgow Site, Bldg. 100, Wilmington, DE 19898. Phone: 302-451-3178.

29. *Inside R&D*

INSIDE THIS ISSUE

DOES AIIM SERVE MEMBERS' NEEDS?

The results of an AM survey of mid- and small-size manufacturers, dealers and service bureaus about how they feel the industry association stacks up. Is it on target to their needs or way off base? What improvements might be made or is it too late for useful change?

see this page

PRODUCT PARADE

A new silver film duplicator, electronic keypunch and ergonomic conversion kit....................5

INTERNATIONAL SCENE

IMC '87 is almost upon us....micrographics is alive and well in Europe. Here are some comments....5

MICROGRAPHICS IN MAGAZINES

Who's writing what where and how to get more information.............6

MICROGRAPHICS MARKETPLACE

Ads for new and used equipment, sales and field engineering jobs, calls for dealers/distributors, and offers to buy.....................7

MICROGRAPHICS STOCKS

How they fared on the NYSE, ASE and over-the-counter....................8

MICRODOTS

The end for Oscar Fisher....financial footnotes....................8

IMAGING TECHNOLOGY REPORT

A monthly insert on happenings in interrelated technologies that affect micrographics.

MICROGRAPHICS NEWSLETTER

the news report for executives who market or use micrographic services and equipment

ISSN 0883-9808

September 1987 · Issue II
Volume 19 · Number 16

AIIM AND THE MICROGRAPHICS INDUSTRY: IS IT SERVING ITS MEMBERS' NEEDS?

Late last spring, after the annual AIIM conference and exposition, MN sent a questionnaire to a representative sampling of micrographics industry trade member leaders --manufacturers, distributors and dealers, service bureaus-- to gauge true feelings as to how well they felt AIIM was meeting their needs. The reason was an undercurrent of discontent picked up in recent months from many mid- and smaller-size manufacturers and dealers.

Those who voiced that discontent essentially felt the association has taken a wrong turn that ignores or largely downplays the microform-based imaging suppliers and those who are the backbone of AIIM. The charge is that AIIM is preoccupied with reaching out to the proliferating other imaging technologies almost to the exclusion of traditional micrographics.

Biting the Hand that Feeds You?

In many ways this is a startling and hard-to-accept argument since, by AIIM's own admission, micrographics today makes up $2.4 billion of the $2.5 billion information and image management industry. Even with that impressive total, micrographics has only 4% of the total U.S. information storage market so there's still room for lots of growth. Further, the overwhelming backing for AIIM --both in terms of vendor support and professional membership --still comes from microfilm-based suppliers and users. With all that in mind, it would be (at the least) foolish for any industry to downplay its largest support base, on much less to threaten its very existence.

MICROGRAPHICS NEWSLETTER is published semi-monthly by Microdata Publishing, Inc., P.O. Box 950, Larchmont, NY 10538-0950. Telephone (914) 834-3644. Subscription rates: $125/year (USA, Canada, Mexico); $145/year air Mail Overseas (Outside USA). Single copies: $6 when available. Michael W. Becker, Publisher-Editor, Dorothy Wright, Circulation Manager. Reid S. Evelhart, Research Associate. Reproduction of information without the prior written permission of the publisher is forbidden. Send correspondence, orders, change of address, classified advertisements to MICROGRAPHICS NEWSLETTER, P.O. Box 950 Larchmont, NY 10538-0950. Microform copies of MICROGRAPHICS NEWSLETTER are available from University Microfilms International, 300 North Zeeb Road, Ann Arbor, MI 48106 (313) 761-4700.

30. *Micrographics Newsletter*

FALL 1987

THE JOHN & MABLE RINGLING

MUSEUM OF ART

Newly Created Work by The Starn Twins Kicks Off *The Projects*

A new contemporary program features works of art created just for the Museum

The Museum is about to introduce a new exhibition concept to its twentieth-century programming: *The Projects*.

Designed as an annual exhibition, *The Projects* will invite a major, or important emerging, artist to create a work or body of works specifically for the Museum. The physical space allotted to this art will generally be small —a single gallery or two in the New Wing— and the work will often be made especially for that limited environment.

Ideally, this mini-exhibition or installation will result in the appearance of important new work whose identity will be inextricably linked to the Museum. A precursor of this concept was the wonderfully zany Judy Pfaff installation, which former curator of modern art Michael Auping showed in the fall of 1981. Pfaff has since been recognized as one of the more important artists of her generation, and the Museum's installation as one of her strongest works.

The Projects will be inaugurated by The Starn Twins, perhaps the most exciting artists of the 1986-87 exhibition season

Collaborating as a single unit in their Boston studio, twenty-six-year-old identical twins Mike and Doug Starn work principally in the medium of photography, although they paint and sculpt as well. Their "photographs" reflect the Starns' interest in these other media; the works look very painterly and sculptural, barely resembling photographs. Their subject matter may sound mundane —horses, boots, a vat, a chair— but their impact is anything but. Often mounted in scale, torn,

'Visions of Faith' Illuminates an Earlier Time

This upcoming exhibition from the graphics collection explores religious thought

Museum members and visitors at last have a chance to see "Visions of Faith." This popular exhibition from the Museum's graphics collection has already traveled to numerous other museums throughout Florida, and was also on view at the College of Charleston, in South Carolina, and the University of Maryland.

The exhibition was curated by former staff member Myron Sprinزwall, who returns to the Museum as a guest curator and lecturer for the show. It was conceived by Professor Timothy Verdon of Florida State University in Tallahassee, where it opened in the spring of 1985 as part of an international symposium on Christianity and the Renaissance he organized, and by Dr. Anthony Janson, the Museum's curator of European paintings.

The exhibition opens to the public on September 4 in the South Wing

The Starn Twins, American, 1961- Mike, Doug (Churchill). II. Toned silver print, 82 x 85 in. Courtesy of the Stux Gallery, New York and Boston

Galleries, and runs through November 2.

"Visions of Faith" is one of the finest exhibitions ever assembled from the Museum's graphics collection," says Dr. Janson. "It offers a visual feast of more than fifty-five prints and drawings of the highest

These works complement the Museum's great strength in paintings of this period.

quality. These works, done mainly between 1550 and 1700, complement the Museum's great strength in paintings of this period."

Among the many beautiful works of art in the exhibition is the warmly human *Tobias and the Angel*, by seventeenth-century Dutch artist Jan van de Velde. The show centers comparisons with well-known Museum pictures, such as Albrecht Dürer's

Continued on page 1

31. *The John & Mable Ringling Museum of Art*

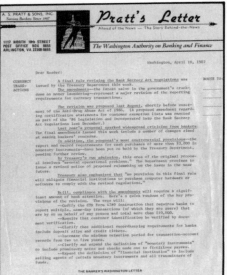

32. Pratt's Letter

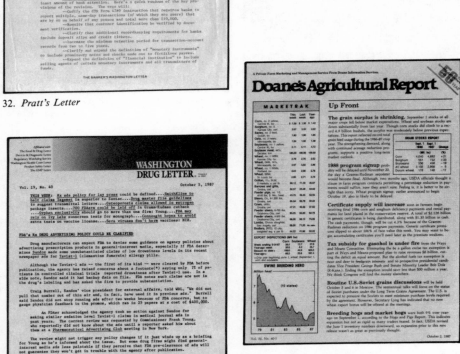

33. Washington Drug Letter

34. Doane's Agricultural Report

35. *Ragan Report*

37. *News-Letter of the American Antiquarian Society*

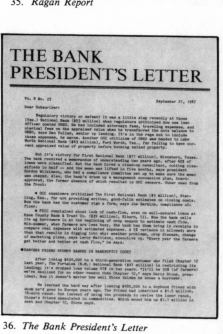

36. *The Bank President's Letter*

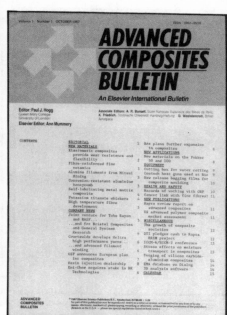

38. *Advanced Composites Bulletin*

Bulletin on Training

Trends · Techniques · Topics

39. *Bulletin on Training*

coal outlook

40. *Coal Outlook*

CARE World Report

CARE Celebrates 35th Anniversary

41. *Care World Report*

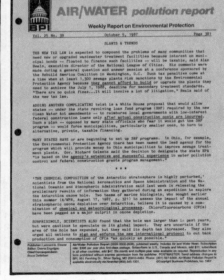

AIR/WATER pollution report

Weekly Report on Environmental Protection

42. *Air/Water Pollution Report*

Recruitment and Retention

Volume 1, Number 10
October 1987

In Higher Education

Recruiting Hispanic College Students

Experts agree that many minority college student recruiting programs fail because they begin too late — in high school. By then, many students have made academic and lifestyle choices which limit their opportunities for higher education. A program at the U. of Southern California aims to reverse that trend by targeting pre-high school students.

USC's Register of Future Hispanic College Students and the Hispanic Students Speakers Bureau focus on junior high school Hispanics with college potential. The aim, says Samuel Mark, director of USC's Office of Hispanic Programs, is to motivate members of this population into thinking about attending college. It's an idea, he says, whose seeds must be planted early.

"We find that many Hispanics lack the motivation to go to college; it's up to USC to seek out and help this population," he says. "Often, they're recent immigrants so they don't know society or how it works. Most don't have the finances to go to school or their parents don't know how to gear them toward an educational background."

Early intervention is needed, Mark says, because many high school students never receive the right information on college preparatory courses.

The Hispanic Speakers Bureau employs eight Hispanic USC undergraduates. The students, who're paid with work-study funds, present workshops at local schools — both public and private — trying to encourage younger Hispanics to pursue a college education.

"The workshops are geared toward the eighth- or ninth-grade students, but we'll make presentations to students from sixth through twelfth grades," Mark says. Speakers use posters and slides to emphasize the advantages of going to college, how to prepare for it, how to finance the college years, and what college life is like.

USC is one of a number of colleges that the speakers highlight in their presentations. "We use the program as a recruiting tool, but it's not exclusively for USC," Mark says. About 8% of USC students are Hispanic, a figure that he would like to double within 10 years.

The Register, a supplement to the speakers bureau, is seen as the school's data base for future Hispanic college students. USC's admissions office mails information to thousands of potential students in the Los Angeles area. The content includes how to prepare for a college education, why

Contents

43. *Recruitment and Retention*

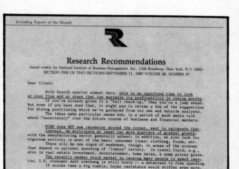

44. *Research Recommendations*

SHIPYARD WEEKLY

45. *Shipyard Weekly*

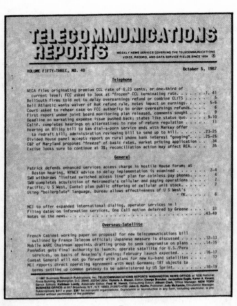

46. *Telecommunications Reports*

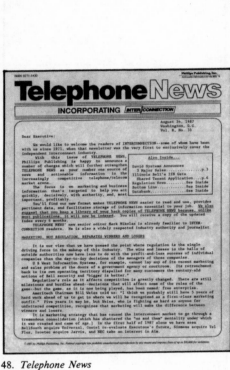

48. *Telephone News*

47. *Mutual Fund Forecaster*

49. *Impact*

51. *AI Nikkei Artificial Intelligence*

50. *Western Tanager*

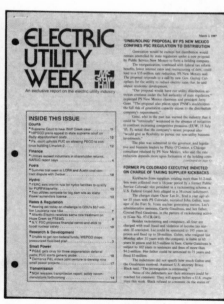

52. *Electric Utility Week*

53. *The Hulbert Financial Digest*

The Hulbert Financial Digest
Volume VII, Number 11 — July 27, 1987

Seven Years... And Counting

55. *Competition*

Reagan Administration Rebuked On Japanese Export Curb

Board Meets in Dallas; Plans Convention

54. *The Gallagher Report*

57. Washington Memo

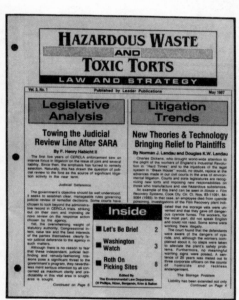

56. Hazardous Waste and Toxic Torts Law and Strategy

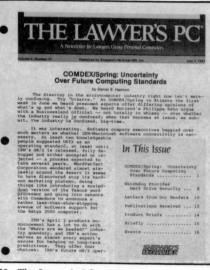

58. The Lawyer's PC

ISSN 0886-7666

Privatization
Strategies and Tactics in Privatization and Contracting Out

Volume 2, Number 15
August 7, 1987

Inside This Issue...

One municipality, a regional authority and the U.S. Air Force contracted for air traffic control tower operations and maintenance at airports in three states........p. 1

Los Angeles County identified **86 active functions** which could be privatized. A recent report shows progress, with data..........p. 2

L.A. County's **privatization law** sets restrictions and conditions under which privatization is sanctioned..........p. 4

Service providers must **sell privatization** to the many groups affected by contracting out. A Privatization Council report outlines the critical concerns....p. 5

New ideas and technologies in urban rail transit hinge on privatization. One innovative system is working in Florida, another is planned for Washington, DC.....p. 6

Here are five real **reasons** why governments turn to contracting out. Cost is far from the only factor..........p. 8

Low-Activity Airports Revived By Tower Contractor

Barton ATC, Inc. operates 11 air traffic control towers under contract through the Federal Aviation Administration's Low Activity VFR Control Tower Contracting Program.

Barton provides control-tower operations, maintenance and other services for municipalities, states, the military and various regional authorities.

The FAA program, which was in danger of folding late last year, affects only Class 1 airports, which are not equipped to guide instrument landings. These are the type of airports for which Barton provides its services. Most serve primarily private aviation, not scheduled commercial airlines.

Barton's most recent contracts, executed in early 1987, are for operation of a control tower at Pendleton Municipal Airport in Pendleton, OR; for continued operation of air traffic control, weather observation and associated maintenance services for the U.S. Air Force at Richards-Gebaur Base in Missouri; and for operation of the control tower and aviation weather-reporting station for the Chennault Industrial Airpark Authority at Chennault Industrial Airpark in Lake Charles, LA.

The Contracting-Out Flight Plan

Barton's contract with Pendleton, OR is for three years. Under the contract terms, Barton is paid a flat sum for each of various "performance periods." The current period runs from January 16 to early September. Pendleton, said Barton spokesman Mike Lynch, in turn contracts with the FAA to provide the funds to pay Barton. According to a 1984 FAA study, privatized control towers can be run for $150,000 annually -- one-half the FAA cost.

The control tower at Pendleton was operated for many years by the FAA until it was closed in 1981. It reopened in 1984 under the FAA's Contracting Program. The airport supports numerous general aviation aircraft, "a significant number" of agricultural operations and hosts a U.S. Army National Guard unit.

59. Privatization

Volume 2, Number 3
March 1987

NASNewsletter
National Association of School Nurses, Inc.

SAY NO TO: "IT'S OK TO SAY NO!"

"Stephanie's Story," which appears on pages 60 and 61 of *It's OK to Say No!* is an insult to school nurses. NASN and The Association of State School Nurse Consultants have written to the editors requesting that these pages are corrected or deleted. School nurses strongly disapprove of this kind of "education."

STEPHANIE'S STORY

One day in school, Stephanie felt sick. Her stomach hurt and she felt a little dizzy. The teacher sent her to the school nurse's office.

The nurse, Mrs. Carmichael, was there alone. She asked Stephanie how she felt and was very sympathetic. She came out from behind her desk and sat very close to Stephanie.

Mrs. Carmichael said, "Here, just let me rub your stomach to make it feel better."

Stephanie knew that rubbing her stomach wasn't going to

make it any better, and she knew that she had the right to say "NO" if anybody wanted to touch her in any way.

Stephanie said, "No, I don't want you to touch me. I think I'd better just go home."

Let the publishers know how you feel. Write to: Tom Doherty Associates, 49 West 24th Street, New York, NY 10010

MOST STUDENTS COMFORTABLE WITH SCHOOL NURSES

The *Weekly Reader National Survey* polls the nation's children twice a year in the pages of various *Weekly Reader* periodicals, and distributed to school children in grades two through nine. Generally, about 500,000 children participate in the surveys, and about 100,000 responses are analyzed. The surveys cover children's attitudes about subjects of importance to them and to adults. The results receive wide publicity in the public press, are regularly reviewed in scholarly publications, and have served as the basis for changes in government policy.

The editors of *Weekly Reader* selected Safety and Health as the subject of the survey conducted in the spring of 1986 because:

• safety and health are subjects about which children have extensive personal knowledge and opinions.

• safety and health are currently subjects of particular adult concern, with an unprecedented level of personal involvement in these areas.

• the attitudes of children about safety and health are likely to have a direct effect on future successes of reforms in these areas.

As school nurses, you will be very pleased by the results of this question in the health section of the survey.

Question: How comfortable would you feel about going to each of these places? (very comfortable, somewhat comfortable, not comfortable): doctor's office, school nurse's office, doctor's office, hospital

Summary of answers

Students feel less and less comfortable about going to places where they receive medical treatment as they progress from fourth grade to sixth grade.

Students feel most comfortable in the school nurse's office and least comfortable in the hospital. In the fourth grade, 38 percent of students feel very comfortable in the school nurse's office; by sixth grade, 30 percent of students feel very comfortable there. Twenty-six percent of fourth graders feel very comfortable in the hospital, with this figure dropping to 20 percent by the sixth grade.

60. NASNewsletter

Health Care Competition Week

Vol. 4, No. 41, October 19, 1987

HCFA to test Medicare insured groups

In a major expansion of the federal government's involvement with private health plans, the Health Care Financing Administration last week announced a preliminary agreement with the Amalgamated Life Insurance Company, New York City, to demonstrate HCFA's "Medicare Insured Group" concept for retirees.

Under the MIG concept, HCFA will pay a fixed amount to ALICO to fund the health benefits of retirees and spouses of certain trusts sponsored by the Amalgamated Clothing and Textile Workers Union. That payment will be less than what HCFA would have spent on the group under traditional fee-for-service Medicare.

ALICO administers health insurance benefits for half a million workers and their families, including about 130,000 retirees and their spouses who participate in certain Taft-Hartley trusts sponsored by the clothing and textiles union.

Mary Kennison, director of the Office of Demonstrations and Evaluations, told HCCW that ALICO has proposed a six-month development phase. After that, the company plans to open one demonstration site in the Philadelphia area where 5,000 Medicare-eligible ALICO retirees reside, she said. In future years, the company would add sites in two or three additional urban areas with high concentrations of eligible retirees.

For the employer or union, MIGs offer better control over their retiree health costs and less worries over their unfunded liabilities, although this point doesn't apply to ALICO. Retirees get more choice, less red tape and a chance for increased benefits at lower premiums.

(more)

IN THIS ISSUE:

Federal workers expected to shift to prepaid plans (page 2)

Major company finds wide differences among HMOs (page 3)

Doctors and contractors don't assume they'll read them (page 4)

Indigent care–will the public foot the bill? (page 5)

REPH, Republic announce elaborate refinancing proposal (page 6)

Marketer's Forum: meshing referrals and marketing (page 7)

Your Competitive Edge–the future of joint ventures (page 8)

61. Health Care Competition Week

63. *Latvian News Digest*

62. *New England Farm Bulletin*

64. *Pulp & Paper International News This Week*

65. *Cardiogram*

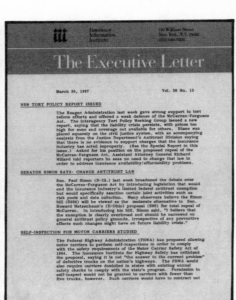

66. *The Executive Letter*

67. *Chamber of Commerce Executive*

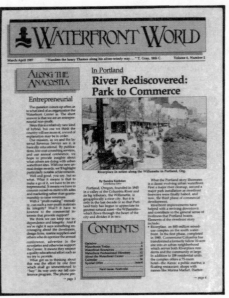

68. *Waterfront World*

Index